TOWER OF BASEL

THE SHADOWY HISTORY
OF THE SECRET BANK THAT
RUNS THE WORLD

TOWER
OF BASEL

ADAM LEBOR

PUBLICAFFAIRS
New York

PUBLICAFFAIRS books are available at special discounts for bulk purchases in the U.S. by corporations, institutions, and other organizations. For more information, please contact the Special Markets Department at the Perseus Books Group, 2300 Chestnut Street, Suite 200, Philadelphia, PA 19103, call (800) 810-4145, ext. 5000, or e-mail special.markets@perseusbooks.com.

EDITORIAL PRODUCTION BY LORI HOBKIRK AT THE BOOK FACTORY
BOOK DESIGN BY DAISY BAUER

A CIP catalog record of this book is available from the Library of Congress.
ISBN 978-1-61039-254-9 (HC)
ISBN 978-1-61039-255-6 (EB)

First Edition
10 9 8 7 6 5 4 3 2 1

*For Justin Leighton
and Roger Boyes,
who ask the right questions*

Contents

"The Bank is completely removed from any governmental or political control."

— Gates McGarrah, first president of the Bank for International Settlements, 1931[1]

Introduction

The world's most exclusive club has eighteen members. They gather every other month on a Sunday evening at 7 p.m. in conference room E in a circular tower block whose tinted windows overlook the central Basel railway station. Their discussion lasts for one hour, perhaps an hour and a half. Some of those present bring a colleague with them, but the aides rarely speak during this most confidential of conclaves. The meeting closes, the aides leave, and those remaining retire for dinner in the dining room on the eighteenth floor, rightly confident that the food and the wine will be superb. The meal, which continues until 11 p.m. or midnight, is where the real work is done. The protocol and hospitality, honed for more than eight decades, are faultless. Anything said at the dining table, it is understood, is not to be repeated elsewhere.

Few, if any, of those enjoying their haute cuisine and *grand cru* wines—some of the best Switzerland can offer—would be recognized by passers-by, but they include a good number of the most powerful people in the world. These men—they are almost all men—are central bankers. They have come to Basel to attend the Economic Consultative Committee (ECC) of the Bank for International Settlements (BIS), which is the bank for central banks. Its current members include Ben Bernanke, the chairman of the US Federal Reserve; Sir Mervyn King, the governor of the Bank of England; Mario Draghi, of the European Central Bank; Zhou Xiaochuan of the Bank of China; and the central bank governors of Germany, France, Italy, Sweden, Canada, India, and Brazil. Jaime Caruana, a former governor of the Bank of Spain, the BIS's general manager, joins them.

In early 2013, when this book went to press, King, who is due to step down as governor of the Bank of England in June 2013, chaired the ECC. The ECC, which used to be known as the G-10 governors' meeting, is the most influential of the BIS's numerous gatherings, open only to a small, select group of central bankers from advanced economies. The ECC makes recommendations on the membership and organization of the three BIS committees that deal with the global financial system, payments systems, and international markets. The committee also prepares proposals for the Global Economy Meeting and guides its agenda.

That meeting starts at 9:30 a.m. on Monday morning, in room B and lasts for three hours. There King presides over the central bank governors of the thirty countries judged the most important to the global economy. In addition to those who were present at the Sunday evening dinner, Monday's meeting will include representatives from, for example, Indonesia, Poland, South Africa, Spain, and Turkey. Governors from fifteen smaller countries, such as Hungary, Israel, and New Zealand are allowed to sit in as observers, but do not usually not speak. Governors from the third tier of member banks, such as Macedonia and Slovakia, are not allowed to attend. Instead they must forage for scraps of information at coffee and meal breaks.

The governors of all sixty BIS member banks then enjoy a buffet lunch in the eighteenth-floor dining room. Designed by Herzog & de Meuron, the Swiss architectural firm which built the "Bird's Nest" Stadium for the Beijing Olympics, the dining room has white walls, a black ceiling and spectacular views over three countries: Switzerland, France, and Germany.[2] At 2 p.m. the central bankers and their aides return to room B for the governors' meeting to discuss matters of interest, until the gathering ends at 5.

King takes a very different approach than his predecessor, Jean-Claude Trichet, the former president of the European Central Bank, in chairing the Global Economy Meeting. Trichet, according to one former central banker, was notably Gallic in his style: a stickler for protocol who called the central bankers to speak in order of importance, starting with the governors of the Federal Reserve, the Bank of England, and the Bundesbank, and then progressing down the hierarchy.

King, in contrast, adopts a more thematic and egalitarian approach: throwing open the meetings for discussion and inviting contributions from all present.

The governors' conclaves have played a crucial role in determining the world's response to the global financial crisis. "The BIS has been a very important meeting point for central bankers during the crisis, and the rationale for its existence has expanded," said King. "We have had to face challenges that we have never seen before. We had to work out what was going on, what instruments do we use when interest rates are close to zero, how do we communicate policy. We discuss this at home with our staff, but it is very valuable for the governors themselves to get together and talk among themselves."

Those discussions, say central bankers, must be confidential. "When you are at the top in the number one post, it can be pretty lonely at times. It is helpful to be able to meet other number ones and say, 'This is my problem, how do you deal with it?'" King continued. "Being able to talk informally and openly about our experiences has been immensely valuable. We are not speaking in a public forum. We can say what we really think and believe, and we can ask questions and benefit from others."[3]

The BIS management works hard to ensure that the atmosphere is friendly and clubbable throughout the weekend, and it seems they succeed. The bank arranges a fleet of limousines to pick up the governors at Zürich airport and bring them to Basel. Separate breakfasts, lunches, and dinners are organized for the governors of national banks who oversee different types and sizes of national economies, so no one feels excluded. "The central bankers were more at home and relaxed with their fellow central bankers than with their own governments," recalled Paul Volcker, the former chairman of the US Federal Reserve, who attended the Basel weekends.[4] The superb quality of the food and wine made for an easy camaraderie, said Peter Akos Bod, a former governor of the National Bank of Hungary. "The main topics of discussion were the quality of the wine and the stupidity of finance ministers. If you had no knowledge of wine you could not join in the conversation."[5]

And the conversation is usually stimulating and enjoyable, say central bankers. The contrast between the Federal Open Markets Committee at the

US Federal Reserve, and the Sunday evening G-10 governors' dinners was notable, recalled Laurence Meyer, who served as a member of the Board of Governors of the Federal Reserve from 1996 until 2002. The chairman of the Federal Reserve did not always represent the bank at the Basel meetings, so Meyer occasionally attended. The BIS discussions were always lively, focused and thought provoking. "At FMOC meetings, while I was at the Fed, almost all the Committee members read statements which had been prepared in advance. They very rarely referred to statements by other Committee members and there was almost never an exchange between two members or an ongoing discussion about the outlook or policy options. At BIS dinners people actually talk to each other and the discussions are always stimulating and interactive focused on the serious issues facing the global economy."[6]

All the governors present at the two-day gathering are assured of total confidentiality, discretion, and the highest levels of security. The meetings take place on several floors that are usually used only when the governors are in attendance. The governors are provided with a dedicated office and the necessary support and secretarial staff. The Swiss authorities have no jurisdiction over the BIS premises. Founded by an international treaty, and further protected by the 1987 Headquarters Agreement with the Swiss government, the BIS enjoys similar protections to those granted to the headquarters of the United Nations, the International Monetary Fund (IMF) and diplomatic embassies. The Swiss authorities need the permission of the BIS management to enter the bank's buildings, which are described as "inviolable."[7]

The BIS has the right to communicate in code and to send and receive correspondence in bags covered by the same protection as embassies, meaning they cannot be opened. The BIS is exempt from Swiss taxes. Its employees do not have to pay income tax on their salaries, which are usually generous, designed to compete with the private sector. The general manager's salary in 2011 was 763,930 Swiss francs, while head of departments were paid 587,640 per annum, plus generous allowances. The bank's extraordinary legal privileges also extend to its staff and directors. Senior managers enjoy a special status, similar to that of diplomats, while carrying out their duties in Switzerland, which means their bags cannot be searched (unless there is evidence of a blatant criminal act), and their papers are inviolable. The central bank governors traveling to Basel for the bimonthly meetings enjoy the same status while in Switzerland. All bank officials are immune under Swiss law, for life, for all the acts carried out during the discharge of their duties. The bank is a popular place to work and not just because of the salaries. Around six hundred staff come from over fifty countries. The atmosphere is multi-national and cosmopolitan, albeit very Swiss, emphasizing the bank's hierarchy. Like many of those working for the UN or the IMF, some of the staff of the BIS, especially senior management, are driven by a sense of mission, that they are working for a higher, even celestial purpose and so are immune from normal considerations of accountability and transparency.

The bank's management has tried to plan for every eventuality so that the Swiss police need never be called. The BIS headquarters has high-tech sprinkler systems with multiple back-ups, in-house medical facilities, and its own bomb shelter in the event of a terrorist attack or armed conflagration. The BIS's assets are not subject to civil claims under Swiss law and can never be seized.

The BIS strictly guards the bankers' secrecy. The minutes, agenda, and actual attendance list of the Global Economy Meeting or the ECC are not released in any form. This is because no official minutes are taken, although the bankers sometimes scribble their own notes. Sometimes there will be a brief press conference or bland statement afterwards but never anything detailed. This tradition of privileged confidentiality reaches back to the bank's foundation.

"The quietness of Basel and its absolutely nonpolitical character provide a perfect setting for those equally quiet and nonpolitical gatherings," wrote one American official in 1935. "The regularity of the meetings and their almost unbroken attendance by practically every member of the Board make them such they rarely attract any but the most meager notice in the press."[8] Forty years on, little had changed. Charles Coombs, a former foreign exchange chief of the New York Federal Reserve, attended governors' meetings from 1960 to 1975. The bankers who were allowed inside the inner sanctum of the governors' meetings trusted each other absolutely, he recalled in his memoirs. "However much money was involved, no agreements were ever signed nor memoranda of understanding ever initialized. The word of each official was sufficient, and there were never any disappointments."[9]

What, then, does this matter to the rest of us? Bankers have been gathering confidentially since money was first invented. Central bankers like to view themselves as the high priests of finance, as technocrats overseeing arcane monetary rituals and a financial liturgy understood only by a small, self-selecting elite.

But the governors who meet in Basel every other month are public servants. Their salaries, airplane tickets, hotel bills, and lucrative pensions when they retire are paid out of the public purse. The national reserves held by central banks are public money, the wealth of nations. The central bankers' discussions at the BIS, the information that they share, the policies that are evaluated, the opinions that are exchanged, and the subsequent decisions that are taken, are profoundly political. Central bankers, whose independence is constitutionally protected, control monetary policy in the developed world. They manage the supply of money to national economies. They set interest rates, thus deciding the value of our savings and investments. They decide whether to focus on austerity or growth. Their decisions shape our lives.

The BIS's tradition of secrecy reaches back through the decades. During the 1960s, for example, the bank hosted the London Gold Pool. Eight countries pledged to manipulate the gold market to keep the price at around thirty-five dollars per ounce, in line with the provisions of the Bretton Woods Accord that governed the post–World War II international financial system. Although the London Gold Pool no longer exists, its successor is the BIS Markets Committee, which meets every other month on the occasion of the governors' meetings to discuss trends in the financial markets. Officials from twenty-one central banks attend. The committee releases occasional papers, but its agenda and discussions remain secret.

Nowadays the countries represented at the Global Economy Meetings together account for around four-fifths of global gross domestic product (GDP)—most of the produced wealth of the world—according to the BIS's own statistics. Central bankers now "seem more powerful than politicians," wrote *The Economist* newspaper, "holding the destiny of the global economy in their hands."[10] How did this happen? The BIS, the world's most secretive global financial institution, can claim much of the credit. From its first day of existence, the BIS has dedicated itself to furthering the interests of central banks and building the new architecture of transnational finance. In doing so, it has spawned a new class of close-knit global technocrats whose members glide between highly-paid positions at the BIS, the IMF, and central and commercial banks.

The founder of the technocrats' cabal was Per Jacobssen, the Swedish economist who served as the BIS's economic adviser from 1931 to 1956. The bland title belied his power and reach. Enormously influential, well connected, and highly regarded by his peers, Jacobssen wrote the first BIS annual reports, which were—and remain—essential reading throughout the world's treasuries. Jacobssen was an early supporter of European federalism. He argued relentlessly against inflation, excessive government spending, and state intervention in the economy. Jacobssen left the BIS in 1956 to take over the IMF. His legacy still shapes our world. The consequences of his mix of economic liberalism, price obsession, and dismantling of national sovereignty play out nightly in the European news bulletins on our television screens.

The BIS's defenders deny that the organization is secretive. The bank's archives are open and researchers may consult most documents that are more than thirty years old. The BIS archivists are indeed cordial, helpful, and professional. The bank's website includes all its annual reports, which are downloadable, as well as numerous policy papers produced by the bank's highly regarded research department. The BIS publishes detailed accounts of the securities and derivatives markets, and international banking statistics. But these are largely compilations and analyses of information already in the public domain. The details of the bank's own core activities, including much of its banking operations for its customers, central banks, and international organizations, remain secret. The Global Economy Meetings and the other crucial financial gatherings that take place at Basel, such as the Markets Committee, remain closed to outsiders. Private individuals may not hold an account at BIS, unless they work for the bank. The bank's opacity, lack of unaccountability, and ever-increasing influence raises profound questions—not just about monetary policy but transparency, accountability, and how power is exercised in our democracies.

WHEN I EXPLAINED to friends and acquaintances that I was writing a book about the Bank for International Settlements, the usual response was a puzzled look, followed by a question: "The bank for what?" My interlocutors were intelligent people, who follow current affairs. Many had some interest in and understanding of the global economy and financial crisis. Yet only a handful had heard of the BIS. This was strange, as the BIS is the most important bank in the world and predates both the IMF and the World Bank. For decades it has stood at the center of a global network of money, power, and covert global influence.

The BIS was founded in 1930. It was ostensibly set up as part of the Young Plan to administer German reparations payments for the First World War. The bank's key architects were Montagu Norman, who was the governor of the Bank of England, and Hjalmar Schacht, the president of the Reichsbank who described the BIS as "my" bank. The BIS's founding members were the central banks of Britain, France, Germany, Italy, Belgium, and a consortium of Japanese banks. Shares were also offered to the Federal Reserve, but the United States, suspicious of anything that might infringe on its national sovereignty, refused its allocation. Instead a consortium of commercial banks took up the shares: J. P. Morgan, the First National Bank of New York, and the First National Bank of Chicago.

The real purpose of the BIS was detailed in its statutes: to "promote the co-operation of central banks and to provide additional facilities for international financial operations." It was the culmination of the central bankers' decades-old dream, to have their own bank—powerful, independent, and free from interfering politicians and nosy reporters. Most felicitous of all, the BIS was self-financing and would be in perpetuity. Its clients were its own founders and shareholders—the central banks. During the 1930s, the BIS was the central meeting place for a cabal of central bankers, dominated by Norman and Schacht. This group helped rebuild Germany. The *New York Times* described Schacht, widely acknowledged as the genius behind the resurgent German economy, as "The Iron-Willed Pilot of Nazi Finance."[11] During the war, the BIS became a de-facto arm of the Reichs-bank, accepting looted Nazi gold and carrying out foreign exchange deals for Nazi Germany.

The bank's alliance with Berlin was known in Washington, DC, and London. But the need for the BIS to keep functioning, to keep the new channels of transna-tional finance open, was about the only thing all sides agreed on. Basel was the perfect location, as it is perched on the northern edge of Switzerland and sits al-most on the French and German borders. A few miles away, Nazi and Allied sol-diers were fighting and dying. None of that mattered at the BIS. Board meetings were suspended, but relations between the BIS staff of the belligerent nations re-mained cordial, professional, and productive. Nationalities were irrelevant. The overriding loyalty was to international finance. The president, Thomas McKittrick, was an American. Roger Auboin, the general manager, was French. Paul Hechler, the assistant general manager, was a member of the Nazi party and signed his correspondence "Heil Hitler." Rafaelle Pilotti, the secretary general, was Italian. Per Jacobssen, the bank's influential economic adviser, was Swedish. His and Pi-lotti's deputies were British.

After 1945, five BIS directors, including Hjalmar Schacht, were charged with war crimes. Germany lost the war but won the economic peace, in large part thanks to the BIS. The international stage, contacts, banking networks, and legit-imacy the BIS provided, first to the Reichsbank and then to its successor banks, has helped ensure the continuity of immensely powerful financial and economic interests from the Nazi era to the present day.

FOR THE FIRST forty-seven years of its existence, from 1930 to 1977, the BIS was based in a former hotel, near the Basel central railway station. The bank's entrance was tucked away by a chocolate shop, and only a small notice confirmed that the narrow doorway opened into the BIS. The bank's managers believed that those who needed to know where the BIS was would find it, and the rest of the world certainly did not need to know. The inside of the building changed little over the decades, recalled Charles Coombs. The BIS provided the "the spartan accommodations of a former Victorian-style hotel whose single and double bedrooms had been transformed into offices simply by removing the beds and installing desks."[12]

The bank moved into its current headquarters, at 2, Centralbahnplatz, in 1977. It did not go far and now overlooks the Basel central station. Nowadays the BIS's main mission, in its own words, is threefold: "to serve central banks in their pursuit of monetary and financial stability, to foster international cooperation in these areas, and to act as a bank for central banks."[13] The BIS also hosts much of the practical and technical infrastructure that the global network of central banks and their commercial counterparts need to function smoothly. It has two linked trading rooms: at the Basel headquarters and Hong Kong regional office. The BIS buys and sells gold and foreign exchange for its clients. It provides asset management and arranges short-term credit to central banks when needed.

The BIS is a unique institution: an international organization, an extremely profitable bank and a research institute founded, and protected, by international treaties.[14] The BIS is accountable to its customers and shareholders—the central banks—but also guides their operations. The main tasks of a central bank, the BIS argues, are to control the flow of credit and the volume of currency in circulation, which will ensure a stable business climate, and to keep exchange rates within manageable bands to ensure the value of a currency and so smooth international trade and capital movements. This is crucial, especially in a globalized economy, where markets react in microseconds and perceptions of economic stability and value are almost as important as reality itself.

The BIS also helps to supervise commercial banks, although it has no legal powers over them. The Basel Committee on Banking Supervision, based at the BIS, regulates commercial banks' capital and liquidity requirements. It requires banks to have a minimum capital of eight percent of risk-weighted assets when lending, meaning that if a bank has risk-weighted assets of $100 million it must maintain at least $8 million capital.[15] The committee has no powers of enforcement, but it does have enormous moral authority. "This regulation is so powerful that the eight percent principle has been set into national laws," said Peter Akos Bod. "It's like voltage. Voltage has been set at 220. You may decide on ninety-five volts, but it would not work." In theory, sensible housekeeping and mutual cooperation, overseen by the BIS, will keep the global financial system functioning smoothly. In theory.

The reality is that we have moved beyond recession into a deep structural crisis, one fueled by the banks' greed and rapacity, which threatens all of our financial security. Just as in the 1930s, parts of Europe face economic collapse. The Bundesbank and the European Central Bank, two of the most powerful members of the BIS, have driven the mania for austerity that has already forced one European country, Greece, to the edge, aided by the venality and corruption of the country's ruling class. Others may soon follow. The old order is creaking, its political and financial institutions corroding from within. From Oslo to Athens, the far right is resurgent, fed in part by soaring poverty and unemployment. Anger and cynicism are corroding citizens' faith in democracy and the rule of law. Once again, the value of property and assets is vaporizing before their owners' eyes. The European currency is threatened with breakdown, while those with money seek safe haven in Swiss francs or gold. The young, the talented, and the mobile are again fleeing their home countries for new lives abroad. The powerful forces of international capital that brought the BIS into being, and which granted the bank its power and influence, are again triumphant.

The BIS sits at the apex of an international financial system that is falling apart at the seams, but its officials argue that it does not have the power to act as an international financial regulator. Yet the BIS cannot escape its responsibility for the Euro-zone crisis. From the first agreements in the late 1940s on multilateral payments to the establishment of the Europe Central Bank in 1998, the BIS has been at the heart of the European integration project, providing technical expertise and the financial mechanisms for currency harmonization. During the 1950s, it managed the European Payments Union, which internationalized the continent's payment system. The BIS hosted the Governors' Committee of European Economic Community central bankers, set up in 1964, which coordinated trans-European monetary policy. During the 1970s, the BIS ran the "Snake," the mechanism by which European currencies were held in exchange rate bands. During the 1980s the BIS hosted the Delors Committee, whose report in 1988 laid out the path to European Monetary Union and the adoption of a single currency. The BIS midwifed the European Monetary Institute (EMI), the precursor of the European Central Bank. The EMI's president was Alexandre Lamfalussy, one of the world's most influential economists, known as the "Father of the euro." Before joining the EMI in 1994, Lamfalussy had worked at the BIS for seventeen years, first as economic adviser, then as the bank's general manager.

For a staid, secretive organization, the BIS has proved surprisingly nimble. It survived the first global depression, the end of reparations payments and the gold standard (two of its main reasons for existence), the rise of Nazism, the Second World War, the Bretton Woods Accord, the Cold War, the financial crises of the 1980s and 1990s, the birth of the IMF and World Bank, and the end of Communism. As Malcolm Knight, manager from 2003–2008, noted, "It is encouraging to see that—by remaining small, flexible, and free from political interference—the Bank has, throughout its history, succeeded remarkably well in adapting itself to evolving circumstances."[16]

The bank has made itself a central pillar of the global financial system. As well as the Global Economy Meetings, the BIS hosts four of the most important international committees dealing with global banking: the Basel Committee on Banking Supervision, the Committee on the Global Financial System, the Committee on Payment and Settlement Systems, and the Irving Fisher Committee, which deals with central banking statistics. The bank also hosts three independent organizations: two groups dealing with insurance and the Financial Stability Board (FSB). The FSB, which coordinates national financial authorities and regulatory policies, is already being spoken of as the fourth pillar of the global financial system, after the BIS, the IMF and the commercial banks.

The BIS is now the world's thirtieth-largest holder of gold reserves, with 119 metric tons—more than Qatar, Brazil, or Canada.[17] Membership of the BIS remains a privilege rather than a right. The board of directors is responsible for admitting central banks judged to "make a substantial contribution to international monetary cooperation and to the Bank's activities." China, India, Russia, and Saudi Arabia joined only in 1996. The bank has opened offices in Mexico City and Hong Kong but remains very Eurocentric. Estonia, Latvia, Lithuania, Macedonia, Slovenia, and Slovakia (total population 16.2 million) have been admitted, while Pakistan (population 169 million) has not. Nor has Kazakhstan, which is a powerhouse of Central Asia. In Africa only Algeria and South Africa are members—Nigeria, which has the continent's second-largest economy, has not been admitted. (The BIS's defenders say that it demands high governance standards from new members and when the national banks of countries such as Nigeria and Pakistan reach those standards, they will be considered for membership.)

Considering the BIS's pivotal role in the transnational economy, its low profile is remarkable. Back in 1930 a *New York Times* reporter noted that the culture of secrecy at the BIS was so strong that he was not permitted to look inside the boardroom, even after the directors had left. Little has changed. Journalists are not allowed inside the headquarters while the Global Economy Meeting is underway. BIS officials speak rarely on the record, and reluctantly, to members of the press. The strategy seems to work. The Occupy Wall Street movement, the anti-globalizers, the social network protesters have ignored the BIS. Centralbahnplatz 2, Basel, is quiet and tranquil. There are no demonstrators gathered outside the BIS's headquarters, no protestors camped out in the nearby park, no lively reception committees for the world's central bankers.

As the world's economy lurches from crisis to crisis, financial institutions are scrutinized as never before. Legions of reporters, bloggers, and investigative journalists scour the banks' every move. Yet somehow, apart from brief mentions on the financial pages, the BIS has largely managed to avoid critical scrutiny. Until now.

PART ONE: **KAPITAL ÜBER ALLES**

CHAPTER ONE

THE BANKERS KNOW BEST

"I rather hope that next summer we may be able to inaugurate a private and eclectic Central Banks 'Club', small at first, large in the future."

— Montagu Norman, governor of the Bank of England, to Benjamin Strong, governor of the Federal Reserve Bank of New York, in 1925[1]

O
ne day in the summer of 1929, Montagu Norman, the governor of the Bank of England, picked up the telephone and spoke to Walter Layton, the editor of *The Economist*. Norman excitedly asked Layton to come to his office as soon as possible to discuss a very important matter.

During Norman's term as governor, from 1920 to 1944, he was one of the most influential men in the world, an apparently permanent bastion of the global financial system. His gnomic utterances were scoured for meaning. When he was re-appointed governor in 1932, the *New York Times* described him as overseeing Britain's "invisible empire of wealth." "Gold standards may come and go," the article noted, "but Montagu Norman remains."[2] Such was Norman's power that a single speech could move markets. When, in October 1932, Norman gloomily proclaimed at a bankers' dinner in London that the world's economic disorder was beyond the control of any man, government, or country, stocks, bonds, and the dollar all slid sharply and quickly in New York.

Layton was not surprised by Norman's agitated manner. The governor was a scion of an old and respected banking dynasty, but his mental state was an open secret among financial insiders. Norman was a mercurial figure, a manic-depressive, and a workaholic, notorious among financial insiders for his mood swings. Shy and hypersensitive, Norman was introverted to the point of neurosis. Before the

First World War, Norman had consulted Carl Jung, the Swiss founder of analytical psychology, to discuss a course of treatment, with no success. Jung had implied that Norman was untreatable, which did not help matters.

The world's most powerful banker abhorred publicity, being recognized or socializing, and was prone to fainting fits. He once threw an inkpot at the head of an underling who failed to meet his exacting standards. "He was a very unlikely banker. He was more like a seventeenth-century nobleman or painter," recalled his stepson, Peregrine Worsthorne. "He was always very neurotic and had very bad nervous breakdowns. He was very shy and a loner. He had no care for conventions. He came down to dinner without socks and traveled to work on the underground, which was very unusual in those days."[3]

Nor did Norman look the part of a sober financier, with his cape, neatly trimmed Van Dyke beard, and sparkling, jeweled tiepin. But despite his own flamboyant dress sense, he disapproved of showy behavior, said Worsthorne. "He lived very austerely and discouraged all signs of ostentation. He hated cocktail parties." Norman's horror of publicity naturally had precisely the opposite effect. Although when he sailed across the Atlantic he used an assumed name because the press covered his every move, hordes of journalists and photographers still awaited when he disembarked in New York.

The balmy months in 1929 were the last hurrah of the Roaring Twenties. The American bull market was still growing. Share prices kept rising. The value of stock in Radio Corporation of America (RCA) rose by almost 50 percent in a single month. Even Wall Street's shoeshine boys were passing on tips to their broker customers. In August a brokerage firm announced a new service for those heading to Europe on ocean liners: on-board trading during the weeklong crossing.

Layton, responding to Norman's summons, quickly made his way to the bank's headquarters at Threadneedle Street, the epicenter of the city, as London's financial quarter is known. Surrounded by a high wall, covering most of a city block, the bank's headquarters were meant to impress, even to intimidate. Behind the giant bronze door lay a complex of courtyards, banking halls, and a garden with a fountain, a veritable Alhambra of money, crowded with clerks and underlings who were bustling along its corridors. Even the terminology was regal: the bank was ruled over not by a board, but by a "court."

Layton was ushered into Norman's office where he sat at a mahogany table in the center of the wood-paneled room. Norman wanted to talk about a new bank, to be called the Bank for International Settlements. The BIS was being set up in connection with the Young Plan, the latest and hopefully final program for implementing German reparations payments for the First World War. But Norman had much more ambitious ideas. The BIS would be the world's first international financial institution. It would be a meeting place for central bankers. Away from the demands of politicians and the prying eyes of nosy journalists, the bankers would bring some much needed order and coordination to the world financial system. But for the BIS to succeed and properly fulfill its potential, Norman explained, he needed Layton's help. A subcommittee would soon meet in Baden-Baden, in Germany, to draw up the bank's statutes. The editor of *The Economist*, Norman said, was just the man to draft the BIS's constitution, one that must, above all, guarantee the bank's independence from politicians.

TO UNDERSTAND HOW and why the BIS wields such influence today, it is necessary to step back to the early 1920s and the arguments about German reparations payments for the First World War. German war guilt was enshrined in the 1919 Treaty of Versailles. But no amount of money could bring back the dead, whose numbers were almost incomprehensible. In July 1916, on the first day of the Battle of the Somme, Britain lost 60,000 men—the equivalent of a medium-sized town, mown down in a few hours. France lost a total of 1.4 million soldiers during the four years of fighting, and Germany lost 2 million. The United States, which did not enter the conflict until 1917, lost 117,000 men.

Reaching agreement on German reparations was a slow, complicated, and politically fraught task. The First World War had internationalized conflict to an unprecedented degree. Its financial fallout was similarly globalized. The war had exacted a terrible cost on Europe's economies, as well as its populations. The fledgling international financial system was ill-designed to deal with the complex demands that were now being placed on it. Where would Germany find the money to pay? What would be the mechanisms by which it would do so? Who would oversee and regulate the reparations payments? These arcane discussions shaped the role, structure, and privileged legal status of the BIS.

In 1919—just as there would be in 1945—there were, broadly, two schools of thought: the punishers and the rebuilders. France led the punishers. "Les Boches," said the French, must, and will, pay for their crimes, many of which were carried out on French soil. Norman and the rebuilders, who included most of Wall Street, believed otherwise. Europe could be reconstructed, but its future lay in trade and financial cooperation. The aim was not to reduce Germany to penury, but to help it fix its economy and start trading again as soon as possible.

In April 1921 the Reparations Commission announced that Germany would pay a total of 132 billion gold marks ($31.5 billion), payable at 2 billion marks a year. The commission might as well have demanded ten times as much. Germany was still reeling from its defeat, society was collapsing, unemployment soared, and there were severe shortages of food. Right-wing extremists—the Freikorps—battled Marxist militants in the streets. Workers' councils took control of Hamburg, Bremen, Leipzig, and central Berlin. This was not the salon Marxism of Greenwich Village or San Francisco, but the real thing—raw and bloody. Hostages were taken, factories were seized, and prisoners were lined up against walls and shot.

Karl Marx's predictions about the inevitable destruction of capitalism seemed to be becoming truer by the hour—especially in his homeland. The bankers' fears that Germany was about to follow Russia into Communism seemed entirely justified. Hyperinflation set in as the government printed money to keep the economy functioning. Shoppers used wheelbarrows to move the bundles of notes needed to buy basic staples. The chaos had to be stopped. On November 13, 1923, five days after Adolf Hitler's failed Beer Hall Putsch in Munich, a tall, imperious German started work as Reich currency commissioner. Hjalmar Schacht demanded, and got, near-dictatorial powers. Working out of a former janitor's closet, he set to work on stabilizing the value of Germany's new currency, the rentenmark. Currencies were usually backed by gold, but the rentenmark was backed by the value of Germany's land and holdings since there was no gold available to back the new currency. This was a somewhat hazy idea—how could the bearer of a rentenmark redeem his money? Would he be given a small piece of a field?

This concern did not matter. As long as Schacht was in office, nobody would want to redeem a rentenmark. He brilliantly understood the key point of the psychology of money, which is as valid today as it was in the hyperinflation of the 1920s: *the appearance of financial stability creates monetary value.* If people believed that someone was in charge, that the chaos would end, and that the rentenmark had value, then it would be valued. The first notes were printed on November 15, 1923. One rentenmark could be exchanged for one trillion old marks (1,000,000,000,000). One U.S. dollar cost 4.2 rentenmarks, a return to the pre-WWI exchange rate. The aim, Schacht said, was to "make German money scarce and valuable." Other than the logistics of printing and distributing the bank notes and convincing Schacht's foreign colleagues that order had been returned to the German economy, there was not that much more to it.

When German reporters asked Clara Steffeck, Schacht's secretary, what he did all day, she replied,

> *What did he do? He sat in his dark room, which smelled of old cleaning rags, and he smoked. Did he read letters? No. And he dictated no letters. But he phoned a lot all over the world, about domestic and foreign currency. Then he smoked some more. We didn't eat much. He usually left late and took public transportation to go home. That was all.*[4]

Not quite "all." Taxes were raised, and four hundred thousand German public employees were sacked. But the rentenmark successfully stopped the German inflation so well that on December 22, 1923, Schacht was promoted to be president of the Reichsbank, while retaining his position as currency commissioner. He could now attend cabinet meetings. "Within a few weeks," notes John Weitz, Schacht's biographer, "he had virtually become Germany's economic dictator."[5]

Schacht certainly looked the part of a strict Prussian banker: his hair was parted precisely down the middle, and his moustache flared briefly under his nose before stopping at a determined mouth. His eyes stared out suspiciously through a pair of pince-nez. He walked with a rigid, almost military manner and wore shirts with high celluloid collars. In fact he was not Prussian at all but was born in North Schleswig, in a land perennially shunted back and forth between Germany and Denmark. Whoever ruled the province, its inhabitants were a stubborn, hardy people. They adapted easily to their alternating masters but retained their tenacity and independence—qualities that would serve Schacht well. His grandfather, Wilhelm, was a country doctor who raised twelve children and charged every patient, rich or poor, sixty Pfennigs. Schacht's father, also called Wilhelm, was a schoolteacher who immigrated to the United States. He worked in a German brewery in Brooklyn and became a naturalized citizen. Hjalmar's mother was a feisty noblewoman, Baroness Constanze von Eggers.

The Schachts settled in New York City, but they did not prosper, and Wilhelm brought his family back to Europe. In 1876 they moved to Tinglev, now in Denmark, and the following year their second son was born. At first they wanted to name him in honor of Horace Greeley, an influential New York journalist and politician who campaigned against the slave trade. The baroness was proud of her radical views—her father had worked to abolish serfdom in Denmark. The infant's grandmother argued that the boy should at least have a proper Danish name first, so the family compromised on Hjalmar Horace Greeley Schacht.

The family was constantly on the move. They lived for a while in Hamburg and then relocated to Berlin. Hjalmar proved to be a diligent student. He enrolled at Kiel University and studied political economy. He worked as a journalist, tried public relations, and then joined the Dresdner Bank. His diligence, attention to detail, and austere manner helped ensure he was soon noticed. Schacht traveled to the United States with other bank officials. They met President Franklin Roosevelt and were invited to lunch in the partners' dining room at J. P. Morgan. Schacht's understanding of the world outside Germany, and his fluent English, proved invaluable. He was promoted to be deputy director of Dresdner Bank and joined the board of the Reichsbank.

So in 1923, with the rentenmark established, the next step was to build a gold reserve to give the new currency real backing. This is why, on the evening of December 31, the Reichsbank president stepped off the train at Liverpool Street station in central London. To Schacht's surprise and delight, he was met on the platform by Montagu Norman himself. "I do hope we shall become friends," said Norman, with a shy smile. Schacht told Norman that he wanted the Bank of England to lend $25 million to a new subsidiary of the Reichsbank, the Gold Discount Bank. The new bank would instantly alter global perceptions of the country's financial prospects. The imprimatur of the governor of the Bank of England would open doors throughout Wall Street and the City of London.

Tenacious as ever, Schacht got his money.

SCHACHT HAD SWEET-TALKED Norman, but the reparations question remained unresolved. America was tired of squabbling Europeans who could not get their houses in order and also recognized that there could be no lasting prosperity while Europe lurched from one financial crisis to another. A new reparations committee was set up under the chairmanship of Charles Dawes, an irascible American banker. The Dawes Committee met in Paris in January 1924. Owen D. Young, the president and chairman of the General Electric Company and the RCA, accompanied Dawes. Young was a consummate diplomat and needed to be. His job was to persuade France to ease the terms of the reparations schedule, which was destroying the German economy, and thus preventing a European recovery, and then to persuade Germany to accept much more stringent external control of its finances.

The Dawes Committee issued its recommendations on April 9. Germany's payments would be reduced for a while, and would increase later, after the economy had stabilized. That stabilization would be based in part on a loan of 800 million gold marks, to be floated on the international market. The German government would hold the funds in marks, which would then paid into an escrow account at the Reichsbank. This account would be controlled by a foreign official known as the agent-general, who could decide how the monies would be used and when they would be released—so as not to flood the markets and affect the value of the Reichsmark. The Reichsbank was placed under the control of a fourteen-man board of seven foreigners and seven Germans.

American companies rushed to invest in Germany. The Great War had triggered an economic boom in the United States. Unlike Europe, mainland America had been spared war damage. Its factories and farms and its mines and industrial plants were all untouched and operating at full capacity. The Dawes Plan loan was floated in New York and London in October and was quickly oversubscribed. American banks soon clamored to finance the companies now investing in the Germany economy.

Between 1924 and 1928, Germany borrowed $600 million a year, half of which was provided by American banks. Much of it swiftly returned from whence it had come. Like modern bailouts, the money swirled back and forth, raising and lowering balance sheets, boosting confidence and keeping the markets happy. As John Maynard Keynes wrote, "The United States lends money to Germany, Germany transfers its equivalent to the Allies, the Allies pay it back to the United States Government. Nothing real passes— no one is a penny the worse. The engravers' dies, the printers' forms are busier. But no one eats less, no one works more."[6] Some, like Schacht, believed that no one was a penny the better—and he was right. The vast sums were merely a financial adhesive strip. And in October 1929, when Wall Street crashed, American investors frantically pulled out of their German investments in droves.

Once again, Germany faced economic disaster. But if Weimar Germany defaulted, the global economy might crash. It was clear that the reparations issue had to be settled. Even Seymour Parker Gilbert, the agent-general in charge of implementing the Dawes Plan, argued that the country needed to take control of its financial destiny. Gilbert was not popular. In 1928 German nationalists staged his mock coronation. Ten thousand people watched his effigy crowned "the new German Kaiser who rules with a top hat for a crown and a coupon clipper for scepter."[7]

The answer to the never-ending German reparations question was, of course, another conference. This one was named after its chairman, Owen Young. The delegations arrived in Paris in February 1929 in the coldest winter for nearly a century. The gap between France and Germany over Germany's reparations bill was as cavernous as ever. Schacht made his opening offer: $250 million a year for the next thirty-seven years. Emil Moreau, the equally stubborn governor of the Bank of France, demanded $600 million a year for sixty-two years. Perhaps even that might not be enough, he informed Young. France might yet settle for nothing less than $1 billion.

Moreau refused to budge, and so did Schacht. Any initial optimism soon soured. The Germans were unnerved by the French secret police, who were tapping the German telephones. Schacht and his colleagues communicated with Berlin in coded telegrams. He traveled back every fortnight to consult with the government. Lord Revelstoke, the second in command of the British delegation, wrote in his diary that Schacht had resumed "his most negative attitude" was "unhelpful to the last degree." With his "hatchet, Teuton face and burly neck and badly fitting collar," he resembled "a sea-lion at the zoo."[8]

Whatever sum was finally agreed upon, there was at least some consensus that a new bank would be needed to manage Germany's reparations. Schacht and Norman argued that the new bank would keep the issue free of politics and manage it on a purely financial basis. This was unlikely, as there were no more politically charged issues than reparations, but it showed how the two governors both saw the benefit of a bank free of political constraints. Years later, Schacht titled his autobiography *The Old Wizard*. He certainly cast his spell over Owen Young. Germany was paying its reparations by borrowing from other countries, Schacht explained to the conference chairman. Such a system was no longer feasible. If the Allies really wanted Germany to be able to pay its obligations, the country needed to become productive again. Instead of lending to Germany, the Allies should lend to underdeveloped countries so they could buy their industrial equipment from Germany.

Young asked how such a plan could be put into practice. Schacht had a ready answer: by setting up a bank. "A bank of this kind," argued Schacht, "will demand financial cooperation between vanquished and victors that will lead to community of interests, which in turn will give rise to mutual confidence and understanding and thus promote and ensure peace." Schacht recalled the setting in his memoirs:

> *Owen Young, seated in his armchair, puffing away at his pipe, his legs outstretched, his great keen eyes fixed unswervingly on me. As is my habit when propounding such arguments, I was doing a quiet and steady "quarter deck" up and down the room. When I had finished there was a brief pause. Then his whole face lighted up and his resolve found utterance in words: "Dr. Schacht, you gave me a wonderful idea and I am going to sell it to the world."*[9]

The Allies then presented their proposal: Germany would pay $525 million a year for thirty-seven years and $400 million a year for the following twenty-one years.

Schacht would have none of it. He proclaimed that to meet these terms Germany must take possession again of all its former colonies, most of which were in Africa. He also demanded the return of the Danzig corridor, which linked Poland to the Baltic Sea, which would tear up the postwar peace treaty. When Moreau heard this he slammed the table with his fist and hurled his ink blotter across the room. A cartoon in a French newspaper summed up the local mood. It showed Moreau asking Schacht, "All right, Excellency, how much do we owe you?"

On April 19, 1929, Lord Revelstoke suddenly died. The Young Conference was adjourned. All sides finally reached agreement on June 7. Germany would pay almost $29 billion, over fifty-eight years. Control of German economic policy was returned to Berlin. A new bank would administer the payments. Schacht wrote of its birth: "In the meantime my idea of a Bank for International Settlements had met with such enthusiastic response from all those taking part in the Young Conference that soon there was not one among them who would not have liked to claim the suggestion as his own."[10] As the delegates signed the final version, the curtains in the meeting hall caught fire.

The Young Plan was accepted in principle at the First Hague Conference, and seven committees were set up to work out the technical details. At Schacht's suggestion, the seventh, the Organization Committee, gathered in Baden-Baden. This was the most important committee, and it was responsible for drafting the statutes of the new bank and its relations with the host country, which would regulate its legal status. The delegates argued about governance, the role of the directors and managers, and even the official language of the new bank's statutes. It was eventually agreed that both the French and English texts would be authentic. The bank would hold central banks' gold and convertible currency deposits. These deposits could be used to settle international payments without having to either physically move the gold between banks or trade the currency through foreign exchange markets. The BIS would be an international clearinghouse for central banks, the world's first. And with the broad outline settled, the next question was where the new bank should be located. Montagu Norman and the British government pushed for London. France objected, on principle, and argued that the new bank should be located in a small country. There was some talk of Amsterdam, and finally the delegates settled on Basel, Switzerland, which was conveniently located on several international railway lines and on the borders of France and Germany.

MEANWHILE IN LONDON, Walter Layton, the editor of *The Economist*, was still grappling with the new bank's constitution. The key point, as Layton recalled, was to "work out some form of words that would place the bank beyond the reach of governments." Layton "struggled hopelessly" and then told Norman that he had failed.

"Why do you insist it can't be done?" Norman demanded, annoyed.

"Because it's the right of every democratic government to reserve its freedom of action," Layton replied—an argument that would resonate through the decades.[11] Layton admitted defeat. The constitution was eventually drafted by one of the many committees set up to establish the BIS. But Norman was victorious: the bank's statutes, still extant today, enshrined its absolute independence from interfering politicians and governments. As for Schacht, chastened and unhappy about the reparations demands of the Young Plan, he traveled to the spa of Marienbad, in Czechoslovakia, to spend time with his wife, Luise. Narrowminded, rigid, and intensely Prussian (as he later described her), Luise met him at the train station. She shouted, "You should never have signed."

But Schacht, and Montagu Norman, had their bank.

CHAPTER TWO

A COZY CLUB
IN BASEL

*"The hangover of secrecy was, indeed, so strong that
the attendants would not permit a look into that sacred
room even after all the directors had left."*

— Clarence K. Streit, on the BIS boardroom after the directors'
meeting, writing in the *New York Times Magazine,* July 1930

In September 1930, a few months after the BIS opened for business, an American lawyer named Allen Dulles sat down in his office at 37 Rue Cambon, in Paris, to write a letter to Leon Fraser. Fraser, a fellow American, was also a lawyer. A former reporter for the *New York World* newspaper, Fraser had served as general counsel for the execution of the Dawes Plan and had taken part in the negotiations at Baden-Baden on the structure of the BIS. Fraser was now a board member of the BIS and the bank's alternating president.

Dulles was confident that his request, which was simple enough, would be granted. After all, he was a scion of one of the most powerful families in the United States. His uncle, Robert Lansing, had served as secretary of state, as had his grandfather, John W. Foster. Born in 1893, in Watertown, New York, Dulles had graduated from Princeton University and joined the US Foreign Service. He was posted to Vienna, Austria, until the United States entered the war in 1917, when he moved to Bern, Switzerland, to work as a junior intelligence officer at the US Legation. Neutral Switzerland, home to squabbling émigrés, businessmen, and revolutionaries, provided a bountiful harvest of information. "It is almost impossible to stop for any length of time in Switzerland," Dulles wrote, "without coming into contact with questionable characters. Bern is just full of agents and representatives of all nationalities."[1]

Dulles relished the world of shadows. Even as a precocious schoolboy, he had shown an insatiable appetite for intrigue and geopolitics. He wrote his first book at the age of seven. *The Boer War* was short treatise on how the Boers, the Dutch settlers, had first claim on southern Africa, as they had arrived there before their British overlords. (Montagu Norman, who fought in the Second Boer War, at the start of the twentieth century, might have disagreed.) Seven hundred copies were privately printed and sold at fifty cents each, with the proceeds being donated to a Boer charity.

But the future director of the CIA did not always know how to assess a potential source. He later loved to recount the story of how one day in April 1917 the telephone rang at the US Legation in Bern. Dulles took the call. A Russian émigré leader urgently wanted to meet with an American diplomat. Dulles refused, as he wanted to play tennis instead. The next day the man who had telephoned left Switzerland on a sealed train for the Finland Station—a railway station in St. Petersburg, Russia. The city would later be renamed Leningrad in his honor. From Bern, Dulles was dispatched to Paris, as part of the US team at the 1919 Paris Peace Conference. Officially, he was included as a member of the commission drawing up the boundary of the new state of Czechoslovakia. In fact, Dulles was running the American diplomatic intelligence operation for central Europe and courting and monitoring its émigrés, exiles, and revolutionaries.

By 1930, when Dulles wrote to Leon Fraser, Dulles had left the Foreign Service. He and his brother, John Foster Dulles, became partners at Sullivan & Cromwell—the most powerful law firm in the United States, if not the world—headquartered at 48 Wall Street, in New York. Allen Dulles ran Sullivan & Cromwell's office in Paris and knew Hjalmar Schacht well. In Paris in 1919, Dulles had learned about diplomacy. And in Paris in 1930, he would learn about the world of high finance and the BIS. Dulles, wrote biographer Peter Grose, was "plunged into a realm where sovereign frontiers were transparent and the trappings of democracies seldom allowed to penetrate. Like beguiled readers of Eric Ambler or Graham Greene, Allen discovered that only a thin line divided respectable high finance from a shadowy underworld."[2]

While Montagu Norman and Hjalmar Schacht had exploited the chaos around the German reparations question to finesse the world's leading powers into creating the BIS, the Dulles brothers used Europe's disorder to broker deals and monetary instruments to refinance Germany that were so complex that few outside their offices at Sullivan & Cromwell could understand them.

Much of this web was connected to the BIS, via the Dulles brothers and their friends on Wall Street and in London and Germany. New York banks had led the way during the 1920s in raising money for Germany, and the City of London had also provided significant funds. Foremost among the British banks was J. Henry Schröder, the London operation of the well-established German banking firm of the same name that was based in Hamburg. Schröder, in London, set up a trust to invest in numerous German firms, including IG Farben, Siemens, and Deutsche Bank. Frank Tiarks, who was a partner in the London branch of Schröder, set up a subsidiary in New York, called Schrobanco. It opened for business in October 1923 and was an instant success. The president of Schrobanco was an American banker named Prentiss Gray, who was a close friend of John Foster Dulles's, whom Gray had met at the Paris Peace Conference. Schröder's historic German connections and contacts made that country a natural focus of Schrobanco's. The company quickly became one of the leading agents for doing business in Germany and later, for processing loans under the Dawes and Young reparations plans. Among Schrobanco's shareholders were a number of German, Swiss, and Austrian private banks, which included, naturally, the Hamburg branch of J. Henry Schröder, as well as a bank called J. H. Stein of Cologne. One of J. H. Stein's partners, who was a scion of the Schröder dynasty, would later join the board of the BIS and use J. H. Stein to funnel money from German industrialists to Heinrich Himmler's personal slush fund.

Frank Tiarks was a director of the Bank of England and a close colleague of Montagu Norman. Tiarks had his eye on an American financier named Gates McGarrah, whom Tiarks wanted to recruit to the board of Schrobanco. McGarrah, whom Tiarks described as "one of the most important American bankers," was a director of the Federal Reserve Bank of New York. He also had excellent connections in Germany—he had represented the United States at the Reichsbank when it was held under international control. McGarrah stayed on the Schrobanco board until 1927 when he returned to the Federal Reserve Bank of New York as chairman. He stayed there until 1930—when he was appointed the first president of the BIS. As for Schrobanco, its complicated German investments were in good hands: the bank's lawyer was Allen Dulles. The links were so close that in 1929 Schrobanco moved into spacious new offices at 48 Wall Street—the same building that housed Sullivan & Cromwell.

ALLEN DULLES HAD a simple request for Leon Fraser that autumn of 1930. His sister, Eleanor Lansing Dulles, had received a scholarship from Harvard University to write a book about the BIS. Eleanor Dulles was a well-regarded academic and currency expert, who had previously written a book about the French franc. Allen Dulles wrote, "Anything you can do for her would be greatly appreciated, and I can assure you she is a very discreet person."[3] Like her brothers, Eleanor Dulles also had easy access to the world's most powerful bankers and financiers.

Allen Dulles's letter was not the first Fraser had received that asked him to assist Eleanor. Owen Young had written in May of that year. And Gates McGarrah, the BIS president, was also getting letters about Eleanor Dulles. Paul Warburg, the eminent banker, had written to McGarrah from the headquarters of M. M. Warburg at 40 Wall Street, in New York. Warburg explained that Eleanor was a "sister of my good friend John Foster Dulles, whose name is well known to you as a writer on international questions and whom you undoubtedly know personally."[4]

Jackson Reynolds, president of the First National Bank of New York, who had chaired the BIS Organization Committee in Baden-Baden, wrote to McGarrah from 2 Wall Street. He asked McGarrah to assist Miss Dulles—especially as she was the sister of Reynolds' friend, John Foster Dulles.

There were few, if any, people in the United States then with a more powerful and influential set of friends than John Foster Dulles, who served as legal counsel to the US delegation at the Paris Peace Conference, where he had specialized in German war reparations. His time in Paris gave him a privileged insight into the workings of international finance and diplomacy and a network of coveted contacts. Dulles's client list during the 1920s read like a who's who of American finance: J. P. Morgan; Kuhn, Loeb & Co.; Harris, Forbes & Co.; Brown Brothers; W. A. Harriman; and Goldman Sachs. Dulles arranged tens of millions of dollars' worth of loans to clients, including to the cities of Munich, Frankfurt, Nuremberg, Berlin, and Hanover, and to the Union of German Mortgage Banks, the Berlin City Electric Company, Hamburg Street Railways, and the State of Prussia. Dulles also worked on the Dawes Plan German Loan in 1924 and the German Government International Loan of 1930 that had been instigated by the Young Committee.[5]

Wall Street in the 1920s was possessed by a near-mania to lend to Germany. In 1923 American banks and finance houses sent abroad $458 million in long-term capital. By 1928 that sum had risen to $1.6 billion. The German credit bubble reached ludicrous extremes. A small village in Bavaria, which needed around $125,000, was persuaded to borrow $3 million.[6] But the real significance of this flow of capital was not just financial. The bonds between the American bankers, businessmen, and industrialists, and their German counterparts, would prove far more durable than the doomed Weimar Republic, and even the Third Reich. With the BIS as the central point of contact, these links would endure during the Second World War and reshape Europe after 1945.

Allen Dulles returned to Bern during the Second World War, as a far more experienced, powerful, and influential spymaster, harvesting much information through his assets at the BIS. John Foster Dulles went on to become US Secretary of State for the Eisenhower administration during the 1950s at the height of the Cold War. The Dulles brothers would help ensure that Nazi bankers, businessmen, and industrialists—many of whom should have been tried for war crimes—were seamlessly integrated back into powerful positions in the new Federal Republic of Germany.

FOR HJALMAR SCHACHT and Montagu Norman, January 20, 1930, was a date to savor: they had created a bank beyond the reach of either national or international law. On that date the governments of the United Kingdom,

France, Germany, Belgium, Italy, Japan, and Switzerland signed an extraordinary document. The Hague Convention guaranteed that the BIS would be the world's most privileged and legally protected bank. Its statutes, which remain in force to this day, essentially make the BIS untouchable. Article 10 of the BIS Constituent Charter noted,

> *The Bank, its property and assets and all deposits and other funds entrusted to it shall be immune in time of peace and in time of war from any measure such as expropriation, requisition, seizure, confiscation, prohibition or restriction of gold or currency export or import, and any other similar measures.*

The BIS enjoys the legal privileges of an international organization, but, arguably, it is not one as usually understood by the term. It is a highly profitable bank that is accountable to, and controlled by, its members: central banks. Under the cover of the Young Plan, as well as the need for an impartial financial institution to administer German reparation payments, Norman, Schacht, and the central bankers had by brilliant sleight of hand created a bank with unprecedented powers and privileges. As Gianni Toniolo, the official historian of the BIS, notes,

> *It was no accident that, although the settlement of the reparations problems had been the immediate cause for setting up the BIS, the bank's statutes defined its actual purpose much more broadly:*
> *To promote the co-operation of central banks and to provide additional facilities for international financial operations; and to act as trustee or agent in regard to international financial settlements entrusted to it under agreements with the parties concerned.*[7]

In February 1930, the governors of the central banks of Britain, France, Italy, Germany, and Belgium gathered with representatives from Japan and three American banks to sign the BIS's instrument of foundation. As the Federal Reserve Bank of New York was not permitted to own shares, for political reasons, a consortium was formed—J. P. Morgan, the First National Bank of New York, and the First National Bank of Chicago—to represent the United States. The BIS formally came into existence on February 27, 1930. The bank's initial share capital was set at 500 million Swiss francs, which was divided into 200,000 shares of 2,500 gold francs. The governors of the founding central banks were ex officio members of the board of directors. Each could appoint a second director of the same nationality. The second director did not have be a central banker. He could be drawn from finance, industry, or commerce—a provision that would later prove crucial in ensuring Nazi influence over the BIS.

The BIS was incorporated under Swiss law. Its authorized activities included the following:

- buying, selling and holding gold for its own account or for central banks
- buying and selling securities other than shares
- accepting deposits from central banks
- opening and maintaining deposit accounts with central banks
- acting as an agent of or correspondent for central banks
- entering agreements to act as a trustee or agent in connection with international settlements

There were some restrictions that were intended to prevent the BIS from becoming a competitor of commercial banks. The bank could not issue banknotes, open accounts for individuals or commercial organizations, own property other than its headquarters or offices, or have a controlling interest in a business. (The immunities granted under international treaty for reparations settlements did not apply to all of its banking operations to ensure that it maintained the confidence of the international markets.)

Even better, although the BIS was protected by international treaty, unlike the League of Nations, it was not dependent on budgetary contributions from its members. It enjoyed a guaranteed revenue stream from the reparations payments that it would manage under the Young Plan, as well as from the highly profitable services it would carry out for its clients, the central banks. In the final analysis, notes Toniolo, the BIS, "although founded by an international treaty sanctioned by national governments, was very much tailored to the views and requirements of the national banks."[8] The key provisions of the bank's statutes were given "protected" status and so could only be changed with the consent of all signatories to the Hague Convention.

The BIS was quickly inundated with job applications, even though it was located in humdrum Basel. Its comparatively modest headquarters at the Grand Hôtel et Savoy Hôtel Univers, next door to Basel main railway station at least offered convenient direct connections to Paris, Vienna, Milan, and Geneva. An article in the *New York Times Magazine*, headlined "The Cashless Bank that Deals in Millions," reported,

> *There is only one bank in Basel that does not look like a million dollars. It is the super-bank. Indeed, it is doubtful if there is anywhere a bank that looks less like a bank than does the Bank for International Settlements. . . . There is no "Bank for International Settlements" stretching in big solid letters across its façade. There is no ostentatiously small bronze plaque at the door. There is nothing at all to reveal its identity to the passer-by.[9]*

Nor did the building sound like a bank. There were no counters where banknotes rustled, no adding machines, nor even the sound of a pen scratching on a ledger. The monies did not physically move through the BIS. When Germany made a reparations payment, it informed the BIS that the Reichsbank had credited the BIS's account in Berlin. The BIS then informed the national banks of those countries receiving reparations, such as, for example, Britain, that the monies were available to draw on, if they so wished. If they did not, in case the movement of substantial sums might affect exchange rates, the funds remained in the BIS's account. In the meantime, the BIS used the funds earmarked for Britain to buy securities—which it could sell if and when Britain wanted to draw its monies.

That was the theory. The practice, at least at first, was not quite so smooth. In February 1931, Gates McGarrah, the bank's American president, wrote to H. C. F. Finlayson, in Athens, asking about the Bank of Greece's gold. Finlayson, a former British financial attaché in Berlin, was now an adviser to the Bank of Greece. Some of the Greek bank's gold may have gone missing. Rather like nowadays, it seemed the accounting at the Bank of Greece left something to be desired. "What has ever happened to the gold of the Bank of Greece, some of which you thought might be left in our custody in Paris or elsewhere?" inquired McGarrah, who, as the president of the BIS might have been expected to know what it held and where.[10] It might, McGarrah suggested, be a good time to find the Greek gold and place it with the BIS.

The BIS, wrote McGarrah, could give the Bank of Greece "all sorts of facilities, rather greater than those of a local Central Bank."[11] For example, if the Bank of Greece held gold at the Bank of France and wanted to buy another currency, it first had to buy francs from the Bank of France. The Bank of Greece then converted the francs to the second currency, with all the usual losses of exchange rates and commissions. However, if the Bank of Greece held gold at the Bank of France in the name of the BIS, the BIS could "give the Bank of Greece any currency it desires at any time and can fix an agreed rate without going through the actual exchange operation."[12] And, the BIS did not charge any commission.

Thirteen thousand people applied for jobs at the BIS, and by the end of 1930 ninety-five people worked there. However, few were bankers—many were lawyers or economists who had previously been employed at international organizations such as the League of Nations or the Dawes Plan Agent General's office. Salaries were comparatively high: the president received $36,000 plus $14,000 entertainment allowance. Heads of department were paid between $15,000 and $20,000 a year, all tax free. (The average American salary in 1930 was about $2,000 a year.) The management reflected the balance of nationalities: the general manager, Pierre Quesnay, was French and a former member of the Young Committee. His German deputy, Ernst Hülse, had worked for the Reichsbank.

But not everyone was happy. Hjalmar Schacht, who loved to refer to the BIS as "my bank," continued to rage over the scale of reparations under the Young Plan. In December 1929 he wrote to J. P. Morgan that he would not take up his directorship at the BIS. The following March, Schacht resigned from the Reichsbank. Hans Luther, a former minister of finance and former German Chancellor, replaced him. Schacht returned to his old métier: public relations. That autumn he went on a lecture tour across Europe and the United States. He passed the time during the journey across the Atlantic by reading Adolf Hitler's *Mein Kampf*. The style was crude and hectoring, he believed, but the author displayed a "keen brain."[13] Wherever Schacht spoke, he gave the same address: fulminating against the Young Plan, the Versailles Treaty, and reparations. He even appeared with John Foster Dulles at a dinner hosted by the Foreign Policy Association at the Astor Hotel in New York. Dulles played down the German elections in September 1930 in which the Nazis won 107 seats, making them the second largest party. The "difficulties" claimed Dulles, "are of a character which are largely psychological and consequently subject to ready reversal."[14]

Dulles's prediction was widely shared by his fellow financiers, especially those in Germany. Hans Luther, the new Reichsbank president, was especially keen to reassure his American colleagues that the surge in Nazi support would not disrupt the smooth flow of international finance. On September 22, eight days after the German election, Gates McGarrah, the BIS president, wrote to his friend and former colleague at the New York Federal Reserve, George Harrison, who was now its president:

> *We have the strongest assurances from Dr. Luther that we need not be disturbed about the result of the election. . . . The German people are not revolutionary and in our opinion anything beyond occasional street brawls will be summarily dealt with.*[15]

Not everyone shared McGarrah's faith. Investors rushed to sell Reichmarks. Paradoxically, the political and financial uncertainty was good for the BIS, giving the new bank an early opportunity to intervene in the money markets. The bank launched a rescue operation for the German currency. The next day, on September 23, McGarrah sent a telegram to Harrison: "Confidentially we intervened today on several markets to the tune of £300,000 with very helpful psychological effect, including cessation of offer of marks."[16] But in thinking that the reparations issue would settle down in Germany under the BIS's influence, Luther and McGarrah were wrong. The Young Plan, like German democracy, was a terminal case.

ON MAY 19, 1931, McGarrah presented the BIS's first annual report to the first general meeting. He noted that the bank had assisted with international financial operations and capital movement, where the "opportunities for constructive service are almost boundless,"[17] then he turned to the numbers. Profit making, noted McGarrah demurely, had "never been a primary object" of the BIS—which surely made him a banker unique in history. But he was pleased to report that thrifty investing during the bank's first ten and half months of existence had brought net profits of 11,186,521.97 Swiss francs. He noted that shareholders had increased from the original seven to twenty-three, including the national banks of Greece, Romania, Hungary, Latvia, Lithuania and Estonia, Sweden, and Czechoslovakia. The small, new European countries such as Czechoslovakia—a fragile construct carved out of the remains of the Austro-Hungarian empire—doubtless hoped that a stake in the BIS would bring stability, credibility, an improved standing in the sinternational community, and even a measure of defense against predatory neighbors. It would prove to be a faint hope.

But for now the bankers were celebrating. Norman and Schacht had invented a perpetual money machine.

CHAPTER THREE

A MOST USEFUL BANK

"The post of Head of Section in the BIS is for Germany's foreign policy definitely as important as the posting of many ambassadors accredited with foreign governments."

— Karl Blessing, Reichsbank official, 1930[1]

S chacht's colleagues in Berlin had a very particular view of the role of the BIS—one quite different to that which the Allies had envisaged when signing the Hague Convention. The bank set up to administer reparations was to be used to wreck them. Karl Blessing, a protégé of Schacht, wrote a lengthy memorandum in April 1930, setting out policy on the BIS. "Opinion on how the Reichsbank should conduct itself in the BIS" called for Germany to gain as much influence at the BIS as possible. German employees of the bank, Blessing wrote, should make sure that "no important business decisions are made without a German representative having knowledge of them or having had an opportunity to express their opinion."[2] Blessing recognized the bank's importance for Germany's national interest. He called for Germany to fill its posts in the bank with the most able and perceptive individuals.

All BIS member states wanted to protect their national interests in the new international forum. But Blessing understood what many bankers did not: that while the BIS might portray itself as neutral, objective, and technocratic, the bank was an inherently political institution, dealing with one of the most contested and bitter issues in politics—German war guilt and reparations. Blessing wrote, "The fact that the reparation question has been delegated to a banking institution naturally turns this bank into a political institution, even if this is officially denied."[3]

France and Britain might believe that the establishment of the bank settled the reparations issue, but Blessing understood that the existence of the BIS actually offered a forum to open up the issue once again. Blessing's savvy ruthlessness was in sharp contrast to Montagu Norman's notion of a cozy club. The Reichsbank, Blessing argued, should certainly cooperate with the BIS in its new role as the bank for central banks. As a trading nation that relied on exports, Germany could only benefit from an improved international economy. Reparations, however, were an entirely different matter.

Blessing called for German officials to undermine the new bank by making impossible demands that would sour the atmosphere and weaken its credibility. He demanded a sophisticated form of psychological warfare against the BIS. German officials there must "time and again refer to the completely utopian objectives of the bank." German bankers should repeatedly ask the BIS to guarantee export credits for high-risk ventures, even when it was clear that the credits would never be granted. The aim was to "gradually create an atmosphere in the Bank in which the anti-reparation bacillus finds fertile ground."[4] If the bank began to lose legitimacy, then so surely would the Young Plan, which the bank was mandated to administer. In 1931 Blessing left the Reichsbank to take up a senior post at the BIS.

But even with Blessing on board, the BIS could not solve the German financial crisis. The elections in 1931, which saw the Nazis and Communists win one-third of the seats in the Reichstag, had made the country almost ungovernable. That political instability triggered capital flight, which caused a further rise in unemployment and a lack of confidence in both government and the banking system and led to further capital flight, higher unemployment, and more support for the Nazis and the Communists. The Weimar Republic had entered its death spiral.

In June 1931 Chancellor Heinrich Bruning declared that he doubted if Germany could meet the next payment due under the Young Plan. The situation was so grave President Herbert Hoover called for a moratorium on all war debts and reparations. It was agreed, for one year. The Bank of England, the Bank of France, the New York Federal Reserve, and the BIS agreed on an emergency loan to Germany of $100 million.

As Toniolo notes, the "newborn BIS was at the heart of the first experiment ever of a multilateral attempt at managing an international financial crisis."[5] It was not successful, but then it was never likely to be. Fixing the German debt crisis was a task far beyond the BIS, even if the BIS had been created expressly for the purpose of facilitating reparations.

In December 1931 the German minister of finance wrote to the BIS, saying that as Germany was suffering a "crisis without parallel" the bank must re-examine the whole question of reparations. The BIS set up a committee, headed by an Italian board member, Alberto Beneduce, to examine the matter. Carl Melchior, a prominent German Jewish banker and vice chairman of the BIS, represented Germany. Melchior had served as a captain in the German army in the First World War, in which he was badly wounded. A skilled diplomat and financier, Melchior had been a member of the German delegation at the Paris Peace Conference in 1919. He had represented Germany on the Young Committee and chaired the finance committee of the League of Nations. His tact and skills had helped Germany re-enter the community of nations. The Beneduce Committee's conclusions, published just before Christmas 1931, were a triumph for Berlin. All intergovernmental reparations and war debts must be "adjusted" to ensure peace and economic stability. "Adjustment" was a euphemism for abolition. Six months later, in 1932, European governments met in Lausanne to consider the Beneduce Committee's recommendations. They agreed to cancel German reparations, except for one final payment.

THE BIS PRESENTED itself as a new and modern institution, but central banks and war had been entwined through history. The Bank of England had been founded in 1694 in part to raise funds for King William III's war against France. The bank accepted deposits and issued personal notes against the funds, which could be redeemed for gold. Clerks added the customer's personal details to the document, the precursor of today's banknotes. A little more than a century later, in 1800, Napoleon Bonaparte founded the Bank of France. The emperor aimed to bring about stability and economic growth after the wars and revolutionary turmoil of the late eighteenth century. The Reichsbank was founded in 1876 in part to finance future German expansionism, after the Franco-Prussian war of 1870 had triggered a liquidity crisis. The German bankers had planned ahead. A law suspending gold convertibility of Reichsmarks in time of war was drafted in1904.[6] By the summer of 1914, the approaching war had triggered a run on the Reichsbank reserves. In July the Reichsbank lost 103 million marks in a week. The bank suspended gold convertibility, which was an illegal act. Parliament passed an act retrospectively authorizing that decision four days later.[7]

Yet there was also an argument in favor of empowering the financial technocrats to get on with running the global economy, unbound by political considerations. It was the politicians and governments, some of them democratically elected—not the bankers—who had led the world to war and caused the deaths of millions. The bankers would finance their political masters' conflicts, as they were required to do, but they had no desire to order men to walk into a hail of bullets to gain an inch of mud-soaked field in Belgium. Rather, the central bankers shared similarly benign aims: stability, economic growth, and increased prosperity for all. The central bankers formed a global brotherhood, united by common bonds that transcended parochial national interests. In an era when nationalism had ripped apart the old European order, perhaps the bankers' transnationalism could bring peace. The BIS, had after all, been specifically designed in the aftermath of war for that purpose. By managing Germany's reparation payments and acting as a trustee for the Dawes and Young loans that had allowed Germany to meet its international obligations, the bank should, theoretically, defuse the explosive German question.

The bankers' personal friendships could be deep and enduring. The bond between Norman and Schacht, for example, lasted for almost thirty years, until Norman died in 1950. It outlasted the hyperinflation of the early 1920s, the stock market crash of 1929, the collapse of the Weimar Republic, the rise and fall of the Third Reich, Schacht's trial at Nuremberg for war crimes, the disintegration of the British Empire, the onset of the Cold War, and the division of Germany. Such deep connections between powerful men were rare and potentially valuable.

Even the BIS's more nebulous mandate of central bank cooperation had its defenders. Economists and bankers had long argued that as the world economy became more sophisticated, and central banks became more powerful, there was a need for some kind of coordinating body to ensure financial stability. Julius Wolff, a professor at the University of Breslau, had proposed in 1892 that a new financial institution in a neutral country be set up to issue an international currency. The new unit would be backed by central banks' gold reserves and be used for emergency lending to countries in crisis. Luigi Luzatti, an Italian politician, wrote in 1907 in the Viennese newspaper *Neue Freie Presse* that central banks were waging an unnecessary "monetary war" by competing for gold supplies by raising interest rates and other devices. It would be far better, he posited, for banks to adopt a policy of "cordial cooperation" by supplying gold to those banks that needed it. He called for a new commission to coordinate "international monetary peace," since even when central banks did lend to each other, national interests colored those loans. Thus there was a need for a technical, apolitical institution to handle these transactions, a financial equivalent of the postal and telegraph unions. The BIS seemed to fit the bill.

The bank was also a creature of its time, of new multilateral institutions run by apolitical technocrats. The League of Nations, which was the forerunner of the United Nations, would defuse the world's political crises, while the BIS would ensure financial stability. Pierre Mendes-France, a French Socialist politician, wrote in July 1930, that the BIS, after administering the Young Plan, "will progressively increase its patch and little by little the experience will show the areas that it may approach safely."[8] Mendes-France, who served as prime minister in the 1950s, praised the BIS and the League as the potential harbingers of peace. "In the mists of the future, the mystical purpose of a union in financial order . . . under wise and prudent management," he wrote, "may become a potent aid for the preservation of world peace."[9]

The US government took a very different view. The BIS was born out of reparations negotiations chaired by two Americans, Charles Dawes and Owen Young. Its first presidents, Gates McGarrah and Leon Fraser, were American.

But Henry Stimson, the secretary of state, proclaimed that the United States did not wish to "directly or indirectly participate in the collection of German reparations through the agency of a bank or otherwise."[10] The United States had never asked for reparations, thus it had no reason to participate in the BIS. It had not even joined the League of Nations, even though President Woodrow Wilson had practically invented the institution. The State Department's opposition to the BIS was so strong that George Harrison, the governor of the New York Federal Reserve, even avoided Basel when he traveled to Europe. Washington, DC, refused the BIS directorship offered to the Federal Reserve. The consortium of American banks—J. P. Morgan, the First National Bank of New York, and the First National Bank of Chicago—that had bought shares at the bank's founding took up the directorship instead.

Eleanor Lansing Dulles, however, was firmly in the internationalist camp. She published her book on the BIS in 1932, despite some difficulties when she was rumored to be an American spy and then lost her office and access to internal documents. McGarrah, the bank's president, wrote of his regret to John Foster Dulles that the bank could not have been more open to her. "I am sorry not to have been able to be more useful to your sister, and we would have been glad to open everything up to her, including an office here, but . . . the work of this bank, like that of any other is in large measure confidential."[11]

Eleanor Dulles was by far the most attractive of the Dulles siblings. She was a feisty career woman with a sharp mind of her own in an age that did not welcome such women. Her personal life was marked by tragedy—a pronounced anti-Nazi, she fell in love with David Blondheim, a Jewish intellectual, and married him, to the dismay of her family. He later committed suicide. Eleanor Dulles went on to enjoy a stellar career in the US Foreign Service, specializing in Germany. In *The BIS at Work*, she described a smooth-running institution, a kind of financial League of Nations, where different nationalities worked in harmonious cooperation. The bank was a future model for the world and should have been granted stronger powers to prevent national interests asserting each themselves. "If the BIS is not given the power and the facilities to work at this problem the result will be the emergence of financial rivalries," she warned.

> *One central bank after another will gain a predominating influence and as this central bank is threatened from time to time by rival financial influence, the stability of the economic system will be strained to the breaking point again as it has been in 1931. It is to avoid such catastrophes that the BIS should be strengthened to meet the urgent needs which lie before it.*[12]

Unfortunately for Eleanor Dulles and her fellow idealists, Blessing and Schacht's plan for the BIS was about to come to fruition. The new regime in Germany would exploit the BIS's supranational reach to advance its own national interests. By April 1933 the Nazi terror had begun in earnest. Legalistic as ever, the German legislators had voted their democracy out of existence. The Enabling Act, passed by the Reichstag the previous month, removed citizens' rights to free speech, assembly, travel, and protest. It permitted arbitrary arrest, torture, and detention. Germany was now a racially based dictatorship. On April 1 Nazi stormtroopers ran riot across the country, barricading the entrances to Jewish shops, daubing them with Stars of David and slogans that called on shoppers not to buy from Jews. The first prisoners began arriving at Dachau, the SS's prototype concentration camp.

Soon after the April pogrom—the clearest signal yet of the Nazis' intentions for Germany—Hitler asked Schacht if he would return to his old job as president of the Reichsbank. Schacht accepted and so regained his seat on the board of directors of the BIS. Schacht was a conservative German nationalist, rather than a believer in Aryan racial supremacy. Jews, he believed, were rather too pushy, but could still be useful for the economy. Schacht tolerated, rather than advocated Hitler's anti-Semitism. Schacht used his privileged position to occasionally speak out against the campaign against the Jews, but he was no anti-Nazi. He wanted a strong, economically independent Germany. If Hitler offered the best chance for that, then so be it. Back in 1930 Schacht had told Bella Fromm, a Jewish society columnist, "Why not give the National Socialists a break? They seem pretty smart to me."[13] Now he had the opportunity to do so.

The Nazis also seemed "pretty smart" to the BIS's American management. "Order and discipline in Germany are at the present time exemplary," wrote Gates McGarrah to Leon Fraser in 1933. "The vast majority of the population has the feeling that the fortunes of Germany are in the hands of strong leaders who are inspired by goodwill, so that an optimistic view as regards the future development is justified."[14] The German order, discipline, and goodwill that McGarrah so admired came at a high price, although he did not have to pay it. Carl Melchior did.

As McGarrah eulogized the new Germany, his colleague Melchior, the vice president of the BIS, was forced by the Nazis to resign. The fate of the eminent Jewish banker was regrettable, they murmured in Basel, especially after three years of loyal service, but there was nothing to be done—and certainly not by the BIS, which must remain neutral in its members' internal affairs. Leonardus Trip, the president of the Bank of the Netherlands, swiftly replaced Melchior. The Dutch banker's elevation left a vacancy on the bank's board, which was filled—as it was noted in the BIS 1933 Annual Report—by "Baron Curt von Schröder of the banking house of J. H. Stein, Cologne."

This terse description rather undersold the German nobleman. Kurt Freiherr von Schröder (his name is usually spelled with a "K") was one of the most powerful and influential bankers in Nazi Germany, a scion of the dynasty whose empire included J. Henry Schröder in London and Schrobanco in New York, whose board Allen Dulles joined in 1937. Sociable, cosmopolitan, and well-traveled, von Schröder was known as a reliable, international financier, part of the new global elite who were equally at home in the gentlemen's clubs of London or the dining rooms of Wall Street. The German banker was especially close to Frank Tiarks, the director of the Bank of England who was a partner in J. Henry Schroder bank in London. Tiarks had set up Schrobanco in New York, recruiting Gates McGarrah to its board. Between 1923 and 1939 Kurt von Schröder regularly traveled to London and frequently met Tiarks. The two men had "many business talks together," von Schröder later testified. While in London, von Schröder arranged loans for the Flick industrial concerns, whose head, Friedrich Flick, was pouring money into the Nazi party. The loans, like most of Kurt von Schröder's arrangements, went through his relative Baron Bruno von Schröder, the head of the London branch of J. Henry Schröder banks. Kurt von Schröder also did business with several other major British banks, including Guinness Mahon, Kleinwort, and Lloyds, all on behalf of J. H. Stein, the influential private bank in Cologne where he was a partner.[15]

Hjalmar Schacht personally appointed von Schröder to the BIS board. The summons came out of the blue. "Mr Schacht called me up one day in Berlin and said that they must have a new man for the BIS and told me he thought I was the right one. . . . I was very surprised," von Schröder told Allied interrogators in 1945.[16] Such modesty was unconvincing. Von Schröder enjoyed close personal links with the highest reaches of the Nazi party. He had helped to bring Hitler to power. In January 1933 von Schröder had hosted a meeting at his villa in Cologne between Hitler and Franz von Papen, the former chancellor, who later served as Hitler's vice chancellor. Rudolf Hess, Hitler's deputy in the Nazi party; Heinrich Himmler, the chief of the SS; and Wilhelm Keppler, Hitler's fundraiser and liaison with German businessmen were also there. Keppler later ran the Himmlerkreis, the circle of businessmen who channelled money to Himmler's slush fund at the J. H. Stein bank.

At the meeting, Hitler outlined his plans for economic autarky.[17] Germany could no longer be dependent on foreign countries for any of its needs. The country must be self-sufficient—especially in synthetic oil and rubber. Without these Germany could not wage war, Hitler announced. Production of synthetic oil and rubber was the responsibility of IG Farben, the giant Nazi chemicals conglomerate, which is why Hermann Schmitz, the CEO of IG Farben, would later join Schacht and von Schröder on the board of the BIS. During the war Schmitz channeled money to Himmler via Schröder into special account "S" at J. H. Stein bank, British intellience documents reveal. In 1941 alone, Schmitz transferred 190,000

Reichsmark into the SS leader's personal account. Himmler appreciated Schmitz's generosity, Schröder wrote to his fellow BIS board member, asking Schmitz to transfer a similar sum:

> *I, therefore, take the liberty of asking you again, this year,*
> *to remit the same amount for the Reichsführer-SS to the Special*
> *Account "S" with the banking firm of JH Stein, Cologne. I would*
> *be grateful to you if you complied with this request. As you know,*
> *the Reichsführer has always particularly appreciated this con-*
> *tribution and you may be sure of his gratitude.*[18]

Carl Melchior, who had served his country and the BIS so diligently, had been long plagued by ill health, and he died in December 1933.

ON WALL STREET, Hitler's rise was watched with fascination and concern. Fascination because the advent of an extreme nationalist, one-party state in Germany seemed to have finally banished the specter of Bolshevism. But were Wall Street's investments and holdings really safe? Substantial sums were at stake, involving the most powerful companies in America, several of which were deeply entwined with IG Farben. The German firm operated in the United States as General Aniline and Film (GAF). GAF's founding board members included Walter Teagle, Standard Oil's president; Edsel Ford, the president of Ford Motors; Charles E. Mitchell, chairman of the National City Bank; and Paul Warburg, of the banking dynasty. Standard Oil was GAF's most important partner, and the two firms signed a research and development agreement on oil production. (Standard Oil was also on excellent terms with the BIS—Robert Porters, the bank's chief administrative officer, left to become an adviser to the oil company.)

Standard Oil owned the patents on synthetic rubber, known as Buna, but had ceded control of them to IG Farben. In 1929 Walter Teagle had agreed to a "division of fields" cartel arrangement with its German partner. "The IG are going to stay out of the oil business and we are going to stay out of the chemical business," explained one Standard official.[19] The Standard Oil–IG Farben agreement set the pattern for a series of powerful cartels. John Foster Dulles carried out much of the pioneering legal work for these. Sullivan and Cromwell represented General Aniline and Film, IG Farben's American subsidiary.

Dulles was a director of the International Nickel Company (INKO), the largest producer of the metal in the world. In 1934 INKO signed a cartel agreement with IG Farben, swapping supplies of nickel sources for the license rights to a newly patented nickel-refining process.[20] Dulles also arranged chemical cartels. He represented the Solvay American Investment Corporation, the American subsidiary of a Belgium firm that was a partner of IG Farben. Solvay American held 25 percent of the stock of the Allied Chemical & Dye Corporation, an American company. In 1936 Allied entered a cartel agreement with IG Farben on dyestuff production. And so it went, all through the 1930s, as American financiers and lawyers—none more than John Foster Dulles—ensured that American money, commodities, and expertise flowed steadily into the Third Reich.

But there was still some unease in the boardrooms and clubs, not because of the persecution of the Jews or the concentration camps, but because the Nazi party seemed to still have some dangerous tendencies: its full name, for example, translated as the German Nationalist Socialist Workers' Party. The Brownshirts, the Nazi "leftist" faction, remained powerful. The bankers and industrialists needed fresh, firsthand reassurance. They needed a meeting with Hitler.

Wall Street's envoy was Sosthenes Behn. On August 4, 1933, the *New York Times* reported that Hitler had held his first meeting with "representatives of American finance." The newspaper noted, "Chancellor Hitler, who is resting at his mountain retreat on the Salzburg, today received Sosthenes Behn, a director of the National City Bank of New York, and Henry Mann, its resident vice president for Germany. . . . There was no hint of the motive." But there did not need to be. Behn had founded the International Telephone and

Telegraph Company (ITT) in 1920. ITT had grown to be one of the most powerful companies in the world. It had substantial holdings in Germany, some of which were engaged in armaments production. ITT needed a well-connected banker there to look after its interests and subsidiaries. It found one—in Kurt von Schröder.

SCHACHT SOON TURNED on the bank he had helped create. The 1932 Lausanne conference had canceled Germany's obligations to pay reparations to the Allied victors. But the loans Germany had taken out under the Dawes and Young plans to meet those obligations were still outstanding. It was of little concern to the Wall Street financiers whether Germany used their funds to pay for reparations or to fund a new armaments drive. They wanted to know that they would get their money back. Schacht told the BIS governors at the June 1933 board meeting that he supported paying the Dawes loan but not the Young loan. Germany simply did not have sufficient resources to pay them both. Schacht was under intense political pressure from the Nazi leaders, who wanted both loans written off, seeing them as the final vestiges of Germany's humiliation at Versailles.

The creditors, naturally, disagreed. Another conference was called, this one chaired by Leon Fraser, the BIS president, and hosted by the Reichsbank in Berlin in May 1934. The Berlin gathering was a total failure. Soon afterward Germany announced a complete moratorium on all medium- and long-term debts, including the Dawes and Young loans. The announcement caused fury as bondholders saw their assets vaporize. J. P. Morgan even suggested that the BIS stake a claim to German funds held in Switzerland. That was neither realistic nor practical. The BIS could do nothing except issue a protest against what Fraser called the "thoroughly arbitrary way in which the German government has disregarded its engagements."[21]

It had no effect, for the old fox, as Schacht was known, had outmaneuvered everybody with a high-stakes game of international poker. The Reichsbank governor understood that a blanket default would severely damage Germany's international standing and credit-worthiness. Yet it was imperative to disentangle Germany from the obligations of the Dawes and Young plans and all the political and emotional baggage that they brought in their wake. The policy of economic autarky outlined at the meeting at Kurt von Schröder's house and the memo written by Karl Blessing back in 1930 demanded no less. So as soon as Germany had broken free from the BIS, Schacht swiftly concluded bilateral agreements with Dawes and Young loan bondholders in seven countries, including Britain, France, and Italy, albeit at reduced rates of interest. It was the old principle of divide and rule, brilliantly applied to the new field of international finance. Just as the rule of law had been torn up in Germany, so had the country's international financial obligations.

Schacht's arbitrary rewriting of Germany's debt obligation proved that Germany's commitments were not worth the paper they were written on. At the same time, the dealings of some of those working in the BIS also seemed less than scrupulous: the combination of secrecy, insider information, and vast amounts of money sloshing around was having unwelcome effects. Some of the BIS staff were, it seems, insider trading. Basel was full of rumors that BIS officials were using their privileged knowledge of the bank's activities to speculate against the Swiss franc. A hard-hitting article in the *Berner Tagblatt*, a Swiss newspaper, in May 1935, had caused uproar, especially as it appeared to be based on documentation or a high-level source inside the BIS. Swiss bankers widely believed that the BIS had no confidence in the Swiss franc. A Swiss MP had even raised the conduct of the BIS in the Swiss Parliament. The situation was getting uncomfortable for the BIS management.

The following month the staff was questioned one by one. Gates McGarrah, who had stepped down as president, but remained on the board, wrote to Johan Willem Beyen, his Dutch colleague and fellow board member, that the investigation had turned up some alarming information. One of the bank's "higher officials" had bank accounts in both London and Switzerland, both of which had been overdrawn on the security of stocks and shares. The staff member had been shorting sterling and Swiss francs—selling the currencies when strong and buying them back when they weakened. "This, of course, is a clear case of currency speculation," admitted McGarrah, but there was no need to take any action, he wrote. If the banks do not object and the overdrafts were long-standing, "it might be difficult to criticize too harshly or to interfere with any vigor in the private affairs of a man of some standing who is endeavoring to look after his own fortune in the way he considers best."[22] In other words, even though the senior BIS official was indeed speculating, nothing should be done, especially as he was a man of "some standing."

Another case, which even the emollient McGarrah noted "calls for comment," involved a member of staff who borrowed money in London to buy gold. Alarmingly, the BIS staffer did this, he explained when questioned, "at the same time as his chief." Such practices were "highly undesirable," argued McGarrah, especially as the staffer's chief was a member of the BIS management (it is not clear who from the documents).[23] Thus, the BIS was in no position to issue an official denial about speculation, McGarrah continued. The bank's best option was to inform the Swiss National Bank that it had received the assurance of its management and staff that no speculation had taken place (even though it had) and that the bank would take measures against the possibility of it happening in the future. Bankers in the 1930s, like many of their present-day contemporaries, wanted any potential scandal about their personal probity shut down as soon as possible. "It might be best to endeavor to let the matter die a natural death outside the house and to proceed only with a further internal investigation," McGarrah noted.[24]

CHAPTER FOUR

MR. NORMAN TAKES A TRAIN

"The above-mentioned young Nazi and his friends believe that the BIS offers them their best contact with the outside world. They want to have capable representatives in the BIS in order to break the way for [an] approach to more normal business and monetary relations with the important countries of the world."

— Merle Cochran, an American diplomat who monitored the BIS, in a telegram to the State Department, May 9, 1939[1]

The *Berner Tagblatt* newspaper's revelations about the murky goings-on inside the BIS highlighted the growing questions about the bank's role and function. Insider trading during the 1930s was often the rule rather than the exception, but there were wider issues at stake. The BIS had been established for three main purposes. The first, and ostensibly the most important, was to manage German reparations payments under the 1930 Young Plan. The second was to facilitate cooperation between central banks. And the third was to act as a bank for central banks. The BIS was barely five years old in 1935, but it had already had lost its primary reason for existence and the second reason was under threat. How long would it be before the third reason—to act as a central bank for banks—was called into question?

The Young Plan had collapsed almost as soon as it was agreed to. The Hoover Moratorium, announced a year later, had paused reparation payments. The 1932 Lausanne Conference had confirmed that Germany's war debts would be written off. Thus, there were no more reparations payments. The BIS was also the trustee for the loans that Germany had taken out under the Dawes and Young plans to make those reparations payments. But Gemany had stopped using the BIS to repay the Dawes and Young plan loans. Instead

Schacht had blackmailed Germany's creditors into signing new bilateral agreements. The Reichsbank, a cofounder of the BIS, had broken its legal, financial, and moral obligations with complete impunity and delivered a serious blow to the BIS's credibility as a neutral interlocutor.

So for what other reasons did the BIS continue to function? It acted as a facilitator of central bank cooperation for countries whose currencies were on the gold or gold exchange standard. (The gold standard valued a national currency at a set amount of gold. The gold exchange standard included the country's holdings in US dollars and British pounds as part of its national reserves.) The statutes of the BIS assumed that international finance was based on the gold and gold exchange standard and so would continue to grow smoothly and steadily, facilitated by the bank. As Toniolo notes, "The gold standard was embedded in the very DNA of the BIS."[2] The bank kept its accounts in Swiss gold francs, with each franc worth 0.29 grams of fine gold. But the central banks were losing their enthusiasm for gold. Even Britain had come off the gold standard. By the end of 1932 only seven of the forty-six countries that had been on the gold standard remained, including France, Italy, and the United States, which left the following year.

With no more reparations and the collapse of the gold standard, why did the BIS stay in business? In part—as others who wished to dissolve the bank would find in later years—because it was founded under an international treaty, and its statutes were essentially immutable. Schacht and Norman had designed their bank superbly. It was not possible to close the BIS. In fact, the end of reparations and the collapse of the gold standard proved a boon for the BIS. It allowed the bank to focus on its founders' intentions: to build a new transnational financial system of large capital movements, free from political or governmental control. Gates McGarrah, the bank's first president, had explained as much soon after the bank was founded. Writing in *Nation's Business* magazine, McGarrah admitted that German reparations payments were a "routine operation," which any trust company could administer.

The conception seems to have formed in the popular mind that the Bank for International Settlements, which began at Basel, Switzerland, May 20, 1930, was organized merely to handle German reparations payments and the so-called inter-allied debt and that its principal operations are concerned with the German debt payments. That is a mistaken, although an understandable, view.

Although the prime reason for the bank's creation was to administer the monthly sums paid into it by Germany, this duty has already become the smaller side of the Bank's activities. The handling of the German reparations payments is a routine operation, which any trust company could carry on. Within six months after opening for business the Bank has developed much larger and more important activities and has become a medium of service, which is one of the saving features in a tense world situation. . . .

The Bank is completely removed from any governmental or political control. No person may be a director who is also a government official. The Bank is absolutely non-political and is organised and operated on a basis purely commercial and financial, like any properly managed banking institution. Governments have no connection with it nor with its administration.[3]

McGarrah, like every international financier, regarded the Bolshevik Revolution with horror. Yet he and Vladimir Lenin had much more in common than either could know. The BIS president and the Russian revolutionary both understood that the twentieth century would be the bankers' century. The new mechanisms of transnational capitalism allowed the bankers to send vast sums of money quickly and easily around the world and harvest vast profits from doing so, free from oversight.

The bankers could save a country from collapse and revive its economy—as they did in Germany in the early and mid-1920s, dispatching hundreds of millions of dollars and underwriting the Dawes loan—or they could help send it into a tailspin, by stopping the flow of cash and then pulling out, as they did at the end of the 1920s.

Massive capital movements were now increasingly common. The BIS, as the bank for central bankers, institutionalized that new power. In the first six months of 1931 the BIS advanced £3 million to the Bank of Spain to stabilize the peseta; gave a credit of 100 million Austrian schillings to the national bank when the Credit Anstalt bank went bust; and advanced $5 million to the Hungarian National Bank and arranged a further $10 million credit for Budapest. A small clique of financiers, unaccountable to any government, most of whom knew each other well, had somehow amassed unprecedented economic and political power. Lenin had understood the rising power of finance capital while he was living in exile in Zürich and working in his epic study of imperialism. "The old capitalism has had its day. The new capitalism represents a transition toward something," he wrote. "Thus the beginning of the twentieth century marks the turning point at which the old capitalism gave way to the new, at which the domination of capital in general made way for the domination of finance capital."[4]

ON JANUARY 5, 1939, almost two months after *Kristallnacht*—the state-sponsored pogrom against Germany's Jews—Montagu Norman stepped off the train at the Zoologischer Garten station in Berlin and was met by Hjalmar Schacht. Norman was the guest of honor at the christening of Schacht's grandson, and he was swiftly driven to Schacht's apartment in the Reichsbank building where the ceremony took place. The baby boy was named Norman Hjalmar. Numerous articles in the German press welcoming Norman to Berlin heightened the friendly atmosphere. The two bankers then traveled to Basel together for the monthly board meeting at the BIS.

As Europe slid inexorably to war, British journalists and politicians were asking increasingly pointed questions about the close ties between Norman and Schacht. The Reichsbank president had been in London just before Christmas and had visited Norman at home. What had been discussed? The *News Chronicle* newspaper, for example, suspected that Norman might be an envoy, not just for the Bank of England, but for the pro-appeasement government, led by Prime Minister Neville Chamberlain. Why had he gone? What was Norman saying to the Nazi leaders in Berlin?[5] The newspaper demanded to know. Ernest Bevin, a powerful trade union leader, also wanted answers. "One cannot enter into financial arrangements between these great central banks involving the economic life of the respective countries, without it having a direct reaction on the liberties and rights of the people,"[6] he thundered—sentiments that are as true today as in 1939.

Bevin and the journalists were right to be suspicious of Norman's relationship with Schacht. The Reichsbank president, more than anyone else, had rebuilt Germany, a country that would soon be at war with Britain. Schacht had wrought a miracle—a centrally planned economy that was not ravaged by inflation, a worthless national currency, or unemployment. In the six years since Hitler had taken power, unemployment had been reduced from six million to around three hundred thousand. Armies of the jobless were diverted to massive programs of public work—building the new network of motorways, gigantic public buildings, and planting forests. Arms production was soaring. Trade unions no longer existed and were replaced by the state-run German Labor Front (DAF). The work-shy, along with Jews, leftists, and others viewed as undesirables were dispatched to concentration camps.

Germany adored its miracle maker. In January 1937, on the occasion of his sixtieth birthday, Schacht had stood for four hours receiving hundreds of guests. Hitler himself sent a personal message praising him. Schacht told Hitler's adjutant, who had brought the message, "Tell the Führer that he has no more loyal co-worker than I." Schacht's admirers believed, correctly, that without him, Germany would still be weak, poor, and, worst of all, humiliated. "Every branch of German finance, commerce, industry, and society and the armed forces was represented. There were bankers, manufacturers, merchants of all grades, big and little," the *New York Times* reported. Hitler gave Schacht a painting by Carl Spitzweg, a German romanticist painter. Montagu Norman sent a mahogany clock.[7]

Schacht's real job was to prepare Germany for war. In his correspondence with Hitler, Schacht repeatedly emphasized the importance of the armaments program. In May 1935 he wrote,

> *The following comments are based on the assumption that the accomplishment of the armament program in regard to speed and extent, is the task of German policy, and that therefore everything else must be subordinated to this aim, although the reaching of this main goal must not be imperiled by neglecting other questions.*[8]

That same month Hitler appointed Schacht General Plenipotentiary for the War Economy. For all his old-world manners and elegant appearance, Schacht was a state-sanctioned crook, licensed by Hitler to tear up contracts, steal, extort, and fiddle the Reichsbank's books, which was why he got the job. Schacht funded rearmament by inventing a piece of financial chicanery known as the "MEFO" bill, which allowed the state to illegally borrow billions of Reichmarks from the Reichsbank—a policy Schacht later described as "daring." He hijacked the blocked funds of foreign depositors in the Reichsbank. He requisitioned German residents' foreign currency holdings and ruled that all foreign currencies received as payments for exports must be sold to the Reichsbank. He fiddled the capital markets so that foreign firms could not compete on equal terms with German competitors. He could outsmart anyone, even the wily Jews, proclaimed Hitler:

> *Before each meeting of the International Bank at Basel, half the world was anxious to know whether Schacht would attend or not, and it was only after receipt of the assurance that he would be there that the Jew bankers of the entire world packed their bags and prepared to attend. I must say that the tricks Schacht succeeded in playing on them really provide that even in the field of sharp finance a really intelligent Aryan is more than a match*

for his Jewish counterparts. In spite of his ability I could never
trust Schacht for I had often seen how his face lit up when he had
succeeded in swindling someone out of a hundred mark note.[9]

Schacht was a creature of his time. The dreams of the internationalists who believed that the BIS, like the League of Nations, would engender global peace and harmony were dead. Invasion, annexation, and mass murder were the new tools of international empire building. The Third Reich was rising and would last a thousand years, proclaimed Hitler. Austria had been forcibly incorporated into the Third Reich in the Anschluss of March 1938—with little objection from its citizens. Italy had invaded Abyssinia (now Ethiopia) and was dropping poison gas on defenseless civilians. Japan was laying waste to Manchuria, having murdered hundreds of thousands during the Rape of Nanking in 1937. Neville Chamberlain, the British prime minister, had signed the Munich agreement that ceded the Sudetenland, a province of Czechoslovakia, to Germany. The Spanish civil war, with its flattened, charred cities, its savage brutality and atrocities, was a precursor of Europe's fate.

Yet even as he rebuilt Germany's economy, Schacht must have asked himself if the price was really worth paying. He did not believe in the Nazis' ideas of racial supremacy and refused to join the party. Rather, he was an authoritarian national conservative. He had made a deal with the devil to see his homeland rise again from, as he saw it, the humiliation of the Treaty of Versailles and the penurious obligations of the Dawes and Young plans. Like many Germans of his class, Schacht tried to rationalize the Nazis' brutality and anti-Semitism until the contradictions could be borne no longer. In the summer of 1938, he turned to his partner at an elegant dinner in Berlin and asked, "Madam, how could I have known that we have fallen into the hands of criminals?" He might have been addressing the question to himself, for after five years of Nazi rule the answer was there in front of him—if he had chosen to look.

By 1938 Schacht had begun to play a perilous game, using the BIS as a secret back channel to Britain to try and bring down Hitler and stop the march to war, or so he claims in his memoirs. Schacht first approached several senior military leaders to encourage them to launch a coup. None would agree. That left the monthly meetings at the BIS. "The more conditions in Germany approached a climax, the greater my desire to make use of my connections in Basel as a means of preserving peace," he wrote.[10] The Reichsbank president took Montagu Norman aside at a BIS meeting and asked him to approach Chamberlain to set up a channel between London and the anti-Nazi Germans. Four weeks later Norman and Schacht met again in Basel. Norman told Schacht that he had discussed his proposal with Chamberlain. Schacht asked what was his reply. Chamberlain had said, "Who is Schacht? I have to deal with Hitler."[11]

After Kristallnacht, even Schacht's self-deception and rationalization began to fade. The attack on Germany's Jews, Schacht proclaimed in his speech to the Reichsbank Christmas party, was "such a wanton and outrageous undertaking as to make every decent German blush for shame. I hope none among you had any share in these goings-on. If any one of you did take part, I advise him to get out of the Reichsbank as quickly as possible."[12] Schacht's indignation, whether real or feigned, was wasted. His Reichsbank was the Nazis' most important instrument for looting the assets of German Jewry. After Kristallnacht, the Nazis imposed a fine of one billion Reichmarks on German Jews, to be paid in four installments.

Schacht then proposed to Hitler a bizarre plan to help German and Austrian Jews to emigrate, the kind that only a banker could dream up. Jewish holdings in both countries would be placed in an international trust. The trust would sell twenty-five-year bonds—which would pay dollar dividends—to world Jewry. Part of the dividend would finance the emigration of German and Austrian Jews, and part would be used to boost German exports. Hitler agreed to the plan, but, not surprisingly, nothing came of it. Schacht did help save Bella Fromm, the high society Jewish journalist. Fromm had continued her acerbic observations of Berlin society, politics, and diplomacy, until the summer of 1938 when it became clear she had to flee. She was packed and ready to go when the paperwork got stuck for the transfer of her personal funds—this was a disaster, as without the monies she would not be allowed into the United States. She asked Schacht for help, and he rushed her case through the Foreign Exchange Office. Fromm immigrated to New York.

MEANWHILE, AS EUROPE slid to war, the atmosphere in Basel between the central bank governors remained "entirely cordial," reported Merle Cochran. Cochran traveled to Basel every month from his base at the United States embassy in Paris, to meet Montagu Norman and Hjalmar Schacht at the governors' meeting. He was not allowed to attend, but Norman and Schacht briefed him afterward on the discussions. Cochran then sent on the information to Henry Morgenthau, the Treasury secretary, and to the State Department. Cochran had excellent sources at the BIS, including Paul Hechler, the German assistant general manager, who signed his correspondence "Heil Hitler." Most of the central bankers had "known each other for many years, and these reunions are enjoyable as well as profitable to them," Cochran reported to Washington on May 9, 1939. "The wish was expressed by some of them that their representative statesmen might quit hurling invectives at each, get together on a fishing trip with President Roosevelt or at a World's Fair, overcome their pride and complexes, and enter into a mood that would make comparatively simple the solution of many of the present political problems."[13]

If only things were that simple. Basel at least was a safe haven from the world's vicissitudes. The governors' monthly meeting took place at 4 p.m. on Sunday, without notes or minutes being taken, after which high tea was served. The rest of the two days were busy with breakfasts, lunches, dinners, concerts, receptions, and walks along the Rhine and in the Black Forest. Bank officials' wives were also drafted to lighten the atmosphere at social events. Each governor—just as nowadays—was provided with his own office. The doors were closed while the governors were in discussions with their staffs but were otherwise left open so that bank staff and other governors could make social calls or drop by to exchange news and information.

The bankers began to see the broader picture—the global linkages between their decisions and their consequences. "As they sat down around the table for two days, you could almost see their point of view change as they began to realize the effect of their own actions," reported W. Randolph Burgess, deputy governor of the New York Federal Reserve.[14] Norman and Schacht were still the star attractions. Johan Willem Beyen, a Dutch banker and BIS president in the late 1930s, recalled,

> *Norman's prestige was overwhelming. As the apostle of central bank cooperation, he made the central banker into a kind of archpriest of monetary religion. The BIS was, in fact, his creation. He came on Saturday night and left on Monday night, accompanied by his retinue. The other governors invariably flocked to his room. He had an unbounded admiration for Schacht (in every respect the opposite of himself) and a thorough dislike for one or two others.*[15]

And Norman also had his hat—a beautifully crafted, black silk Homburg with a red silk lining embroidered with a golden bee. When Beyen commented on the detail, Norman quipped, "Oh yes, that's the bee I wear in my bonnet."[16]

In 1939 the BIS board welcomed one of the world's most powerful industrialists: Hermann Schmitz, the CEO of IG Farben—the giant German chemical conglomerate. IG Farben was much more than an ordinary business. It was a virtual parallel state, which would soon evolve into an unprecedented synthesis of finance capital and mass murder. Born out of a merger in the 1920s between Bayer, BASF, Hoechst, Agfa, and other companies, IG Farben was the fourth-largest concern in the world (after US Steel, General Motors, and Standard Oil). It produced pharmaceuticals, chemicals, high explosives, film, plastics, fuel, rayon, paint, pesticides, car tires, poison gases, lightbulbs, aspirin, margarine, detergents, fertilizer, and much more. IG Farben provided the nickel for the engines of the Heinkel and Stuka bombers, the aluminum for their bodies, the magnesium for their wings, and the artificial rubber to hold the windshields together.[17] It refined the fuel, oils, and greases that let the Wehrmacht unleash the Blitzkrieg. The firm once attacked by the Nazis as "Isadore G. Farber"—a macabre reference to the former presence of prominent Jewish financiers such as Max Warburg on its supervisory board—was now the centerpiece of the Nazi war machine.

IG Farben had a liaison office with the Wehrmacht to plan its takeover of competitors in newly occupied countries. It ran its own intelligence service, known as "Buro IG," from its headquarters on the Unter den Linden in Berlin. During the war, IG Farben managers built and ran the company's private concentration camp at Auschwitz, known as "IG Auschwitz," which manufactured Buna, or synthetic rubber.

The presence of Hermann Schmitz on the BIS board highlighted how deeply the bank was entangled with the Third Reich. Nazi Germany benefited immeasurably from its relationship with the BIS. By 1939 the BIS's investments in Germany totaled 294 million Swiss gold francs ($96 million), a substantial sum. But the BIS brought much more than money. As the "Young Nazi" quoted at the start of this chapter in Merle Cochran's telegram explained, the BIS gave the Third Reich the chance for a more "normal" type of business relations with foreign countries. It provided the Reichsbank with a ready-made network of contacts and business channels. It gave Schacht, the architect of the German war economy, a regular opportunity to meet his peers and gain intelligence, both financial and political. It legitimized a national bank engaged in state-sponsored financial chicanery, theft, and appropriation of Jewish businesses through state-organized terror. The BIS thus ensured that the Reichsbank, which should have been a pariah institution, remained a central pillar of the global financial system. Schacht's status and prestige and his regular attendance at the Basel meetings made the criminal actions of the Reichsbank seem acceptable. The personal connections of the central bankers, fostered at the BIS's lunches, dinners, cordial receptions, and strolls in the woods, were crucial in this acculturation of Nazi methodology.

The BIS reports during the 1930s and the buildup to war are especially illuminating in this respect—for what they do not discuss, as much as the information they do impart. The bank's access to figures provided by the world's leading central banks allowed it to collate and analyze statistics, to dissect global trends, and to make policy recommendations in a unique, new format. The BIS annual reports, wrote John Maynard Keynes, the influential British economist, were now "the leading authority for certain statistics, not easily obtainable," and the staff were to be congratulated. The reports were supervised and written by Per Jacobssen, who had joined the bank in 1931 as economic adviser.

Born in 1894, in Tanum, Sweden, Jacobssen had made his name while working at the Economic and Financial Section of the League of Nations from 1920 to 1928. He was far more than an adviser. He shaped the bank's policy recommendations of laissez-faire economics and the importance of individual responsibility over state provision. He supported European federalism and supranationalism. His legacy has shaped our world. Jacobssen was also a kind of global economic troubleshooter with a much-envied contacts book. During his time at the BIS, he oversaw numerous financial and economic inquiries into troubled countries and was especially well connected in the United States. As a perceptive observer, Jacobssen also co-wrote two thrillers, fusing his knowledge of international finance and diplomacy. *The Death of a Diplomat*, which was set in the League of Nations, was published in eight languages, and the film rights sold to a German company. *The Alchemy Murder* was macabrely prescient— especially when Hermann Schmitz, the CEO of IG Farben, joined the board of the BIS. The book's storyline focused on chemical companies producing poison gas.

But Jacobssen's reports for the BIS, no matter how detailed on economic and financial analysis, gave scant attention to the wider context in which the central bankers operated. It was their job, the bankers believed, to focus on finance, rather than on the complex moral and political issues that shaped nations and the world's economy. In this they succeeded so well that an article in the *Bankers' Magazine* in 1943 described the BIS reports as documents "whose emotionless neutrality would do credit to a visitor from Mars." The Nazi persecution of the Jews and the systematic, state-organized theft of Jewish-owned firms and businesses is reported purely as a technical question. Page 101 of the 1939 annual report notes that some

German firms had experienced a reduction in liquidity and were asking banks for credit to improve their liquidity. But this was not the only cause of the growth in requests for loans. "Other reasons for the demand for advances are to be found in the changes in the ownership of private enterprises due to the Aryanization of private firms." There is not a word of condemnation, merely a dry noting of the changed circumstances.

The Anschluss, the Nazi annexation of Austria, is noted on pages 100 and 101 of the 1938 report as follows: "In connection with the incorporation of Austria in the German Reich in March and April 1938, the Austrian National Bank entered into liquidation and a series of measures were promulgated transferring most of its assets and liabilities to the Reichsbank." These assets included the Austrian National Bank's gold reserves and their 4,000 BIS shares. The BIS accepted their "transfer" to Berlin, the first of many decisions that the bank's leadership would take to legitimize Nazi plunder and looting.

The BIS's 1939 report does devote more space to the Third Reich's methods, but mainly as a question of technical banking interest. The report notes with typical understatement that "Territorial changes in Europe in 1938 left their impress on the banking and credit structures of the countries concerned." There was perhaps a note of relief in the statement that "the absorption of Austria into the German Reich presented comparatively few difficulties for the German banking system as Austria itself had a unified banking structure." However, the report observed, "much more intricate questions were involved in the taking over of the Sudetenland," the border province that Czechoslovakia had been forced to cede to the Nazis in September 1938. The Czechoslovak banks had 143 branches in the Sudetenland. These banks had to change their currency from crowns to Reichmarks. These 143 branches, the report notes, had to be "severed from their old head offices and adapted to the German system"—an adaptation that the BIS was finding very easy indeed.

The bankers gathered at Basel were not burdened with idealism except in one respect: they wanted to work together to facilitate the free flow of international capital. They sought economic stability, low inflation, and global free trade that would provide political stability and control unemployment—reasonable aims that were shared by much of the world. The bankers may not have been immoral (apart from Schacht), but they were certainly amoral. They believed that financial considerations existed in a vacuum, away from troublesome politics and national interests. Ethical considerations of right and wrong simply did not exist in their universe. What counted was the bottom line and the interest of the banks themselves, especially, now, the BIS. As Merle Cochran noted, "The Directors prefer to view the BIS as a long-term proposition, and insist that its field of usefulness need not be analyzed or altered with every shift in world monetary and economic conditions."[18]

It was a peculiar arrogance that granted such self-belief to a clique of unaccountable financiers. A clique that had, by sleight of hand, built its own bank that was untouchable and beyond the reach of any government—and then proclaimed its existence to be something of virtue for the rest of mankind. The most important thing, the bankers agreed, was that transactions were properly authorized and formal procedures followed. It was not the bank's business to ask where the money came from or how it had arrived. It was this obsessive formalism, repackaged as "neutrality," that would soon lead the BIS to become, in the words of Henry Morgenthau, the US Treasury Secretary, "a symbol of Nazi instrumentality."[19]

TRANSNATIONAL CAPITAL HAD decided the fate of Spain. The Spanish civil war lasted from July 1936 to April 1939, when the Nationalist army, led by General Franco, finally captured Madrid, the capital, from the left-wing Republicans. Spain is often described as a trial run for the Second World War. It was an exceptionally savage conflict, marked by atrocities on both sides. The airplanes of Germany's Condor Legion bombed Spanish cities and strafed civilians, perfecting the strategies that would soon be deployed in the Blitzkrieg. But the conflict was also a trial run for newly honed techniques of economic warfare.

Money, as much as superior numbers and military forces, helped Franco to victory. Nazi Germany and Fascist Italy provided hundreds of millions of dollars worth of aid. The nationalists understood that finance was a weapon as effective as bullets. They set up their own rival economy, complete with a separate national bank that issued its own currency, also called the peseta. This was a psychological as well as economic assault on the Republic. It was chillingly effective. By July 1937, a year into the war, the Republican peseta was worth three times less in French francs than the fascist version, even though the Republicans were the legitimate government of Spain and controlled the national economy, its currency, and the country's gold reserves.[20] Inflation was far higher in the Republican zone. Between July 1936 and March 1937 prices doubled in the Republican zone, while in the nationalist zone they rose by only 15 percent. The nationalists steadily corroded the Spaniards' belief in their currency and, by extension, in their government.

Yet arguably, the Republican government's peseta should have been worth three times the nationalists' scrip. At the end of 1935 Spain had the fifth-largest gold reserves in the world, after the United States, France, Britain, and the Soviet Union. The BIS annual report for 1936 notes that Spain had gold reserves of 2,225 million gold Swiss francs, nearly three times that of Italy. Much of this had been accumulated during the First World War when Spain remained neutral. For the previous four years the country had enjoyed a current account surplus, much of which had been invested in gold.

The country should have been in a prime position to issue bonds, backed by the abundant gold reserves, to finance the economy and the war. Yet as Pablo Martín-Aceña, Elena Martínez Ruiz and María A. Pons, the authors of the paper "War and Economics: Spanish Civil War Finances Revisited," note the Spanish government did not do so. "The reasons for this decision are controversial: either they were not able to do so because of the political aversion of international banks and financiers, or it was a deliberate policy decision."[21] Probably it was a mix of both. The country was under an arms embargo. And where would the bonds have been sold? Allen Dulles and his friends on Wall Street had no desire to buttress a government that—from their perspective—was composed of dangerous leftists. Nor would London have been more enthusiastic. Britain also preferred Franco's fascists to the Republic.

So Spain simply sold its gold reserves. France bought 175 tons and the remainder was purchased by Moscow. The BIS report for 1937 records a fall in Spain's holdings to an estimated value of 1,600 million gold Swiss francs.[22] The money was used to pay for weapons, aircraft, tanks, food, and other supplies. As neither Spain nor the Soviet Union were members of the BIS, they were not able to use its special facilities for crediting and debiting national banks' accounts. Instead the gold was physically moved. Spain's gold reserves were held in the subterranean vaults of the Bank of Madrid. As Franco's forces advanced on the capital the reserves were transferred to a naval store in Cartagena, on the Mediterranean coast. From there the reserves were loaded onto four Soviet ships and taken to the port of Odessa, to be transported to Moscow on a special train. When the gold was gone, the Bank of Spain sold its silver reserves of 1,225 tons to the United States and France.

The Republicans' chaotic politics also weakened their economy and currency. The nationalists were centralized, authoritarian, well-organized, and united around one ideology—fascism—with one leader: General Francisco Franco. The Republicans were a kaleidoscope of competing creeds: socialism, communism, and anarchism. Numerous local, regional, and revolutionary authorities printed their own banknotes, which had no credible backing. The Republican government did not centralize the issuing of bank notes until autumn 1937. In contrast, the nationalists fought a currency war as well organized as their military campaigns. They declared all Republican banknotes issued since 1936 to be illegal. The only legal tender was to be the notes issued by the nationalists' own rival Bank of Spain. The Republicans blocked all current and deposit accounts in their zone that had been opened or increased in value since the start of the war. So as Franco's troops advanced, bank account holders cashed in their savings and quickly spent the money on whatever they could. One bank, Banco Zaragozano, even sent its chairman to the front. As soon as each city fell, he entered the newly captured territories with the military leaders to reorganize the local banks.[23]

This, as much as the Blitzkrieg, was the real lesson of the Spanish Civil War: the nationalists' sophisticated fusion of financial and military power. The Nazis would hone this model, using the BIS to underpin their economic empire.

CHAPTER FIVE

AN AUTHORIZED PLUNDER

"The Bank for International Settlements is the bank which sanctions the most notorious outrage of this generation—the rape of Czechoslovakia."

— George Strauss, Labor MP, speaking in the House of Commons, May 1939[1]

When Nazi Germany annexed the Czechoslovak border province of the Sudetenland in September 1938, it immediately absorbed a good part of the country's banking system as well as most of Czechoslovakia's strategic defenses. By then the country's national bank had prudently transferred most of its gold abroad to two accounts at the Bank of England: one in the name of the BIS, and one in the name of the National Bank of Czechoslovakia itself. (Countries had deposited some of their gold reserves in a sub-account at the BIS account in London to ease gold sales and purchases.) Of the 94,772 kilograms of gold, only 6,337 kilograms remained in Prague. The security of the national gold was more than a monetary issue. The Czechoslovak reserves, like those of Republican Spain, were an expression of nationhood. Carved out of the remains of the Austro-Hungarian Empire in 1918, the Czechoslovak Republic was a new and fragile nation. A good part of the gold had been donated by the public in the country's early years. Josef Malik, the governor of the national bank, and his fellow Czechs believed that, even as the Nazis' dismembered their homeland, if the national gold was safe, then something of the country's independence would endure.

They were wrong. The Czechoslovaks' faith in the probity of the BIS and the Bank of England was tragically misplaced. The gold was sacrificed, with barely a second thought, to the needs of transnational finance and the Third Reich.

The Nazis' first demand came in February 1939 when Berlin ordered Prague to transfer just over 14.5 metric tons of gold, supposedly to back the German currency now circulating in the Sudetenland. This was certainly an innovative idea—first invade a neighboring country, annex part of it, and then demand that the newly truncated state supply the gold to pay for the loss of its territory. The following month the question became academic. On March 15 the Wehrmacht marched into Prague. The German protectorate of Bohemia and Moravia was declared, and Czechoslovakia no longer existed. But the gold reserves did. Three days later a Reichsbank official was dispatched to the National Bank of Czechoslovakia and ordered the directors, under the threat of death, to issue two orders. Thanks to diligent detective work by Piet Clements, the BIS archivist, we have a clear picture of what happened next. The first order instructed the BIS to transfer the 23.1 metric tons of Czechoslovak gold held at the BIS account at the Bank of England to the Reichsbank BIS account, also held at the Bank of England. The second order instructed the Bank of England to transfer almost 27 metric tons of gold held in the National Bank of Czechoslovakia's own account to the BIS's gold account at the Bank of England.

Malik and his fellow directors hoped that it would be obvious that the instructions had been issued under duress and so would not be implemented. The Nazis had just invaded Czechoslovakia and would obviously target the national gold reserves. But Malik had not reckoned on Montagu Norman. The governor of the Bank of England had no interest in whether Czechoslovakia was free or a Nazi colony. "Political" considerations must not affect the BIS's transactions. The transfer order, he said, must go through.

Meanwhile, in Basel, Johan Beyen, the Dutch president of the BIS, wavered. Beyen discussed the matter with the BIS's legal adviser, Felix Weiser. But like Norman, Weiser took the most formalistic approach possible. As long as the paperwork was in order, the monies must go through. Weiser argued, somewhat bizarrely, that there could be no legal grounds to claim that the transfer order had been issued under duress, as such a plea could be brought before a Swiss court only by the persons who had acted under duress. Clearly, the directors of the National Bank of Czechoslovakia were unlikely to travel to Switzerland to present their case. Therefore any decision not to authorize the transfer would be one of BIS policy, rather than administration. The board of the BIS made policy. Thus Beyen would have to consult the board to stop the payment. (This was poor advice for another reason—under the terms of the BIS statutes the Swiss authorities anyway had no jurisdiction over gold transfers between states.)

Beyen was unwilling to take a decision without authorization. But who could he ask? The chairman of the BIS board, Sir Otto Niemeyer, of the Bank of England, was traveling to Egypt and so was incommunicado. At 6 p.m. on March 20, Roger Auboin, the bank's general manager, told Beyen that the governor of the Bank of France had discussed the matter with London. The Bank of England and the Bank of France would not be taking any action to stop the transfer, because they felt that there were no grounds for action. The BIS transfer order went through.

With London, Paris, and Basel's compliance, Nazi Germany had just looted 23.1 metric tons of gold without a shot being fired. More than two-thirds of that gold was traded with the Dutch and Belgian national banks and was eventually transported from Amsterdam and Brussels to the Reichsbank's vaults in Berlin. Czechoslovakia's diligent planning to safeguard its national gold reserves, together with its misplaced faith in the integrity of the new international financial system, had come to nothing. The second transfer order for the 27 metric tons held in the National Bank of Czechoslovakia's own account at the Bank of England did not go through. Sir John Simon, the chancellor of the Exchequer, had instructed banks to block all Czechoslovak assets. But Czechoslovak gold held in a BIS account at the Bank of England, it seemed, was not defined as a national asset and was beyond the reach of UK laws.

Norman and Beyen's decision caused despair and incomprehension in Prague and uproar in London. The loss of the Czechoslovak gold was all "Norman's fault," exclaimed the *Daily Herald*.[2] Paul Einzig, of the *Financial News*, ran a stream of stories exposing the complicity of both the treasury and the Bank of England in the affair. Einzig demanded to know why the treasury had not stopped the transfer, as it was in clear violation of the law known as the Czechoslovakia Act. Brendan Bracken, a journalist and ally of Winston Churchill, declared in the House of Commons that "the Bank of England after what has happened may no longer be looked on as the safest place in the world and the phrase 'Safe as the Bank of England' may no longer apply."[3] Churchill himself demanded to know how the government could urge people to enlist in the military when it was "so butter-fingered that six million pounds of gold can be transferred to the Nazi government."[4]

The real villain of the affair was Norman. Beyen, who later served as Dutch foreign minister and as executive director of the International Monetary Fund, was an ineffectual bureaucrat, paralyzed by the idea that he might have to take responsibility for a decision. Norman could have stopped the transfer immediately. He was the governor of the Bank of England, which held the two BIS accounts involved. At the very least he could have asked for the transfer to be referred to the BIS board for a decision, which would also have been a face-saving measure. He chose not to do so. It was clear that war was coming, one that Britain would have to fight. The Nazi invasion of Czechoslovakia had destroyed the last hopes of peace. That country's gold reserves, held in London, were now a British national security issue.

Yet Norman's priority was not the best interests of his homeland, but rather the independence of his beloved BIS. Even as the shells were loaded into the German tanks, Norman still believed that for the bankers it could be business as usual. Nothing could interfere with the bankers' sacred neutrality and gentlemanly trust in one other, not even the coming conflagration with a regime whose evil was now plain to see. The Bank of France had refused to stop the transfer but had also asked Norman to block it. Norman was adamant. There could be no political interference in the operations of the BIS, even, it seemed, when they were ordered at gunpoint.

Norman did not express any regret at all over the Czech gold transfer. In fact, he was positively indignant at the very idea that the British government might have some say in the bank's actions. He wrote, "I can't imagine any step more improper than to bring government into the current banking affairs of the BIS. I guess it would mean ruin. I imagine the Germans would never have paid any interest to the BIS, and at the board we would have then likely have found the Germans, Italians, and Japs standing together!"[5] Norman then lied to Sir John Simon, the chancellor of the Exchequer, albeit with a very telling falsehood. Simon asked Norman if he could not have warned the government that, thanks to the BIS, Germany was about to acquire "large additional financial strength." Norman told Simon that while the Bank of England held gold for the BIS, it did not know if the gold was actually owned by the BIS or was held by the BIS for other central banks. This was untrue, as Norman later admitted. Norman then made a significant, even shocking, admission. He told Simon that "he was very doubtful that he would have thought it his duty, as Director of the BIS, to make a statement about its transactions to the British government."[6]

Norman even wrote to Beyen to clarify the matter and to assure the BIS president where his ultimate loyalties lay in Basel. Norman did not want to publicly correct the minutiae of what was being reported in the press and *Hansard*, the British parliamentary journal—that the Bank of England did not know whose gold was held in the BIS accounts—as that would expose him. "The difficulty is that if I point out to the Treasury that this is incorrect, I lay myself open to being asked details of BIS transactions, which I do not consider the Treasury are entitled to know."[7] This was little short of treason. As Norman's compatriots were enlisting in the military, preparing to risk their lives for the freedoms and luxury that he enjoyed, as his country prepared for the war against the Nazis that all knew was coming, Norman blithely announced that his primary loyalty was not to Britain, but to a hyper-privileged, international bank that was not even a decade old.

The mistake of Malik, the director of the National Bank of Czechoslovakia, was to believe that either Norman, Beyen, or indeed any of the BIS management could conceive of any moral or political dimension to their decisions. The world's most powerful international bankers were not only unwilling to obstruct the Nazi seizure of Czechoslovak—or Austrian—assets. They simply could not conceive of any reason why they should do so. As long as the formalities were observed, the necessary papers were stamped and the gold was re-assigned. Norman's precious independence for both the Bank of England and the BIS had been bought at a high price—in mountains of gold ingots to pay for steel to build bombs that would soon rain down on London.

THE SAME OBSESSIVE legalism governed the response of the US Federal Reserve to requests from American banks to transfer Czechoslovak assets. On March 16, 1939, the day after German tanks rolled into Prague, Henry Morgenthau, the US Treasury secretary, called George Harrison, the president of the New York Federal Reserve, to say that the principal banks in New York had been asked—voluntarily—not to make any "important or unusual" transactions involving Czechoslovak assets until Monday, March 20, when the situation might become clearer.

By Tuesday, March 21, the situation was as clear as Bohemia's famed crystal: Czechoslovakia no longer existed. The country had been absorbed into the Third Reich. Harrison called Morgenthau to find out what the US position was. Morgenthau consulted the State Department and told Harrison that the banks and the lawyers should decide for themselves what to do if they were asked to move Czechoslovak funds. On Thursday, John Wesley Hanes, Morgenthau's undersecretary, called Harrison and asked him to inquire from the New York banks about the deposits they held for the Czech National Bank. The information would be passed to the State Department, which would give it in turn to the Czechoslovak ambassador. Harrison did not agree with the banks' handing over the information voluntarily. That would not be a good idea, as it might trigger retaliation in Germany against American interests. The treasury should compel the banks to surrender the information rather than request it. And if the Czechoslovak ambassador wanted the information, he could look it up himself, in Thomas Skinner's *Bankers' Almanac and Yearbook*.[8]

A few days later, on April 1, the New York Federal Reserve received a cable that ordered the transfer of $35,000 from the Czechoslovak National Bank account into the BIS. Harrison wrote Marriner Eccles, the chairman of the Federal Reserve Board, in Washington, DC, and set out the chain of events. The request, he wrote, was "properly tested in every way." For most observers, the simplest test showed that as Czechoslovakia no longer existed, it was obvious that the request should be blocked. But not to Harrison and Eccles. For them, like Norman in London and Beyen in Basel, the most important thing was to keep the money moving. Harrison could see "no reason, regardless of the possible motive for the transfer, for refusing to honor it." Even worse, was the possibility that there "might be greater liability on us for refusing to honor the transfer than in honoring the order."[9]

The Czechoslovak ambassador thought otherwise. He wrote a letter pointing out that the transfer requests may have been made under duress and asked that such requests not be honored. Ever the bureaucrat, Harrison made sure to guard his back. Just as Beyen had done in Basel, Harrison consulted a lawyer on how to proceed further. The crucial issue was not the Nazi takeover of Czechoslovakia, but the potential risk to the New York Federal Reserve. All drafts against the account of the Czech National Bank's account were to be honored, provided they were properly drawn and tested. "It is our opinion that there is less risk to the bank in following this procedure than in refusing to honor a draft merely because, as the Czechoslovak minister says, it might or might not have been drawn 'under duress.'"[10]

UNUSED TO PUBLIC scrutiny of their decisions, the BIS bankers were taken aback by the depth of the anger against them over the Czechoslovak gold affair. There were recriminations and buck-passing at the BIS board meeting in June that year. Fournier, the governor of the Bank of France, protested that the decision had been taken without consulting the board—which was rich, considering that he had told Beyen that neither the Bank of France nor the Bank of England had any objections to the transfer. Sir Otto Niemeyer, the chairman of the BIS board, defended himself, falling back on the usual excuses. "The Bank had satisfied itself that there was no legal reason why the instructions should not be executed, and the transaction was therefore carried out in the usual manner. There had, in fact, been no alternative but to carry out the instructions received."[11] One director (unnamed) suggested that in future the board should be consulted on "important matters," as the board was responsible for policy. Niemeyer quickly shot down the proposal. Not surprisingly, Niemeyer wholeheartedly took Norman's position. As the BIS was an international institution, it could not concern itself with "political questions." This was nonsense, for the decision to authorize the transfer was profoundly political, executed in a Europe that had never been more politicized and which was about to erupt in war.

Malik left Prague in August 1939 and fled first to Basel, to explain the facts of the Czechoslovak gold transfer to the BIS management before eventually finding refuge in London. There remained the question of the Czechoslovak National Bank's four thousand shares in the BIS. By the end of that year their status, the bank's 1939 report noted, had not still "yet been determined." After the war ended, Malik claimed that he had to dissuade Paul Hechler, the German head of the BIS banking department and Nazi loyalist, from distributing the Czechoslovak BIS shares to the Reichsbank, the Hungarian National Bank, and the national bank of the new Slovak Nazi puppet state (the banks of the three states that now controlled the former Czechoslovak territories). The "plan was then contemplated by him in all seriousness," Malik wrote.[12] In the end, the BIS took a more judicious approach to the Czechoslovak BIS shares than it had toward the country's gold reserves. After seeking legal advice, the BIS suspended them.

But the affair had highlighted the deeply unsettling connections between the Bank of England, the British government, and the BIS. There was a good deal of cross-party feeling in Britain, reported the *New York Times*, that "the Bank for International Settlements should be liquidated before it furnished any more sinews of war to Germany, and that the odd relationship between the British government and the Bank of England should be re-examined without delay."[13] The *New York Times* then was able to assume that its readers would understand a classical allusion. The word "sinews" was a reference to an epithet of Cicero, the Roman philosopher, who had said, "The sinews of war are infinite money." Cicero's observation was as prescient then as during the late 1930s. But those who wanted the BIS to be liquidated were too late. Thanks to the BIS the "sinews of war" and the flow of near-infinite money were about to be immeasurably strengthened.

THE CZECHOSLOVAK GOLD affair also highlighted how the bank's increasingly sophisticated gold operations were growing in reach and importance. The BIS's gold trades were a primitive forerunner of today's globalized economy where vast sums instantly fly back and forth at the touch of a keyboard. The technology available in the 1930s was far more primitive, but the principle of buying and selling assets sight unseen and without taking physical possession is the same. This development of a free gold market between central banks via the BIS was significant. Had all the Czechoslovak gold been held in an account at the Bank of England in the national bank's own name, rather than at a BIS account, it is doubtful that any would have reached the Reichsbank.

The BIS offered central banks a unique service, one unavailable to private companies or individuals who were not allowed to hold accounts there. The BIS held two kinds of gold deposits: bank deposits and earmarked gold. The first was gold deposited there by central banks. In 1936 this accounted for around 14 percent of deposits. (The actual bars of gold were held at the Swiss National Bank in Bern.) The second category was known as "earmarked" gold—gold that was physically held in another bank but that was credited to the BIS's account (as the Czechoslovak gold in London had been).

The BIS held collective gold accounts at the Bank of England and the New York Federal Reserve. These accounts were subdivided into subaccounts for central banks, which owned the gold, although the gold was physically stored in London or New York. Neither the Bank of England nor the New York Fed was supposed to know which central bank owned the sub-accounts held in the name of the BIS, although as Norman's correspondence over the Czechoslovak gold affair shows, they did. So if the Bank of France (sub-account X) wanted to transfer funds to the Bank of Hungary (sub-account Y), the BIS simply instructed the Bank of England to make the necessary deposit from sub-account X to sub-account Y. Earmarked gold, as Toniolo notes, "allowed for cheap and confidential transactions between central banks, as the transfer of property merely entailed a bookkeeping change by the BIS."[14] This was a growth industry for the BIS—in 1935–1936 earmarked gold movements totaled more than 1,121 million Swiss gold francs. By 1938–1939 that sum had increased to more than 1,512 million.

BIS managers and directors were immensely proud of the bank's innovative, new mechanisms for gold and foreign currency trades. But the principle behind earmarked accounts was not nearly as new as they believed. Few, if any, of the BIS directors had ever heard of the island of Yap, in Micronesia. But centuries ago its inhabitants had invented a similar system, one based on large limestone discs. The discs, known as *fei*, were quarried on a neighboring island and brought back to Yap by boat. The discs, the islanders decided, represented substantial wealth—enough, for example, to pay for a daughter's dowry. But the "currency" was extremely heavy and almost unmovable. So it stayed in its place, and only the ownership changed with the agreement of the buyer and seller. In fact the stone did not even need to be present on the island. The locals' oral tradition tells of one disc that fell off the boat into the sea. Rather like the gold deposits at the BIS accounts in London or New York—or indeed any bank nowadays—the physical existence of the submerged *fei* was taken as a matter of faith. The islanders simply passed the ownership of the submerged disc back and forth—until 1899 when the Germans arrived and colonized the island of Yap.

The islands' new rulers demanded that the inhabitants repair the walkways that linked the different settlements. The locals ignored their orders, and eventually the Germans decided that they must be fined. Painting a large black cross on the most valuable fei and declaring them to be the property of the government exacted the fine. It worked. The islanders quickly fixed the paths, the German officials removed the crosses, and the islanders once again had possession of their capital assets.

To the sophisticated financiers of the twentieth century, such an episode would have seemed charming but irrelevant. But as Milton Friedman later noted, it was very relevant indeed. Neither gold nor stone discs have any inherent value. Their worth is completely arbitrary, the worth that we give them. The painting of the Yap islanders' stone discs had precise parallels in 1932 when the Bank of France decided to sell its dollars. The bank feared that the United States would not adhere to the traditional gold standard at $20.67 for an ounce of gold. It asked the Federal Reserve of New York to use its dollars held there to buy gold. As it was expensive and risky to ship the gold across the Atlantic, the Bank of France asked the New York Fed to simply store the Bank of France's newly acquired gold at its account there. Friedman described what happened next:

> *In response, officials of the Federal Reserve Bank went to their gold vault, put in separate drawers the correct amount of gold ingots and put a label or mark on those drawers indicating that they were the property of the French—for all it matters they could just have done so by marking them "with a cross in black paint" just as the Germans did to the stones.*[15]

This event—or arguably non-event—had serious consequences. The French sale of dollars drove the exchange rate down, while the franc strengthened, even though nothing had actually happened. What was the difference, asked Friedman, between "the Bank of France's belief that it was in a stronger monetary position because of some marks on drawers in a basement more than 3,000 miles away and the Yap islander's conviction that he was rich because of a stone under the water a hundred miles or so away?"[16] Evidently, not very much.

PERHAPS NORMAN AND Schacht sensed, as they traveled together from Berlin to Basel that January 1939, that this would be the last meeting at the BIS they would attend together. By then Schacht realized that he had created a monster. The German war economy and state spending were out of control.

If things carried on as they were, Schacht and his fellow Reichsbank board members believed, the country would go bankrupt. On January 7, Hitler received a memo signed by all eight members of the Reichsbank board, including Schacht. Uncontrolled expenditure would soon cause the "national financial structure" to collapse, the memo warned. "It is our duty to warn against this assault on the currency."[17]

Two weeks after Hitler received the Reichsbank directors' memo, Schacht was summoned to the Chancellery in Berlin. Hitler handed him the official notification that he was relieved of his position as president. Most of Schacht's fellow directors resigned. Walther Funk, who also took his place on the BIS board, replaced Schacht. Funk, a former journalist, was an ardent Nazi and had joined the party in 1931. He was the point man for big business and industrialists, including IG Farben, who used him to channel funds to the Nazis, and was also one of Hitler's key economic advisers. Funk had replaced Schacht as economics minister in 1937, and as Plenipotentiary for the War Economy in 1938, so his appointment as Reichsbank president surprised nobody. What was a surprise was how Funk's dissolute personal life had not stalled his steady rise through the highest reaches of the Nazi state. Funk was a scruffy drunkard and homosexually active at a time when gay men were sent to concetration camps.

Schacht retreated home to his villa in the Berlin suburb of Charlottenburg for a while, and then set off in March on a trip to India. In July 1939 he returned to Basel where he had a secret meeting with Montagu Norman. Schacht made a bizarre offer to the British government. Fearing for his life, and less protected by Hitler from his enemies in the SS, who had always envied his power over the economy, Schacht proposed that he go to east Asia to report on the economy for Britain. Norman met with Neville Chamberlain and told the prime minister of his friend's request. Schacht's offer was met with some bewilderment, but Frank Ashton-Gwatkin, a foreign office official, was dispatched to Italy. He and Schacht spent three days closeted in a luxury hotel above Ancona. Ashton-Gwatkin recalled, "I listened to Schacht's odd-sounding scheme, and, allowing for the fact that he was anxious to get as far away from Hitler as possible, I had to confess that I had heard of more promising ventures." Still, he told Schacht that he would write a report on his proposal and submit it to London.

Schacht then demanded to see what Ashton-Gwatkin had written. The Foreign Office man handed over his notes. Schacht, imperious as ever, informed him, "This won't do at all." Schacht rewrote the report and then demanded that the original be destroyed. Ashton-Gwatkin handed over his notes, which Schacht, with great theater, proceeded to set on fire, sheet by sheet and then drop into the toilet. Schacht was less adept as a spy than a banker. The toilet cracked, and water gushed the wet ashes all over the floor. "We spent what seemed to me a long time mopping up the water and fishing for sodden bits of charred paper," recalled Ashton-Gwatkin. Schacht's mission never took place.[18]

Just over a month later, on September 1, Germany invaded Poland.

CHAPTER SIX

HITLER'S AMERICAN BANKER

"The business affairs of the bank, which are run on a greatly reduced scale, virtually rest in the hands of Mr. McKittrick, the president of the bank. "

— John Gilbert Winant, the US ambassador to Britain, July 1941[1]

Merle Cochran, the American diplomat whom Henry Morgenthau had dubbed the "unofficial ambassador" to the BIS, had some inside information for the treasury secretary. The main business at the "usual Sunday informal and secret meeting" of the bank's governors that May 1939 was the appointment of the next president. Johan Beyen, the hapless Dutch incumbent who had handed over the Czechoslovak gold to the Nazis, was due to retire in 1940. There were three main contenders to succeed him: a Dutchman, a Swede, and an American. "Chances are best for the American, so far," Cochrane reported.[2]

The American was Thomas McKittrick. On the surface McKittrick seemed a curious choice. He was a lawyer by training with no direct experience of central banking. But that mattered little, for war was coming. All sides already agreed that the financial channels must be kept open during the conflict. In that sense, McKittrick was the perfect candidate. He was citizen of both a neutral country— the United States— and of the world's newest hinterland—transnational finance.

McKittrick had worked for Higginson & Company, the British subsidiary of Lee, Higginson & Company—a renowned Boston investment house. The bank no longer exists, thanks in part to McKittrick, but in its heyday it was richer and more prestigious than Goldman Sachs and Lehman Brothers. Born in St. Louis, McKittrick had graduated from Harvard in 1911. He moved to Italy where he worked for the foreign arm of the National City Bank of New York, before joining the US Army in 1918. He was sent to Liverpool, where he was seconded to British military intelligence, to check that there were no spies using the docks to pass in and out of Britain. After the armistice in November, McKittrick was dispatched to France to work with the Allied occupation forces.

He returned to New York in 1919 and started work at Lee, Higginson. McKittrick's foreign experience in Italy and France made him unusual in the more parochial world of American bankers. He was sent to London in 1921 to work for the company's British wing, and was made a partner in charge of foreign operations for both London and New York. Although McKittrick was a lawyer rather than a banker by training, he soon found his way around the City of London and built up an impressive network of contacts with international connections. Much of his time was spent working on German loans and investments, including the Dawes Plan German External Loan of 1924, which had been arranged by John Foster Dulles and Sullivan and Cromwell. McKittrick became a kind of honorary Englishman, regarded in Europe as an envoy from the City, complete with a butler who ironed his copy of *The Times* before he read it. "I was leading the life of an Englishman," he later recalled. "My associates were all British, and toward the end of that time I was frequently spoken to by people who assumed I was British."[3]

McKittrick had come to the BIS in 1931 when he joined the German Credits Arbitration Committee, which adjudicated over any disputes of credits granted to German private banks. The other two members were Marcus Wallenberg, of Sweden's Enskilda Bank and Franz Urbig, the chairman of the Deutsche Bank supervisory board. Wallenberg and his brother, Jacob, were two of the most powerful bankers in Europe. The Wallenberg family enjoyed a network of lucrative connections to bankers in London, Berlin, and Wall Street. During the Second World War, the Wallenberg brothers would use Enskilda Bank to play both sides, always making sure to harvest enormous profits along the way. Their relative, Raoul, would later save tens of thousands of Hungarian Jews during the Holocaust before disappearing into the Soviet gulag, abandoned by his uncles.

McKittrick had long been a good friend of Allen Dulles, whom he had first met when Dulles was working at the American Legation in Bern and Dulles assisted him with a visa matter. McKittrick well understood that Sullivan and Cromwell offered an entrée in the covert world where politics and diplomacy met transnational finance. In September 1930 McKittrick wrote to a colleague, "We are seriously considering throwing some legal work to Sullivan and Cromwell in order to get benefit of Dulles services in many directions."[4] McKittrick also arranged short-term loans to the German government. McKittrick's German loans were watched appreciatively at the BIS and Sullivan and Cromwell. In October, Gates McGarrah, the BIS president, wrote to John Foster Dulles expressing how glad he was that the "Lee Higginson [German] credit got itself through."[5]

So were McKittrick and his partners at Lee, Higginson. At least something was going right, for the firm had become embroiled in the affairs of one of the greatest swindlers in history, Ivar Kreuger, a Swedish industrialist. Kreuger had built up a fortune—on the simple safety match—that would now be worth billions.

Wall Street had welcomed Kreuger with open arms and checkbooks. Thanks to McKittrick and his colleagues, Kreuger's reputation had preceded him. The London Higginson partners told their American colleagues that Kreuger had already made them a fortune. But it was a fortune built on fraud. Kreuger had constructed a massive Ponzi scheme that demanded a never-ending stream of new investors to pay their predecessors. In 1931 one of the brokers at Lee, Higginson wrote to Kreuger that some of his bank creditors would like more information about the company and how it worked. The broker asked Krueger to explain what he meant by "loans secured by real-estate mortgages," which was an eerie precursor of the bundled mortgages that triggered the subprime meltdown in 2007.

What Kreuger meant was that he could no longer pay his creditors. He frantically tried to arrange a bailout with Sosthenes Behn of ITT. Behn wrote a check for $11 million on the condition that Price Waterhouse, the accounting firm, could check Kreuger's finances. It did, and it quickly found a hole of $6 million. Kreuger's empire began to collapse. ITT wanted its money back. Kreuger returned to Europe in March 1932 to meet his bankers, but he made it only as far as his apartment on Avenue Victor Emmanuel III in Paris. There, according to most accounts, he lay down on his bed and shot himself in the heart. Lee, Higginson, the venerable Boston bankers who had backed Kreuger for a decade, went bust. The partners were ruined. "I suddenly knew we had all been idiots," an anonymous source told investigators. But McKittrick kept his job at the bank's London branch, as well as his position as vice chairman of the BIS's German Credits Arbitration Committee. It seems there were no recriminations or questions in Basel about McKittrick's judgment—or lack of. McKittrick himself later claimed that he had been selected as president of the BIS without his knowledge or participation. In March 1939, he recalled, "People began whispering—primarily on the continent—'we hear that you're going to BIS as president.' And that continued. The normal grapevine operation." The following month Charles Dalziel, McKittrick's fellow partner at Higginson & Co., told him that "he had heard on an unquestionable basis that I was going to be offered the presidency in the BIS and he wanted me to know that I would make a great mistake if I didn't accept it."[6] Sir Otto Niemeyer, the chairman of the BIS board, made the formal offer in May. McKittrick readily accepted. At first the State Department refused to allow McKittrick to travel to Europe, but after what McKittrick later described as the "principal European countries," doubtless including Britain, applied sufficient pressure, he was allowed to leave. McKittrick moved to Basel and started work in January 1940 on an annual salary of SF175,000 (US$40,000). He immediately traveled to Berlin, Rome, London, and Paris to meet the German, Italian, British, and French BIS directors and central bankers.

But before McKittrick moved from London to Basel he had another task: to help Hitler's former propaganda chief get released from a British prison camp. In October 1939 Ernst Hanfstaengel's lawyers asked McKittrick to provide a character reference for their client. Hanfstaengel, a Harvard graduate, had lived in New York and was well connected in American high society. He returned to Germany to become one of Hitler's earliest backers. Hanfstaengel lent the Nazi party $1,000 dollars during its early years—an enormous sum during the Weimar hyperinflation—which paid for the publication of the *Völkischer Beobachter*, the party newspaper. Appointed foreign press chief in 1931, Hanfstaengel's job was to present a moderate, sophisticated face to journalists. However his eccentric mannerisms, dry sense of humor, and close connection to Hitler made him enemies, and he fled in 1937. Hanfstaengel's detention as an enemy alien was especially badly timed, explained his lawyers, as he had just signed a contract with an American magazine to write a series of articles about his relations with Hitler—at one dollar a word. McKittrick replied that he would do all he could. McKittrick was ready to declare that the former Nazi spin doctor would not act against British interests if he were set free—although it is unclear how McKittrick could know this.[7] Hanfstaengel was duly released and returned to the United States, where he compiled psychological profiles of Nazi leaders for American intelligence.

McKittrick was not a Nazi, but he was certainly a friend of the new Germany and, like many in his social and business circles at that time, had an ambivalent attitude toward Jews. In November 1938, two weeks after Kristallnacht, he used his contacts to help Rabbi Israel Mattuck, of the Liberal Jewish Synagogue in London. McKittrick introduced Rabbi Mattuck to the US Consul General in London to try and help arrange the immigration of German Jews. Mattuck wrote a grateful note thanking McKittrick "most heartily." The meeting had been very useful. "As a result, I hope that I may, by means of a fund that we have here, help at any rate a few German Jews to find a way of escape."[8] Later on, during the war, in August 1942, Paul Dreyfus, a Basel banker, asked McKittrick to write a letter of introduction to Leland Harrison, the American ambassador to Switzerland. McKittrick obliged but made his feelings about Dreyfus clear in a separate letter to Harrison. "He is, as you will surmise, a Jew, but a good sort who is doing everything he can to help his unfortunate countrymen."[9]

THE OUTBREAK OF war brought existential choices for the BIS's management. There were three options: liquidate the bank, downsize and become dormant until the end of hostilities, or remain as active as possible within the bounds of the declared policy of "neutrality." The directors were unanimous—and already thinking ahead of the needs of transnational capital: the BIS must be kept going to assist with postwar financial reconstruction. McKittrick gave an under-taking to the Swiss authorities that all staff would not "undertake political activities of any sort whatsoever on behalf of any governments or national organizations." Any such departures, he noted in a memo to staff, would be "particularly regrettable at present when special privileges are being sought on behalf of the bank and its staff."[10] A safe passage home would be arranged for anyone who wanted to leave.

The BIS declaration of neutrality meant the following: the bank would not grant credit to central banks of belligerent countries; it would, when op-erating on neutral markets, ensure that belligerents did not profit from such operations; it would not carry out any transactions, either direct or indirect, between countries at war with each other; it would not sell assets in one coun-try to make a payment to another if they are at war, and it would not hold as-sets of one belligerent country secured against another. Badly burned by the Czechoslovak gold affair, the BIS said it would not make decisions implying recognition of what it delicately called "territorial changes not universally accepted." When the central bank of the German Protectorate of Bohemia and Moravia (the illegitimate Nazi regime ruling Czechoslovakia) requested the transfer of its remaining gold held at the BIS to the Reichsbank, it was blocked. When the Belgian government in exile proclaimed that the National Bank's official seat was in London, the Nazi occupation regime responded that the bank's headquarters were in Brussels. The BIS said it was neutral and would not recognize either. The Belgian vote on the board of directors remained unused. The BIS took the same position with regard to Yugoslavia, when faced with competing claims from Belgrade and London.

The bank's declarations of neutrality soon proved worthless. McKittrick and the rest of the bank's management turned the BIS into a de facto arm of the Reichsbank. This was not a result of inertia, passivity, or bureaucratic sloth. It followed from a series of deliberate policy decisions. The BIS carried out foreign exchange deals with the Reichsbank. It accepted looted Nazi gold until the final days of the war, when even neutral countries such as Sweden had begun to refuse it. It recognized the forcible incorporation of occupied countries, including France, Belgium, Greece, and the Netherlands, into the Third Reich. By doing so, it also legitimized the role of the Nazi-controlled national banks in the occupied countries in appropriating Jewish-owned assets. The BIS allowed the Nazi occupation regimes to take ownership of BIS shares, so that the Axis block held 67.4 percent of the bank's voting stock. Board meetings were suspended, but Annual General Meetings continued. Shareholder banks voted by proxy. The case of Poland is telling. In April 1940, Leon Baranski, the Polish representative to the BIS, asked for the government in exile in London to take control of the Polish shares. McKittrick refused. He told Baranski that he did not want to have to issue a ruling, but if he was forced to, the "result may necessarily be an adverse decision" for Poland. McKittrick was determined to avoid raising "a question of this sort," for "once political discussion gets underway, even without publicity, one never knows where it will end."[11]

While Nazi territorial annexations were accepted, Soviet ones were not. In June 1940 the Red Army invaded Latvia, Lithuania, and Estonia. The Soviets ordered the three central bank governors to instruct the BIS to transfer their gold reserves to the Soviet Union's state bank. The parallel with the Czechoslovak gold was clear—but the outcome was very different. The BIS's management, as legalistic as ever, argued that the bank had to accept the instructions. But this time the president refused. "I had to fight my whole management—particularly my legal adviser, saying that we had to accept these instructions and turn the gold over to the Russians. But I just couldn't do it," McKittrick recalled.[12]

Instead, McKittrick commissioned an outside legal opinion from Professor Dieter Schindler of Zürich University. Schindler argued that neither the governors nor the banks of the Baltic States were free agents, but had probably acted under the instructions of the Soviets. He quoted Article 10 of the BIS charter, which prohibited coercive measures against depositors. Thus, Schindler argued, it was the duty of the BIS management to "resist, as far as lies in their power" any attempts by governments to interfere with the BIS's assets. McKittrick was vindicated. He sent a copy of Schindler's memo, which was accepted by the bank management, to Merle Cochran. The BIS president asked him to keep Schindler's legal opinion confidential. "My one serious concern is that it should not get into the press. After the damaging campaign of publicity regarding the Czech gold, it is of the greatest importance to the BIS to remain in the background at this time."[13]

UNTIL THE OUTBREAK of war, the BIS was a congenial place to work. The staff were well paid, intelligent, and cosmopolitan in their outlook. The BIS, like the League of Nations, was an international oasis. Managers regularly traveled to meet their counterparts in London, Paris, Berlin, and other capitals. The governors' meetings were the high point. Some of the most powerful people in the world traveled to Basel, sprinkling the staid BIS with a little stardust. The staff enjoyed the glamour, the sense of being on the inside track, and the social whirl of dinners, receptions, and teas.

That idyll ended with the fall of France in May 1940. Axis-controlled territory now surrounded Basel on two sides where the borders reach almost to the city limits. Bank officials worked to a backdrop of gunfire. The Swiss authorities feared a German invasion and made plans to evacuate the city. Meanwhile, McKittrick's patrons in London were keeping a very close watch on their protégé. The BIS president was in regular contact with Sir Frank Nelson, the British consul in Bern. Nelson, who was an experienced international businessman, later became chief of the Special Operations Executive, the British wartime sabotage organization. One day, around May 20, as tension soared, Nelson called McKittrick at home at 7 a.m. The British diplomat told him, "Things look very bad indeed. They couldn't look worse." Nelson explained that he must be able to reach McKittrick at any time. He told him, "Don't go out without telling somebody where you are going, and don't leave the next place without telling me where you're going."

At 7 p.m. that evening, McKittrick had returned home when Nelson called again. He instructed the BIS president to evacuate all French and British staff from Basel immediately. The Nazi invasion was imminent, expected to commence at any moment. McKittrick returned to the bank's headquarters and summoned his senior staff, including Roger Auboin, Rafaele Pilotti, and Paul Hechler. They contacted as many French and British employees as they could. Hechler then told McKittrick, "You're the only man who alone can dispose of the assets of this bank. I think you're the most important man for us to get out of Basel." McKittrick agreed and quickly abandoned his colleagues. He called his chauffeur, and went home and grabbed some clothes. The chauffeur, McKittrick recalled, "didn't pack them but stuffed them into the car." They headed for Bern and were stopped on route fourteen times by Swiss soldiers or police.[14]

The German invasion of Switzerland never happened. Swiss francs, Swiss banks, and the BIS were far more use to the Third Reich than another stretch of mountainous territory, where a stubborn, hardy population would have likely waged guerilla warfare against the Nazis. The BIS relocated to Château d'Oex, in the southwest of the country. McKittrick and Per Jacobssen moved into the Chateau de Rougemont, kindly loaned by its American owner. The rest of the staff had to make do in the village. There were few decent houses, schooling was basic, and the village was tiny. By the end of the autumn, as the war ground on, relations between the different nationalities were near-poisonous. Morale was collapsing, recalled McKittrick. "There was only one movie house in town, and if a Frenchman and his wife went to the movies, and a German and his wife went to the movies, and they walked into each other, it was an embarrassment for all concerned."[15]

Everyone was relieved when the BIS returned to Basel in October 1940. There, despite the conflict, the BIS continued to enjoy immense financial as well as legal privileges. It could buy and sell unlimited amounts of Swiss francs. This was the most important currency in wartime Europe, accepted everywhere. The BIS, thanks to its charter, did not have to report foreign exchange transactions. Its exchange rate against the Swiss franc was not subject to the same restrictions as Swiss commercial banks. Until 1942 the BIS could buy and sell gold at better rates than the Swiss National Bank. This bizarre setup, where Allied and Axis bankers worked together so profitably, drew increasingly hostile attention in London and Washington, DC.

The State Department asked the American embassy in London to investigate the state of the relationship between the British government and the BIS, noting that "many problems" have come up. John Gilbert Winant, the ambassador, met with Sir Otto Niemeyer, the former chairman of the BIS board. Niemeyer was as adamant as ever about the BIS's immunity. He pointed to article 10 of the BIS's charter that guaranteed that in the event of war, the property and assets of the bank shall be immune from seizure. Niemeyer had even made arrangements with the British government that BIS communications to London could pass directly through the censor. "It is Niemeyer's belief," wrote Winant, "that the British should continue their association, as well as lend the bank their tacit approval, if only for the reason that a useful role in postwar settlements might later have an effect."[16] While the BIS was operating in such a restricted manner, "it was felt that it would be of no use at this time to raise difficult legal questions with respect to the relationship of the various countries overrun by the Germans." Niemeyer argued that McKittrick should stay in Switzerland as he was "the guardian of the bank against any danger that might occur."[17]

McKittrick was far more than a guardian of the BIS. He repeatedly passed economic and financial intelligence to the Reichsbank leadership. McKittrick was especially close to Emil Puhl, the vice president of the Reichsbank and BIS board member, whom McKittrick described as his "friend." Puhl, a gold and currency specialist, was a regular visitor to both the BIS at Basel and the Swiss National Bank in Bern. He had close links with the financial wing of the SS that managed its extensive business interests. Puhl, rather than Walther Funk, his nominal superior, was the real boss of the Reichsbank. In autumn 1941 McKittrick gave Puhl a tutorial on the Lend

Lease program, under which the United States supplied the Allies with arms, ammunition and other war material. The act, passed in March of that year, effectively marked the end of the United States' policy of neutrality. McKittrick later recalled the conversation. Puhl asked the BIS president,

> *"What does this Lend Lease thing mean? We don't understand it. Is there anything you'd be willing to tell me about it?" And I [McKittrick] said, "Yes. I'll give you this. It's my own idea but there's no reason I shouldn't tell it to you. I think that if America is going to be in the war something will happen to get us in. Just the way it did in the first war. And what is happening is that we're getting our industrial organization into shape for our entry into the war." I've never seen a man's face drop more than his did. I though he was going to faint or something. He said, "My God. If you're right, we've lost the war."[18]*

McKittrick's prediction proved correct. But America's entrance into the war in December 1941 caused him further problems. The BIS president was no longer a neutral, but a citizen of a belligerent nation—in daily contact with his German, French, and Italian colleagues. But the advent of hostilities between the United States and Nazi Germany did not change his cordial and productive relationship with the Reichsbank. Puhl wrote of McKittrick in September 1942, "Neither his personality nor his manner of conducting business have been any cause for any criticism whatsoever."[19] Puhl even described the BIS as the "only real foreign branch" of the Reichsbank.[20] Some of the BIS dividend payments to its shareholders in Nazi-occupied countries went through the Reichsbank, thus giving Berlin access to the foreign exchange transactions and allowing it to charge a fee for its services. During the war the Reichsbank continued to pay interest on BIS investments in Germany, even though that interest contributed to the bank's dividends, which were paid to its shareholders, including the Bank of England. Thus, through the BIS, Nazi Germany was contributing to Britain's wartime economy.

It was a price worth paying, Puhl believed. For despite Hitler's bluster and Schacht's planning, Nazi Germany had not achieved autarky. It needed to buy vast amounts of raw materials to manufacture armaments and to feed, heat, and clothe its population. Swedish steel, Romanian oil, Portuguese tungsten, even South American beef, all had to be purchased and paid for in hard currency. Nazi Germany needed a financial channel to the neutral countries it ran through Basel. Which is the main reason why Nazi Germany did not invade Switzerland or Sweden. These neutral countries were far more use to the Third Reich as monetary hubs on the transnational financial network than as extra swathes of German-controlled territory.[21]

When questions were raised at the German Foreign Ministry as to why the Reichsbank remained a member of a bank with an American president, Puhl was the BIS's most influential advocate. The BIS was one of Germany's most important external trading partners, he argued. It carried out gold and foreign exchange transactions and gave the Reichsbank a mechanism for buying vital war materials. It was a listening post, providing useful intelligence on enemy financial transactions. The Germans working there, such as Paul Hechler, the assistant general manager, were loyal and efficient. If Germany pulled out and the BIS closed down, it would be an enormous loss to the Nazi war effort. And the BIS needed the Reichsbank—and Puhl—just as much. Per Jacobssen, the BIS's economic adviser, had lunch with Puhl on December 7, 1942, at Puhl's office in the Reichsbank. The two men always enjoyed each other's company. They had a pleasant meal, just a short walk from the bank's vaults that held the wealth of a looted continent and of its exterminated Jews. Puhl, Jacobssen believed, was the BIS's most important ally in Nazi Germany. Without his support the bank would collapse. Jacobssen later wrote in his diary, "I know full well to what extent the future of the BIS depends on Puhl's possibilities of holding the fort in Berlin."[22]

THE WAR WAS not good for the BIS's balance sheet. By 1943, its business volume fell to less than 5 percent of the average for prewar years. But the BIS had 294 million Swiss gold francs ($96 million) invested in Germany in the form of state bank funds, bills, and bonds. The bank was kept going by the interest payments it received from the Reichsbank, which eventually accounted for 82 percent of its income. At first Germany paid its dues in currency. But after March 1940 it changed to gold, much of it looted. During the war Germany added $603.5 million worth of gold to its reserves, more than 80 percent of which was plundered from the central banks of occupied countries. $88 million-worth was seized from citizens of Germany and Nazi-occupied territories. Around $3 million worth was taken from concentration camp victims, including the macabre category of "dental gold." This was also credited to an account at the Reichsbank, overseen by Emil Puhl, the confidant of Thomas McKittrick and lunch partner of Per Jacobssen.[23]

Thanks to research by Piet Clements, we know that during the war years a total of 21.5 metric tons of gold passed in and out of the Reichsbank gold account at BIS, of which 13.5 metric tons was acquired during the war. Some of the new gold—much of which was looted—was used to pay the interest on the BIS's loans and investments to Germany. Six metric tons were used to pay the Reichsbank's debts through the BIS payments system for international railway and postal traffic, which the bank also handled.

The fate of the Belgian gold reserves is the most extraordinary. At the end of 1939 the National Bank of Belgium sent more than 200 metric tons of its reserves to France for safekeeping. As the Nazis advanced, France transported the Belgian gold and some of its own to the port of Dakar in West Africa. Fearing an Allied raid, the French authorities then moved the gold inland. After the fall of Paris, Germany ordered the collaborationist French government based in Vichy to send the gold to Marseilles to be taken into the "custody" of the Reichsbank. The gold was then transported by boat, truck, train, and camel train through the Sahara Desert to Algiers. From there it was flown to Marseilles and eventually deposited in the vaults of the Reichsbank.

In the summer of 1943 Yves Bréart de Boisanger, the governor of the Bank of France, now under Vichy control, traveled to Basel to warn McKittrick about the fate of the Belgian gold, some of which would doubtless end up in Basel.

McKittrick dismissed de Boisanger's concerns. All the gold received at the BIS had been stamped with the proper markings, he said, and was German, not Belgium. Whether or not he believed this, McKittrick understood that if the bank were to stay in business there was probably no other option than to accept the Reichsbank's gold shipments. But Auboin, the French manager, sided with his compatriot. The BIS should no longer accept German payments in gold, but demand Swiss Francs instead.

Auboin was right. The Belgian gold had been melted down at the Prussian Mint and stamped with false identifying numbers and dates between 1934 and 1939. About 1.6 metric tons was used by the Reichsbank to meet its BIS interest payments, as well as 2 metric tons of looted Dutch gold.

However, not all the gold melted down at the Prussian Mint originated in the vaults of national banks. The Nazis set up a network of informers and torturers, called the Devisenschutzkommando (DSK), to track down private gold holdings in occupied territories. The stated purpose of the special unit that was handpicked by SS soldiers was to control currency traffic across the Third Reich. Its actual purpose was "the acquisition of gold by any means, including deceit and brutality," according to British intelligence records. In Paris alone the DSK employed eighty informers, from the "lowest levels of society to the highest circles."[24] Each received a 10 percent commission, as well as false identity cards and counterfeit American and British currency. Victims were lured with supposed sales of property or land. They were then arrested, beaten, and tortured to reveal how they would pay for such a purchase. The favorite interrogation method of Hugo Doose, who ran the DSK for the Channel Islands, was to break a beer glass over his victim's head. Ludwig Jaretski, an Austrian living in Paris, "employed burning matches on stripped victims."[25] Some of the BIS gold had an even more grisly origin, which came from the watches, spectacles, jewelry, and gold teeth of concentration camp victims. This was why, after the war, Emil Puhl, vice president of the Reichsbank and BIS director, would be found guilty of war crimes.

Under McKittrick's leadership, the BIS also carried out a significant number of gold transactions for other Axis powers. It sold gold for the Bank of France (Vichy) to Portugal for escudos, which France needed to pay for Portuguese imports. It organized three gold shipments from Bern to Bulgaria. It sold almost nine metric tons of gold to Romania, by undercutting the Swiss National Bank. All of these were direct breaches of the policy of neutrality. The BIS also carried out thirteen gold swaps with Turkey—a total of 8.6 metric tons—exchanging gold that Turkey had held at the Swiss National Bank for BIS gold that was held in New York, Paris, and London. Turkey was technically neutral but had strong trade relations with Germany and was the Third Reich's main supplier of chromium. Nor was the BIS was alone in its acceptance of looted Nazi gold, and the failure of its managers to check the gold's provenance. Swiss commercial banks and the Swiss National Bank (SNB) also readily accepted looted Nazi gold. The bankers' policy of "business as usual" with the Nazis was led from the top. Ernst Weber, the chairman of the BIS board from 1942 to 1947, was also the president of the Swiss National Bank. Weber, like McKittrick and Jacobssen, enjoyed cordial relations with Puhl. Even as the Allies fought their way through Nazi-occupied Europe to the Swiss border, Weber and Puhl were still arranging gold shipments. The two bankers had dinner together on December 10, 1944, to discuss their latest arrangement: Switzerland would buy German gold, and in exchange Germany would sell Switzerland coal. The negotiations took place in what Otto Köcher, the head of the German legation in Bern, called the "usual atmosphere of trust."[26]

The cozy relations between the BIS, the SNB and the Third Reich stayed buried until the late 1990s, when the scandal broke that Swiss commercial banks were still holding the assets of Holocaust victims. The BIS and the SNB were soon dragged in. A report commissioned by the Swiss government, published in 1998, said that Swiss National Bank officials followed an "ethic of the least effort" to check the origins of the gold sent to Switzerland, some of which had been looted from Holocaust victims. During the war the SNB bought $280 million of gold from the Nazis. By 1943 the SNB knew about the extermination of European Jewry, but bank officials did not take measures to distinguish looted gold from other Reichsbank holdings.[27]

DESPITE MCKITTRICK'S SAFE and privileged existence, he was often lonely. His wife and four daughters were far way in the United States. Travel remained difficult and slow. There were few visitors in Bern, apart from Emil Puhl, and the postal service was erratic. McKittrick kept an account at a bookshop on Charing Cross Road and took refuge in non-bankerly works including, *Will Europe Follow Atlantis*, which examined the coming cataclysm of European civilization; a work of Sufi devotion called *At the Gate of Discipleship*; and even *The Occult Causes of the Present War.* McKittrick went walking in the woods and mountains with Erin Jacobssen, the daughter of the bank's economic adviser. A keen botanist, McKittrick taught Jacobssen about the region's rich flora. Other correspondence doubtless cheered the BIS president. Hermann Schmitz, the CEO of IG Farben and BIS board member, for example, sent his sincerest New Year wishes on January 3, 1941. Schmitz wrote, "For their friendly wishes for Christmas and the New Year, and for their good wishes for my 60th birthday, I am sending my sincere thanks. In response, I am sending you my heartfelt wishes for a prosperous year for the Bank for International Settlements."[28] It would certainly be another prosperous year for IG Farben, whose profits were soaring and whose plans were well advanced for the construction of IG Auschwitz, the firm's own corporate concentration camp.

Most of the BIS staff stayed, but Charles Kindelberger, an American with a young wife, returned home. His departure left a vacancy. Leon Fraser, now president of the First National Bank of New York, had a suggestion for his old friend McKittrick. In November 1940, Fraser met with a young man named Henry Tasca in Washington, DC. Tasca was working at the National Defense Commission, specializing in foreign trade and Latin America. "He has a pleasing personality, a manifestly keen mind, and is ambitious and hard-working."[29] Tasca could leave for Switzerland on thirty days' notice. "He makes a much more favorable impression than did Kindelberger, both in appearance and seriousness of purpose."[30] And Tasca, fortunately, had the right answer for the most sensitive question, reported Fraser. Merle Cochran had asked it, "and the reply was that Tasca was not Jewish."[31]

As the war ground on, the Czechoslovak gold affair still haunted the BIS. Once again, there were angry questions in the House of Commons about Britain's continued membership, the bank's role, and its connections to Nazi Germany. The government stayed firm in its support. Sir Kingsley Wood, the finance minister, declared in October 1942 that with McKittrick at the helm, there was nothing to worry about. "The conduct and control of the bank have been and are today in the sole hands of the President of the Bank, an American citizen. . . . This gentleman has our complete confidence."[32]

In Washington the Treasury Department was increasingly hostile, especially after the United States entered the war in December 1941. McKittrick's first term of office ended in December 1942. Many argued that it should not be renewed. Montagu Norman was certainly worried. In June 1942, Norman wrote to McKittrick to assure him of his continuing support. "We certainly hope that means can be found for you to continue your presidency of the Bank, indeed it is not too much to say that we regard it as *essential*."[33] Perhaps McKittrick could simply "carry on without any formal steps at all." Bearing in this mind, it would be helpful for McKittrick to visit the United States. "We would at any rate do our best to make that possible."[34]

Norman and his allies had a plan: to appoint Ernst Weber, the president of the Swiss National Bank and a BIS board member, as chairman, as long as he agreed to re-appoint McKittrick as president. Weber would be a neutral figurehead for the BIS and provide cover for its activities. As Ivar Rooth, the governor of the Swedish Rijksbank, wrote to Norman, it was "important" that the Bank should be safeguarded by "putting in as authoritative position as possible a personage of neutral nationality."[35] Weber's discretion was guaranteed. In 1940 McKittrick had mentioned the Czechoslovak gold to Weber. The BIS president explained that the conversation went like this: "I asked him not to tell me where the gold would go, and he did not do so."[36] McKittrick was in close contact with Weber, whom he met in Zürich or Bern two or three times a month.

In Berlin, Joachim von Ribbentrop, the former German foreign minister, did not understand McKittrick's value to the Third Reich either. McKittrick should resign, he thought, and be replaced by a neutral, or Germany should sever its links with the BIS. Emil Puhl and Paul Hechler swiftly went into action. Both were great admirers of McKittrick, whom they described as "professional and loyal."[37] They told von Ribbentrop that if McKittrick went, Ernst Weber, once appointed chairman of the board, would take control. Even if McKittrick was deposed as president, the United States would still have a representative in the bank's management. Such a person would undoubtedly disrupt the "until now smooth functioning of the BIS and its use by us for conducting gold and foreign exchange transactions."[38]

McKittrick himself lobbied Marcel Pilet-Golaz, the Swiss foreign minister. The two men met in October 1942. There were several items to discuss. The unpleasant articles about the BIS in the British press unsettled McKittrick. The BIS president was hypersensitive to criticism or any hint that the British government might withdraw its support for the bank. As the bank depended on its neutrality for its continued existence during wartime, a British withdrawal would spell the end. The Swiss legation in London had taken the matter up with the Foreign Office and the Treasury. The articles did not reflect British governmental opinion, Pilet-Golaz said, reassuringly. Pilet-Golaz also confirmed the Swiss government's support for the BIS. The Swiss attitude to the numerous international organizations it hosted "varies very much."[39] He complained the League of Nations was the worst. The conduct of its staff left much to be desired, and it had created "numerous political difficulties."[40] The International Labor Organization (ILO) was somewhat better regarded, while the BIS had never "given cause for severe criticism."[41] It would certainly be a "cause for regret" if the bank would leave Switzerland.[42]

McKittrick then raised the delicate matter of the Weber plan. The chairman of the board, he explained, was very different to being president of the bank. The board dealt mainly with the bank's internal governance. The big questions of transnational capital flows, loans, and currency support were dealt with at the governors' meetings, which were anyway suspended for the war. Pilet-Golaz was agreeable, noted McKittrick. "He thinks it desirable that Switzerland should assist in the maintenance of international organizations and as an intermediary between belligerent countries when this can be done without undue publicity and when it does not interfere with the general policy of neutrality."[43]

It worked. Weber was appointed chairman of the BIS board. And on January 1, 1943 the Swiss banker re-appointed McKittrick for a further three years. By then, the BIS president—just as Norman had suggested—was in the United States.

CHAPTER SEVEN

REASSURING WALL STREET

"He believes that the Germans—at least those connected with the Reichsbank—desire his return [to Basel] and that some way will be found to make it possible."

— American intelligence report on Thomas McKittrick and the BIS, December 14, 1942[1]

The BIS had pioneered swift movements of international capital but could do little to speed its president across the Atlantic with enough cash in his pocket. In late 1942 Thomas McKittrick planned to travel to France, Portugal, Spain, and Britain, and then head to the United States. But even with his privileged status, he was still subject to currency control laws that allowed him to take a maximum of 1,000 French francs into France. "Can French franc banknotes be sent by registered mail to Spain from Switzerland?" he wondered in a note to himself. Such postal smuggling might be a better option, as he could use the French francs to buy pesetas on the black market. "Spanish currency can be obtained on better terms than by exchanging dollars or Swiss francs in Spain at the official rate," McKittrick mused to himself. Food might also be problematic, especially perhaps for someone used to the BIS dining room. "Take sandwiches to supplement food available in France. On arrival in France, ask for bread coupons. Use these to purchase bread on leaving France, as bread in Spain is very scarce and bad."[2]

McKittrick left Basel in early November and arrived in Lisbon some days later. There, while checking into his hotel, he had a pleasant surprise. He recalled, "The first thing I knew, somebody grabbed me from behind and said, 'Is that you Tom McKittrick?' I said, 'Yes' without seeing who it was. He said, 'Well, my gosh, I've got to see you. You're the first man I wanted to see in Switzerland.'"[3] It was

Allen Dulles, who was on his way to Bern to set up the Swiss station of the Office for Strategic Services, the embryonic American foreign intelligence service. The two men spent some enjoyable time together before McKittrick flew to London. There he spent two weeks ensconced with Montagu Norman and Sir Otto Niemeyer. McKittrick then traveled to Ireland, took a flying boat back to Lisbon, and eventually reached New York via Portuguese Guinea, Liberia, Brazil, Trinidad, and Puerto Rico.

There was much to think about on the long and arduous journey. The BIS now had a suitably neutral chairman in the shape of Ernst Weber, the president of the Swiss National Bank, and McKittrick had secured himself another three years as president. McKittrick had lobbied hard for a second term, using his extensive network of diplomatic contacts to make sure he was acceptable to both the Allied and Axis powers. The world was at war, but the one thing both sides could agree on, it seemed, was that the BIS should stay in business, with Thomas McKittrick in the president's chair. The American banker carefully cultivated his friends at the foreign legations in Bern. He was so successful that the foreign diplomats even sent his letters in their embassies' diplomatic pouches, McKittrick later recalled. "I made it my business to keep on good terms with their ambassadors or ministers in Bern, and they were all of them kind enough to send letters that were of certain importance and secrecy in the diplomatic pouches—so they were all informed of this and they all agreed to do it."[4]

The American Legation in Bern also encoded communications from the BIS to McKittrick while he was in the United States. In February 1943 Roger Auboin, the BIS's general manager, asked the US Legation to send a coded cable to McKittrick inquiring about the arrangements for his return journey to Basel, via Lisbon:

> *Please communicate as soon as possible approximate date arrival Lisbon to enable us to settle material details of your journey regarding which we shall cable you in due course care American Legation Lisbon.*[5]

It seemed that Leland Harrison, the American ambassador to Switzerland, even allowed McKittrick to write his cables for him—in exchange for a substantial sum of money. On November 15, 1943, McKittrick wrote to Harrison about "the draft cable of which we spoke on Thursday." The cable had been "recast," noted McKittrick, who admitted he had "gone rather far in putting words" into Harrison's mouth. "My purpose has not been to tell you what to say but to avoid leaving blanks in the picture, and if I have used the wrong color anywhere you will please make the necessary correction." McKittrick then promised Harrison a "reward" for his services, of three million Swiss francs (around US$700,000).[6]

The Treasury Department did not share the State Department's enthusiasm for McKittrick and the BIS. Henry Morgenthau, the Treasury secretary, and his colleague, Harry Dexter White, loathed the BIS, seeing it, correctly, as a channel for the perpetuation of Nazi economic interests in the United States. They ensured that the bank was facing ever more obstacles to doing business in the United States. Under wartime legislation Swiss banks, including the BIS, could operate only under special license in the United States. At first, McKittrick's friends at the New York Federal Reserve had obtained a general license for the BIS, so most routine transactions could be executed without delay. But that was revoked in June 1941, which caused substantial difficulties. The bank's dividends to its American shareholders, and other planned transactions, were blocked. The Treasury Department believed that Swiss banks were being used to transfer ownership of Italian and German firms to Swiss or American front companies. Their investigators were unraveling the links between New York, Berlin, and Bern. For example, Felix Iselin, a Swiss banker, was the chairman of IG Chemie, the Swiss subsidiary of IG Farben, the industrial conglomerate that drove the Nazi war machine and whose chairman, Hermann Schmitz, sat on the BIS board. Iselin also sat on the board of the Swiss Bank Corporation and the Credit Suisse bank.[7] IG Chemie was a holding company for General Aniline and Film, IG Farben's American subsidiary.

Morgenthau was a doughty foe, drawn from a very different world to McKittrick's WASP friends on Wall Street. Born into a prominent Jewish dynasty in New York, Morgenthau was an intellectual and a farmer who grew Christmas trees. His father, Henry Morgenthau Sr., had served as American ambassador to the Ottoman Empire during the Armenian genocide and had loudly condemned the extermination. A close friend of Franklin and Eleanor Roosevelt, Henry Morgenthau had a strong sense of social justice and was a key architect of Roosevelt's New Deal. White, like Morgenthau, was also Jewish, but his parents were poor Lithuanian immigrants. Born in Boston, White worked for a while for his father's hardware business and served in the US Army during the First World War. White was a prize-winning Harvard economist and had a solid understanding of the new global financial architecture emerging under the aegis of the BIS. He left academia to work at the Treasury, where Morgenthau placed him in charge of international affairs. Morgenthau and White would prove to be McKittrick's most powerful enemies in the United States. McKittrick later recalled that White "hated me, because I was doing things that he couldn't get done because I could get in all sorts of places in Europe that he couldn't get his people in."[8] This was largely because many of the things that McKittrick was doing, such as gold and foreign exchange deals with the Reichsbank after Pearl Harbor, were treasonable.

Once McKittrick had safely arrived in Manhattan, he set up an office at the Federal Reserve, with the help of his old friend Leon Fraser, the former BIS president who was now president of the First National Bank of New York. McKittrick needed a lawyer to persuade the Treasury to unblock the BIS's funds. His choice was never in doubt: John Foster Dulles. Meanwhile, McKittrick made the rounds of government departments, trying to show how the BIS could help with the American war effort by offering financial services and helping in the postwar reconstruction of Europe. The BIS president was much in demand as a fresh, first-hand source on wartime Europe. "I had a lot of questioning to go through in Washington, because everybody wanted to know everything about the war in Europe, everything about political affairs in Europe."[9] McKittrick also met Henry Morgenthau. The encounter did not go well. McKittrick laid out his arguments for paying dividends to American BIS shareholders and the bank's position on other contentious matters. Morgenthau walked out after twenty minutes, recommending that he consult Treasury experts.

But the worst was to come. In April 1943, while McKittrick was still in the United States, Congressman Horace Jeremiah Voorhis demanded an investigation into the BIS. Voorhis wanted to know why the bank's president was an American and whether the bank was being used to help the Axis powers. Voorhis, McKittrick believed, was being fed information by Paul Einzig, the BIS's journalistic nemesis, who ever since the fiasco of the Czechoslovak gold, had lambasted the bank in the British financial press. Einzig was a dogged reporter, whose criticisms of the bank struck a nerve, so much so that McKittrick, always hypersensitive about press coverage, referred to him in one letter to Leon Fraser as a "swine."[10]

McKittrick then found he could not get permission from the US authorities to return to Basel. He was stranded, his requests for help unanswered. "I talked to the State Department and they made believe they didn't know what I was talking about."[11] McKittrick asked Col. Bill Donovan, the OSS chief and Allen Dulles's boss, for help. Donovan also stonewalled the BIS president, repeatedly promising him to sort out his passport. But the passport did not arrive. The OSS did not want McKittrick to go anywhere until he had told them everything he knew about Nazi Germany's economy, the Swiss connection, the role of the BIS, the progress of the war, in-fighting among the Nazi leadership, conditions inside Germany, and anything else of interest. McKittrick was called in for several interviews. He was, it turned out, a fantastic source, if somewhat delusional about the centrality of his own role. Even with all that we now know of the BIS's wartime record, the OSS report of McKittrick's explanations of why an American should run an international bank that was under de facto control of the Nazis is still eye opening.

The Weber plan—to install the president of the Swiss National Bank as BIS chairman—McKittrick explained, had been carried out with the full knowledge of the Reichsbank and the German Foreign Office. Both also knew that the Swiss banker would name McKittrick as the next BIS president and were satisfied with that. Hitler himself, though, was not involved, and the plan to extend McKittrick's term as president avoided mentioning the American banker in detail, in case Hitler "heard of the matter" and became angry. The

OSS memo reveals how much high-grade economic intelligence McKittrick had access to: the governor of the Hungarian National Bank explained to him how Hungary had deliberately obstructed a new trade agreement with Germany; Vichy France, had been sending gold into Switzerland by a roundabout route to avoid occupied France; Switzerland was awash with Romanian oil, as Romania preferred to sell there rather than to its ally Germany; Walther Funk, the Reichsbank president, had failed to persuade Germany's allies in the Balkans that their debts would eventually be paid. There is an intriguing glimpse into the morale of the BIS's staff: the bank employed fourteen British staff and eight Italians. The Italians were "morose and depressed." They felt that Italy was already defeated and would not "have a friend in the world."

McKittrick's Reichsbank contacts made him an excellent source for news about life inside the Third Reich. Hitler, McKittrick revealed, had become indecisive. "Instead of having a definite plan laid out, and pursuing it relentlessly, he switches from one plan to another," the OSS document noted.[12] There were even rumors that he had started drinking. Despite the soaring casualties on the Eastern Front, and the surrender at Stalingrad, most Germans, McKittrick explained, still believed state propaganda. He related how one friend of his in the Reichsbank said he had to get out of Germany every now and again or he would start to believe the propaganda himself. McKittrick was also in contact with Hjalmar Schacht. The BIS president was not a fan of Schacht's and regarded him as a "political crook and entirely untrustworthy." Schacht still saw Hitler every couple of months, and when the Nazi leader asked numerous technical questions Schacht proffered his advice. Sometimes Hitler took it, other times not. As for Basel, McKittrick believed that there were twenty thousand Germans living in the city, who were "well-organized under Nazi leadership." He did not believe he was under observation by the Gestapo.

Some of most intriguing material the OSS obtained from McKittrick detailed his role as a back-channel between anti-Nazi Germans and the United States. This doubtless explains why the State Department eventually allowed him to return to Basel and the BIS to stay open. McKittrick told the OSS that he received "peace feelers" from non- or anti-Nazi Germans twice a month. All of them, however, argued that, even if a deal was made, Germany would remain the dominant European power "with a free hand in the east and a large measure of economic control in western Europe." These envoys included a "Berlin lawyer" and a "retired diplomat" Adam von Trott zu Solz. A former Rhodes Scholar at Oxford University, von Trott was a German nobleman and diplomat. He had lived in the United States and was active in the resistance against Hitler. McKittrick's personal papers include the record of a meeting with von Trott in June 1941. Von Trott asked McKittrick to arrange for five hundred dollars to be transferred by the Institute of Pacific Relations (a liberal think tank based in New York) to Switzerland, so von Trott could keep in touch with the IPR's European members. Communications for von Trott should be sent through Werner Karl von Haeften, the German consul in Basel, McKittrick noted.[13] Von Trott was a leading figure in the July 1944 plot against Hitler. Had it succeeded, he would have become foreign minister and led negotiations with the Allies. After it failed, von Trott was hanged.

McKittrick, like his colleagues in London and Berlin, strongly emphasized the BIS's future use in planning the postwar order. "While it does not concern itself with political affairs, it does offer facilities for the discussion of postwar financial and economic questions," wrote the author of the OSS memo, "and he thinks that a year or two can be saved in getting Europe back to work by informal international conversations under its auspices."[14]

McKittrick's return to New York was the talk of Wall Street. On December 17, 1942, Leon Fraser hosted a dinner for him at the University Club. Thirty-seven of the United States' most powerful financiers, industrialists, and businessmen gathered in his honor. The Treasury was stonewalling him, his passport was stuck on a bureaucrat's desk, and the OSS was grilling him, but here at least friends and admirers surrounded him. They included the presidents of the New York Federal Reserve, the National City Bank, the Bankers' Trust, the New York Life Insurance Company, the New York Clearing House Association, and General Electric, as well as a former undersecretary of the Treasury and a former US ambassador to Germany. Standard Oil, General Motors, J. P. Morgan, Brown Brothers Harriman, several major insurance companies, and Kuhn Loeb also sent senior executives. It was probably the greatest single gathering of America's war profiteers.[15] Many of these companies and banks had, like McKittrick, made fortunes from their connections with Germany, connections that carried on producing massive profits long after Hitler took power in 1933 and certainly after the outbreak of war in 1939. Some have been accused of continuing links with the Nazis after December 1941, through subsidiaries in Germany—accusations they deny. The three most powerful sectors were oil, cars, and banks.

Jay Crane, Treasurer, Standard Oil

Walter Teagle, Crane's boss, was a founding board member of General Aniline and Film, IG Farben's American subsidiary. When in 1929 Standard Oil entered into a "division of fields" arrangement with IG Farben—a cartel—IG Farben retained supremacy in the chemicals field, including in the United States, in exchange for giving Standard Oil its oil patents for use anywhere— except Germany, according to a Senate investigative committee.[16] Further agreements followed over the next decade to share technical information and patents. In 1938 Standard sent the full specifications of its processes for synthesizing Buna—artificial rubber—to IG Farben. In exchange, the German chemical combine promised its latest research—once it had permission from the government. Not surprisingly, this was not forthcoming. Thus IG Auschwitz, the firm's massive chemical and Buna factory, run by slave labor and concentration camp inmates, was based partly on American scientific knowledge.

When war broke out in 1939, IG Farben assigned its Buna patents to Standard Oil—to prevent them being seized as enemy property. This was not illegal. But Standard's obstructive policies over development of the Buna industry were. By the time the United States entered the war in December 1941, the country was facing a desperate shortage of artificial rubber. Standard had deliberately delayed the development of the domestic artificial rubber industry by repeatedly telling other American companies that it would share its expertise, even though it had no intention of doing so, to prevent them developing alternatives, according to the US Department of Justice, which brought a lawsuit against the company.[17] In March 1942, six Standard Oil subsidiaries and three company officials were fined five thousand dollars each by a federal judge for violating anti-trust laws. IG Farben was named as a co-conspirator. Thurman Arnold, the assistant attorney general in charge of the Antitrust division, accused Standard of "treason" and entering an "illegal conspiracy" to prevent the development and distribution of artificial rubber. In its defense, Standard claimed that its agreement with IG Farben had resulted in the release of new information about synthetic rubber production, fuel, and explosives.

British Security Coordination, the British intelligence service operating in the United States, was closely monitoring the connections between Standard Oil, GAF and IG Farben, whose CEO, Hermann Schmitz, sat on the board of the BIS. GAF and Chemnyco, another American subsidiary of IG Farben, were the headquarters of Nazi industrial espionage in the United States. British intelligence believed that before the outbreak of war, IG Farben's spy service, "Buro IG," had dispatched deep cover agents to settle in the United States, to make business contacts, and to glean American scientific know-how. Some had married American women and become citizens. Chemnyco was also investigated by the US Department of Justice, which reported that it was a spying operation: "The simplicity, efficiency, and totality of German methods of gathering economic intelligence data are exemplified by Chemnyco, Inc., the American economic intelligence arm of IG Farbenindustrie. Chemnyco is an excellent example of the uses to which a country with a war economy may put an ordinary commercial enterprise."[18]

Donald MacLaren, a BSC operative based in New York, had been working for months on an operation against GAF. MacLaren's plan combined dirty tricks with very public exposure of the firm's links to Nazi Germany. MacLaren, an ebullient Scot and bon viveur, was a forensic accountant by training and an expert in economic warfare. He had untangled the web of connections linking Standard Oil and Sterling Products, an American pharmaceuticals firm, with GAF and IG Farben. GAF, he wrote, was a "supply depot" for the Latin American subsidiaries of IG Farben and sought to "camouflage its German ownership."[19] MacLaren knew that there were two factions in GAF's board of directors. He infiltrated both groups under a false name and gained their confidence. He then persuaded each of his contacts to reveal their faction's plan to outmaneuver the other grouping—information that he promptly passed on to the other side, which produced "an outright quarrel between the two." The result was most satisfactory, he wrote, with "one faction racing the other to Washington to report the wicked activities of their colleagues to the Department of Justice, thereby exposing their German instructions to the United States government."[20]

MacLaren and his colleagues in British Security Coordination also set up a company called Booktab. The firm published a seventy-page pamphlet entitled *Sequel to the Apocalypse: The Uncensored Story—How Your Dimes and Quarters Pay for Hitler's War*. With a trenchant foreword by Rex Stout, the popular mystery novelist, the pamphlet described, in forensic detail, "the hidden corporate relationships between American organizations and German monopolies." The pamphlet, published in early 1942, demanded the "the full penalty" for German industrialists and bankers, including Hermann Schmitz and Hjalmar Schacht. Two hundred thousand copies were printed. Despite the best efforts of the companies exposed to sabotage the project by buying up as many copies as possible, tens of thousands were sold. The facts about American business links with the Nazis were now out.

Sequel to the Apocalypse caused a nationwide furor. It was certainly a public relations disaster for Standard Oil. The Treasury Department took control of GAF in February 1942 and soon after handed the stock to the newly established Alien Property Custodian. One hundred members of staff known to be sympathetic to the Germans were sacked, from directors to engineers. GAF's research arm was turned over to war production. By 1944 the Custodian had also seized a total of twenty-five hundred patents from Standard Oil and its affiliates. Standard Oil eventually released all its patents for artificial rubber for free.[21]

Meanwhile, in Nazi-occupied Poland, the slave laborers at IG Auschwitz were enduring a living hell of backbreaking work, extreme brutality, and starvation rations. Among them was a teenage boy named Rudy Kennedy.

Rudy and his family were deported to Auschwitz in 1943 from the ghetto in Breslau, now Wroclaw, in Poland, when he was fourteen. When the train arrived at the selection ramp, Rudy took his father's advice and lied about his age, claiming to be eighteen:

> *My father and I went to the right, my sister and my mother to the left. The guards kicked and beat us, and we went into a room with showers and basins at one end. My father was naked with hundreds of older men. Everyone was very agitated. They shaved our hair and told us to go into the shower. I was very disturbed by the shoes. All the shoes were piled up and jumbled together in a big heap. I wondered how they were going to sort them out, if we would ever wear them again. We went into the shower. Water came out. By then my mother and my sister were dead. The temperature was about minus ten and we were chased naked and barefoot down a frozen path to a blockhouse. We were given a red blanket and a piece of bread and salami. In the morning we were given clothes, everything at random, nothing fitted. They called out our names and we had numbers tattooed on our arms. The tattoo needle was very thick, like a knitting needle and the blood of the previous prisoner was still running down it.[22]*

Rudy and his father were sent to the IG Farben factory, where he worked at installing electric motors. The extremely harsh conditions were designed to kill off the laborers in a couple of months. Rudy survived because of his specialist knowledge of electrical systems, which meant he had access to food. He became a kind of mascot. One day a supervisor dropped his sandwich on the floor and told Rudy to pick it up. He would not eat it, he told the starving boy, because it was dirty. But Rudy could have it. This counted as an act of kindness. The IG Farben managers were fully aware of what was happening in their factory, Rudy later recalled. "We saw the civilians from IG Farben all over the place. We worked very near a site where they were building a chemicals factory. We could see people dragging sacks of cement, then they would collapse and die. The IG Farben civilians had to go past that on the way to their canteen. They absolutely knew what was going on. There is no question."[23]

When IG Farben's managers judged their slave laborers to be *gebraucht*, or used up, they were dispatched to Auschwitz I or II, to be dispatched by Zyklon B. Degesch, the German pest control company, which manufactured the poison gas capsules was a subsidiary of IG Farben. Rudy Kennedy survived. His father, Ewald, endured for about two months before being killed by an injection of prussic acid, which fit with IG Farben's planners' calculations about how long a slave laborer could live on his own body fat reserves.[24]

Walter Teagle resigned from the board of Standard Oil in November 1942. Bruised and disappointed by the pillorying he had received in the media, in 1944 he set up the Teagle Foundation with a mission to "advance the well-being and general good of mankind throughout the world." The foundation's reach did not extend to Nazi-occupied Poland but it still exists today.25

Donaldson Brown, Vice Chairman, General Motors

War had brought enormous profits to the American car industry. Opel, General Motors' German division, produced the "Blitz" truck on which the Wehrmacht invaded Poland. Ford's German subsidiary produced almost half of all the two- and three-ton trucks in Nazi Germany. There is a strong argument that without General Motors' and Ford's German subsidiaries the Nazis would not have been able to wage war.[26] Hitler was certainly an enthusiastic supporter of the American motor industry's methods of mass production. He even kept a portrait of Henry Ford by his desk.

In July 1938, Henry Ford was awarded the Grand Cross of the German Eagle, the highest honor Nazi Germany could bestow on a foreigner. The following month James Mooney, who ran General Motors' overseas operations, was also awarded a high Nazi honor. Mooney was a regular visitor to Berlin, where he met numerous Nazi officials, including Hjalmar Schacht, to negotiate

Four of the world's most powerful central bankers gather in New York in 1927: Hjalmar Schacht (Reichsbank), Benjamin Strong (New York Federal Reserve), Montagu Norman (Bank of England), and Charles Rist (Bank of France). (Courtesy BIS)

The first informal meeting of the Board of Directors of the Bank for International Settlements, in April 1930. The gatherings were so secretive that the room remained closed to outsiders, even after the central bankers had departed. (Courtesy BIS)

The first headquarters of the BIS was a former hotel near the Basel central railway station. It was intended as a temporary site, but the bank remained there until 1977. (Courtesy BIS)

The Board of Directors meeting in May 1935. Those in attendance included Montagu Norman, Hjalmar Schacht, and Kurt Freiherr von Schröder, a powerful Nazi private banker. (Courtesy BIS)

Hjalmar Schacht (center) with Adolf Hitler. Schacht, the architect of the German war economy, once described himself as Hitler's "most loyal co-worker." (Süddeutsche Zeitung/ Northfoto)

Donald MacLaren, a British intelligence agent, ran a sabotage operation against the American subsidiary of IG Farben, the giant Nazi industrial conglomerate. Hermann Schmitz, the CEO of IG Farben, sat on the board of the BIS. (Courtesy MacLaren family)

Allen Dulles, the American intelligence chief in Switzerland during the Second World War (right). Dulles was friends with Thomas McKittrick, the president of the BIS, who supplied him with information as codename 644. (Süddeutsche Zeitung/ Northfoto)

Karl Blessing (left), the president of the Bundesbank and BIS board member from 1958–1969. Blessing, like many German bankers, was a loyal Nazi during the Third Reich. He oversaw an empire of concentration camps and slave laborers. (Süddeutsche Zeitung/ Northfoto)

Thomas McKittrick, the American banker who served as BIS president from 1940–1946. The BIS acted as the foreign branch of the Reichsbank, accepted Nazi looted gold and was a back channel for secret contacts between the Allies and the Axis powers. (Courtesy BIS)

Roger Auboin, the general manager of the BIS from 1938–1958. The French banker embodied the continuity of transnational financial interests before, during, and after the Second World War. (Courtesy BIS)

Alexandre Lamfalussy, the Hungarian-born economist known as the "Father of the euro." Lamfalussy served as BIS general manager from 1985–1993 before leaving to set up the European Monetary Institute, which became the European Central Bank. (Courtesy BIS)

Andrew Crockett, a well-regarded British economist, succeeded Lamfalussy as BIS general manager. Crockett oversaw the transformation of the BIS from a primarily European institution to a global one, thus ensuring its survival. (Courtesy BIS)

Per Jacobssen, the bank's influential economic adviser from 1931–1956. Jacobssen used his status as a neutral Swede to pass economic information from Washington, DC, to Berlin during the war. (Courtesy BIS)

The 1980 Annual General Meeting. After fifty years of existence, the bank had made itself an essential pillar of the global economy. (Courtesy BIS)

The Governing Council of the European Central Bank in January 2013. The ECB, like its parent bank the BIS, is protected by an international treaty, and remains opaque and unaccountable. (Courtesy ECB)

deals to produce vehicles for the military. In 1939 Mooney even held talks with Hermann Goering on converting the General Motors plant at Russelheim to production of the Junker Wunderbomber.[27]

George Messersmith, the U.S. Consul-General in Berlin, who later served as ambassador to Austria, was watching Mooney's enthusiasm for the Nazis with alarm. Messersmith, despite his German origins, was an ardent anti-Fascist. His reports through the decade detail Mooney's unwavering determination to build up General Motors' links with the Nazis. Mooney, like Sosthenes Behn (the president of ITT whose German partner was the BIS director Kurt von Schröder) believed that the Nazi regime was here to stay in Germany and was "well established," wrote Messersmith in November 1934.[28] Thanks to Schacht's policies and the armaments drive, the German economy was booming. "It is curious that he and Colonel Behn and some other factories in Germany give this opinion. The factories owned by the ITT in Germany are running full time and in double shifts and increasing their capacity for the simple reason that they are working almost entirely on government orders and for military equipment."[29]

Numerous American business leaders traveled to Berlin to ingratiate themselves with the Nazis. Thomas Watson, the president of IBM, arrived in 1937, to be decorated with the Merit Cross of the German Eagle. That was one grade down from Henry Ford's honor. But Watson could comfort himself with the fact that Schacht himself had hosted the ceremony and given a speech in Watson's honor.[30] The following year, after the Nazi annexation of Austria, the SS used one of IBM's prototype computers, known as a Hollerith machine, to keep a record of Jewish properties and their subsequent Aryanization. The Vienna Nazi party newspaper boasted that thanks to the Hollerith machine, "within six weeks we shall have laid hands on all Jewish fortunes over 5,000 marks; within three years every single Jewish concern will have been Aryanized."[31] The historian Edwin Black argues that IBM's technology, used for cataloging and identifying the Jews of Europe, was crucial for the organization of the Holocaust.[32]

Mooney's medal was certainly a good investment by Hitler. In late 1938, Mooney was still pressing for a trade agreement with Nazi Germany, noted Messersmith, claiming that it would "help the conservative elements in Germany and therefore improve the prospects for a more reasonable regime in Germany," as though a wealthier Third Reich would somehow become more benign. Messersmith dismissed Mooney's claim. His real aim was to "in some way or other help along the important General Motors interests in Germany."33

Even in April 1941 Mooney refused to get rid of Axis supporters in the company's overseas subsidiaries, Messersmith wrote to Breckinridge Long at the State Department. "There are some cases like the General Motors, which are not giving us any cooperation in our program to get rid of anti-American agents of American firms abroad. This is due to the fact that there are certain people in the General Motors, such as Jim Mooney, and some of the men whom he brought into the organization over the years, who are really betting on a German victory and who hope to be the big boys in our country if there is a Nazi victory."34

Siegfried Stern, Vice President, Chase National Bank

Chase National Bank was the world's largest private bank in terms of assets and deposits. Its New York headquarters was a key hub in the Nazi's global financial network and held accounts for the Reichsbank and Germany's Gold Discount Bank. Chase was so close to the Reichsbank that after the war, Thomas Dodd, a prosecutor at Nuremberg, claimed the bank had once offered Emil Puhl, the vice president of the Reichsbank and BIS board member, a job in New York.35 The Treasury closely monitored Chase's transactions for its Nazi clients. On October 3, 1940, Merle Cochran sent a note to Henry Morgenthau detailing trans-fers from Chase's German accounts. In the previous two days alone, $850,000 had been debited from the Reichsbank account, of which $250,000 was sent to the Wallenbergs' Enskilda Bank in Stockholm. A further $1.13 million was transferred from the account of the Gold Discount Bank to Topken and Farley, a firm of lawyers at 17 Battery Place, New York.36

Chase National was of special interest to the Nazis because of its over-seas branches in London, Paris, Mexico City, and Shanghai. A wartime in-vestigation of the bank's Nazi links, by Paul Gewirtz, a US Treasury official noted, "The Chase Bank, like the other American banks in France, operated on a relatively small scale. The attitudes of the Germans, however, when they came into France, indicates that they looked beyond the activities in France and were more interested in the international character of an organi-zation like Chase with its established branches through the world and its his-tory in international banking which including a friendly intercourse with the Germans."[37] In other words, Nazi Germany valued Chase National, like the BIS, for its transnational reach.

After the German invasion of France in May 1940 the Paris headquarters of Chase National had enthusiastically collaborated with the country's new overlords—with the knowledge of the bank's headquarters in New York, re-ported Gewirtz.

> *Investigations conducted at the Paris Branch and at the Home Office in New York of Chase Bank disclosed that the bank operated in Paris throughout German occupation and engaged in sundry activities indicate an over-riding desire to continue operating even though this required a close collaboration with the German authorities. There is evidence that the Home Office in New York was fully informed of these activities, at least until late in 1942, but took no steps to discourage them, at the same time withholding pertinent information from United States Gov-ernmental authorities.*[38]

Carlos Niedermann, the manager of Chase's Paris office, was an ardent Nazi sympathizer. He closed Jewish-owned accounts and transferred the assets to Nazi-owned ones. In May 1942, Hans Caesar, a director of the Reichsbank, was put in charge of American banks in France. Niedermann met with Caesar. Caesar held the bank in "very special esteem" because of its New York headquarters. Niedermann recorded, "It is a fact that the Chase Bank enjoys special prestige in the banking circles in question owing to the international activities of our head office."[39]

Thomas Lamont, J. P. Morgan

Thomas Lamont was a senior partner at J. P. Morgan, one of the BIS's founding banks, a veteran of the reparations negotiations and, naturally, a friend of John Foster Dulles. Lamont had represented the US Treasury at the Paris Peace Conference in 1919 and later sat on the Young Plan committee. Like Chase National, J. P. Morgan encouraged its French subsidiary, known as Morgan & Cie, to continue trading with the Nazis, according to declassified US intelligence reports. As the Germans advanced on Paris, the French authorities ordered Morgan & Cie to liquidate their accounts and destroy their stocks of banknotes. Morgan & Cie ignored the order. Instead, like Chase National, the bank opened a new office in Vichy, France, at Châtel-Guyon to service its Nazi clients.

A Treasury investigation reported that "the primary loyalty of the Morgan partners was not to the US or France, but to the firm. Regardless of national considerations, they invariably acted in what they deemed to be the best interests of Morgan et Cie."[40] Morgan & Cie even gained permission to handle payments from German accounts to the European subsidiaries of American firms that were building military equipment for the Third Reich—such as General Motors. This ran so smoothly that Morgan & Cie's American lawyers cabled the firm's French managers to thank them: "The office at Châtel-Guyon has proved to be of great practical utility; without it we could not have carried on any business with the outside world."[41]

SWEDEN, ONE OF the Nazis' most important trading partners, was also represented at McKittrick's dinner, by Lars Rooth, the son of Ivar Rooth, the director of the Rijksbank. Ivar Rooth was one of the world's longest-serving central bankers and a founding member of the new transnational financial elite. He was important enough to be elected unanimously to the BIS board in 1931, even though Sweden was only a shareholder and not a founding member of the BIS. Rooth stayed until 1933 and returned in 1937, praised in the BIS annual report for that year as a banker well known for his "constructive work of collaboration." Working with the Wallenberg brothers at Enskilda Bank, Rooth helped steer Sweden through a neutrality whose profitability was rivaled only by Switzerland's. Swedish firms supplied the Nazis with millions of tons of iron ore to be turned into tanks, guns, and ammunition, with vital ball bearings, foodstuffs, and timber. Rooth, it seemed, was indeed a highly skilled collaborator, although not only in the meaning referred to in the BIS report.

Thomas McKittrick was the third American president of the BIS, after Gates McGarrah and Leon Fraser. The American connection had shaped the BIS since its foundation in 1930. The bank had been ostensibly set up to administer the Young Plan for German reparations, named for the American diplomat who had brokered the deal. The BIS was the trustee for the loans Germany took out from Wall Street to meet those obligations. The bank's American presidents stood at the center of the network of connections between Wall Street and American industry and Nazi Germany. Standard Oil had formed a cartel with IG Farben, whose CEO, Hermann Schmitz, sat on the board of the BIS. The French subsidiary of J. P. Morgan, a founding member of the BIS, traded profitably with the Nazis after the invasion of France. ITT had gone into partnership with Kurt von Schröder, the powerful Nazi banker who was a director of the BIS. For the new class of transnational financiers, war was merely an interruption in commerce, albeit a highly profitable one. Both McKittrick and his guests were already planning how to maximize their profits in the postwar era. Meanwhile, the money channels had to be kept open, and they ran through Basel. McKittrick embodied the American-Nazi financial network, which is why dozens of the United States' richest and most powerful businessmen and industrialists gathered in New York that freezing December evening to honor Hitler's American banker.

MCKITTRICK REMAINED MAROONED in New York, unable to return to Basel, until Montagu Norman came to the rescue. Meanwhile the BIS president was still a man in demand. Thomas Watson, the president of IBM who had been honored by Hitler, could not attend McKittrick's dinner at the University Club. Instead, Watson, who was also the president of the International Chamber of Commerce, arranged a luncheon in McKittrick's honor. Aware that not all of the American public shared the financiers' enthusiasm for the BIS, McKittrick limited himself to three private formal engagements while in New York. On January 12, 1943, he wrote to Ernst Weber, the president of the Swiss National Bank and chairman of the BIS board, that "it seemed to me best, however, for the BIS not to take part in public or semi-public gatherings."[42]

One day, McKittrick paid a call on a diplomat at the British embassy in Washington, DC. He had reassuring news for the BIS president. The Bank of England and the Treasury were "very interested in the BIS," the British diplomat said. "I've got to take this up with London. I'll be surprised if I can't get you back."[43] Calls were made, cables were sent, and the wheels of transitional finance started turning. Rafaelle Pilotti, the BIS's Italian secretary general, told McKittrick to travel to Lisbon and report to the Italian Legation, which would help him get to Rome, and from there he could travel on to Basel. McKittrick eventually received permission to leave the United States and arrived safely in Lisbon. After a stop in Madrid, he flew to Rome.

The United States was at war with Italy, and McKittrick was a citizen of an enemy nation, but none of that mattered. The BIS president still received a regal reception, he recalled. "I was met at the airport as if I was the king of something. Nobody looked at my passport; they just waved their hands at it." McKittrick was then taken to a comfortable hotel where Pilotti met him. Understandably, the Italian authorities did not want an American banker wandering freely around Rome. Pilotti arrived, to act as McKittrick's minder. The two men sent out for a sumptuous dinner. "That was the best meal that I ever had in the war, and Italy was really short of food, but good gracious they gave me a wonderful meal," recalled McKittrick. Soon after, at 11 p.m., McKittrick was put on a train to Switzerland.[44]

McKittrick finally arrived back in Basel in April 1943. His trip to the United States had produced mixed results. Despite his lobbying and John Foster Dulles's legal advice, the BIS's request for exemption was denied. The bank's funds in the United States remained frozen. But if that battle was lost, a far larger one loomed: for the bank's very survival. This time Henry Morgenthau, rather than McKittrick, would find himself outgunned.

CHAPTER EIGHT

AN ARRANGEMENT WITH THE ENEMY

"The bearer of this letter, Mr. Thomas McKittrick,
President of the Bank of International Settlements, is a
close friend of a prominent member of the State
Department stationed in Switzerland, Mr. Allen Dulles."

— OSS *laisser-passer* for Thomas McKittrick, June 15, 1945, request-
ing the provision of US Army billet and mess facilities[1]

T here were many in Washington, DC, especially in the Treasury department, who asked why the State Department had renewed McKittrick's
passport and allowed him to return to Basel, when it was clear that
the BIS was aiding the Nazi war effort. The answer lay in Bern, at Herrengasse,
23. Here McKittrick's old friend and protector, Allen Dulles, ran the Swiss
branch of the Office of Strategic Services, America's foreign intelligence service—a complex network of bankers and businessmen, scholars and spies, and
refugees and émigrés. Some of Dulles's assets and agents traded information
out of principle, others for money. McKittrick, also known as OSS codename
644, traded information out of loyalty—not to the Allied cause or the national
interest of the United States, but to transnational finance, a creed shared by
America's spymaster.

Back channels between the Allies and the Axis powers existed throughout
the war in neutral capitals such as Stockholm, Berne, and Lisbon. The BIS was
one of them. Its multinational staff and neutral, privileged status made the bank
an ideal place for gathering and disseminating intelligence. Switzerland was
its natural home. As the cynical wartime saying noted, "For six days a week
Switzerland works for Nazi Germany, and on the seventh it prays for an Allied
victory." After his return to Basel in 1943, McKittrick regularly met with Allen

Dulles and American ambassador Leland Harrison. The three men, McKittrick recalled, talked more freely "in those meetings than at any other time." Dulles and Harrison wanted to know everything McKittrick knew, especially about Nazi money channels—which was a lot, McKittrick later recalled,

> *And I did know, for instance, the way the Germans were obtaining the money with which they maintained their organisation for sabotage, subversion, as well as political and military intelligence, especially in South America. The Allies were very anxious to stop this, but no way was found to do so without risking a loss of good will among the neutral nations which would be too serious to provoke.*[2]

The Portuguese connection was key, McKittrick explained to Dulles and Harrison. The Germans needed a steady supply of Portuguese escudos to pay for vital war materials such as tungsten. The Portuguese escudo was then a hard currency, accepted by the Allies, the Axis powers, and of course, South American countries. Some German companies were still connected to their American partners or parent firms through subsidiaries in South America. The key players were the Bank of Portugal, the Reichsbank, the Swiss National Bank, and the BIS. The Bank of Portugal bought gold bullion from the Reichsbank, which was delivered to the Swiss National Bank and credited to the Bank of Portugal's account. The Bank of Portugal then credited the requisite amount of escudos to German accounts in Lisbon, allowing German purchases to take place there.

Germany was also shipping gold to the BIS, McKittrick explained,

> *You see we had a lot of German investments, which were made in '31 in accordance with the statutes of the bank. We had to help Germany with loans to pay for reparations payments in the first years . . . they had to pay us about a million Swiss francs a month and that is what we lived on. And in order to give us that money they*

would ship gold to us. Now, we had no vaults. We had no place to handle gold. We had none of the necessary devices to assay gold or weigh gold. They [the SNB] have a scale as big as that chimney breast there, and you can weigh the weight of your signature on a piece of paper. So we had the Bank of Switzerland do all our gold handling and gold storing for us in Switzerland.[3]

The American government knew this. A source referred to as "A" passed intelligence about BIS gold movements to American officials in Bern. It was sent to the State Department in a cable dated June 23, 1943:

German gold shipments (gold bars) arriving here, which were referred to recently, seem to be for the account of the Bank for International Settlements. The value involved is small, approximately Swiss francs 750,000 at a time. The gold, upon the arrival at the National Bank of Switzerland, Bern, is passed to the credit of the Basel bank.[4]

The BIS also held gold for the Reichsbank so sometimes, when the interest was due on the bank's investments, the BIS simply helped itself to the Nazi gold it held to make up the payments, McKittrick explained. At other times, the Germans borrowed BIS gold for their dealings with Swiss banks. This cozy arrangement caused no concern at the BIS, said McKittrick, as "we knew that they'd replace it." McKittrick's close relationship with Emil Puhl, the vice president of the Reichsbank, was especially valued by Dulles and the OSS. Puhl, whom McKittrick described as a "friend," passed on important information about German morale, the country's economy and political intrigue. OSS telegram 3589-90, sent on May 25, 1944—at a time when thousands of Hungarian Jews were still being deported every day to Auschwitz, where most were immediately murdered—records Puhl's fears—not that the war was lost, but that the Reichsbank might lose its privileged position during the reconstruction.

Not long ago our 644 [McKittrick] had two lengthy conversations with Puhl of the Reichsbank. The latter was extremely depressed, not so much by the idea of Nazi defeat, but by the situation, which Germany will have to contend with later. The Reichsbank has been engaged in work on plans for the reconstruction, and evidently they are unable to see where an effective beginning can be made.[5]

Roger Auboin, the BIS manager, was known as OSS codename 651. Auboin naturally had excellent connections in France. OSS telegram 3401, sent on May 11, 1944, warns that the Nazis planned to plunder what remained of French national assets:

I have been informed by 651 that he is the recipient of secret information from Paris pointing out the danger of an attempt to seize both the French Treasury and Bank of France's gold and foreign exchange.[6]

McKittrick also had excellent connections in neutral Sweden. The Stockholm OSS station closely observed Jacob Wallenberg and his brother Marcus, of Enskilda Bank. Jacob, the author of the Swedish-German trading agreement, was the most powerful banker and businessman in Sweden. He had strong links with both the Nazi leadership and the German resistance. His brother Marcus was McKittrick's mentor at the BIS since the two men worked together on the German Credits Committee during the 1930s, when Wallenberg had taught McKittrick about the intricacies of international finance.

When Marcus fell ill in June 1943, McKittrick wrote an appreciation of the Swedish banker, which was hand delivered by Ivar Rooth, the governor of the Rijksbank. "During the three years I have been in Basel," wrote McKittrick, "your method of approaching international problems, of which I gained some understanding during our work together in Berlin, has helped me more than I can tell you in dealing with the intricate and delicate questions which have presented themselves to the Bank for International Settlements by reason of changes wrought by the war." Marcus Wallenberg was his most important teacher, McKittrick concluded. "The thought of following in your footsteps will provide spur to my will and a goal for my ambition."[7]

The most important lesson the Wallenbergs could teach McKittrick was how to play both sides at once: ensuring that Sweden remained one of Nazi Germany's key trading partners while feeding intelligence to the Allies—and thus guaranteeing that regardless of whoever won the war, the Wallenberg banking and business empire would survive and thrive. Jacob Wallenberg managed the bank's channel to Berlin while Marcus looked after connections with the Allies. As the managing director of the Enskilda Bank, Jacob Wallenberg was the "principal financial figure in Scandinavia" and was "vigorous, shrewd, and cautious," Abram Hewitt, an OSS agent based in Stockholm, reported.[8] Outside the Swedish foreign office, Jacob Wallenberg was the country's "principal representative" dealing with Nazi Germany. "Wallenberg frequently goes to Germany and most Germans of importance visiting Stockholm are in touch with him."[9]

Sometime in 1943, Wallenberg had asked Hewitt if he would like to meet representatives of cells forming in Germany who planned to overthrow Hitler. Nothing came of this as the cells were subsequently "liquidated." In 1944 Wallenberg claimed to know the names of German generals who were now opposed to Hitler—because of German defeats—and were ready to overthrow him. However, he would share the names only when "in his opinion conditions would justify it." Wallenberg "probably has better sources of information about Germany and the continent in general than any man in Sweden," Hewitt continued. However Wallenberg was a "very difficult" man to approach, except by someone whom he had known for a long time. Jacob Wallenberg was still a bachelor at the age of fifty-four, and one possible approach of getting to know him was the time-honored one of the honey trap, preferably on a yacht. "It is important for anyone dealing with Jacob Wallenberg to know that he is very interested in sailing and in attractive women." Marcus Wallenberg, his young brother, was quickly dismissed, as a "man of less integrity and less weight."

Meanwhile, in Washington, DC, the Treasury was also closely monitoring the Wallenberg brothers and Enskilda Bank. A Treasury report in December 1944 made numerous accusations of economic collaboration with the Nazis: "Jacob Wallenberg recently indicated that he was willing to sell to the Germans a Swedish plant in Hamburg for gold, provided the price was high enough to compensate for possible future complications from the Allies."[10] Enskilda Bank acted for the German interest in the American branch of the Bosch company and had also worked with the Swiss Bank Corporation to conceal German interests in Schering, a chemical company in New Jersey—which had since been vested by the Alien Property Custodian, the report noted.[11]

J. Holger Graffman, Wallenberg's point man for foreign currency deals, was regarded as a high-value asset by the OSS. Graffman, an engineer by training, had worked as Latin American representative of Ivar Kreuger, the Swedish fraudster bankrolled by Lee, Higginson, the former employers of Thomas McKittrick. After Wallenberg had taken control of the remains of Kreuger's empire, Graffman returned to Sweden and joined Enskilda Bank, working on currency transfers, foreign credit, and blocked accounts. "In my opinion this man is the most useful single contact there is for us in Sweden. He is very pro-American and is married to a Dutch woman whose feelings toward the Germans are what you would expect," noted Hewitt.

But Graffman was also friends with Felix Kersten, an Estonian-born masseur who now lived in Stockholm. Kersten's most important client was Heinrich Himmler and he frequently returned to Berlin to treat him. Graffman introduced Hewitt and Kersten over coffee and cakes at his house. Kersten began treating Hewitt for his back problems. But Kersten was much more than a masseur: soon afterward he brokered a meeting between Hewitt and Walter Schellenberg, the Nazi intelligence chief, in Stockholm. Schellenberg and Hewitt met in Kersten's office in November 1943. Schellenberg hoped to arrange a separate peace with the Western Allies to prevent a Soviet takeover of Eastern Europe. The plans came to nothing.[12]

The Wallenberg business empire was the most important transnational finance channel between Sweden and Nazi Germany. Not just money but vast amounts of intelligence flowed back and forth between Stockholm and Berlin. Much of the State Department and the OSS—especially Allen Dulles—shared Jacob Wallenberg's desire to keep links with German industry so that business could resume as swiftly as possible after the end of the war. An OSS psychological warfare operation known as the "Harvard Plan" specifically utilized Thomas McKittrick for this purpose. The Stockholm OSS office published a wartime newsletter for German businessmen filled with snippets of intelligence and news. The purpose of "Information for German Business," was to suggest that cooperation now would pay handsome dividends after the Allied victory. OSS officials believed that the newsletter was seriously affecting the morale of German businessmen, many of whom were now planning for their future in a post-Nazi Germany.

On February 1, 1945, David Williamson, a senior official in the OSS Morale Operations department, wrote to codename 110—Allen Dulles. Williamson suggested to Dulles that he set up a similar psychological warfare operation in Switzerland, or find another way to use the Harvard Plan material to erode German morale. Williamson enclosed some draft material for Dulles's perusal. Notably, all the information in the OSS Stockholm newsletter had been passed by the State Department before it was to be distributed. The newsletter included this paragraph:

> The direct negotiations, which have been taken up by the business interests on both sides thanks to the mediation of Mr. McKittrick, the American who lives in Basel, have already led to a number of detailed agreements. Thus, we learn that representatives of the German potash industry have contacted and entered into binding agreements with the new and expanded potash industries overseas . . . it is expected that the postwar demand permanently will be materially higher than pre-war consumption.

The new agreement will guarantee the German export interests during this second period an export income at least equal to their pre-war revenues regardless of the expected break in the German cartel control.[13]

Once again, the German chemical industries were key. In 1925 Lee, Higginson, McKittrick's employers, had been part of a syndicate, including Enskilda Bank, that had issued an £8 million bond on behalf of the German Potash Syndicate. Nineteen years later, McKittrick was still ensuring that supplies of the mineral, vital for agriculture, would continue after the war's end. A second paragraph, also datelined Basel, outlines how, even as Allied airmen were bombing Germany, McKittrick had already concluded an agreement to "preserve the industrial substance of the Reich." Anyone who questioned the wisdom of such backdoor accords was merely a "leftist radical":

Mr. Thomas H. McKittrick, the American president of the BIS, has announced his decision to continue his efforts for a close cooperation between the Allied and German business world, irrespective of the opposition of certain leftist radical groups; in these efforts he counts on the full assistance of the American State Department. "After the war such agreements will be invaluable," said McKittrick. We learn that certain German interests have received assurances that their negative attitude toward the National-Socialist regime will be fully be considered by the Allied political and economic leadership after the war. Negotiations are under way to bring hostilities to a speedy conclusion and to preserve the industrial substance of the Reich.[14]

Thus, while American and Allied troops were fighting their way across Nazi-occupied Europe, Thomas McKittrick, an American citizen, was using his position at the BIS—with the knowledge of the State Department—to try and bring Allied and Nazi businessmen together, to plan for a post-war Germany that preserved as much as possible of the country's industry. McKittrick was even brokering agreements to guarantee German companies' postwar profits and to help German industrialists avoid the financial consequences of the break-up of prewar cartels.

THE OSS MEMO on the Harvard Project also noted how profitable Cicero's "sinews of war" had been for the American oil industry, most of all for Standard Oil. Oil industry dividends in 1944 reached a new high of almost $300 billion, the memo noted, quoting the *Wall Street Journal*—nearly a fifth more than in 1943. Standard Oil alone would pay out $68.3 million.

With such enormous sums moving around the increasingly globalized economy, it was becoming more clear that the world would need a new international financial system to finance postwar reconstruction and stabilize trade. In July 1944 more than seven hundred delegates from the forty-four Allied nations gathered at the Mount Washington Hotel in Bretton Woods, New Hampshire, for the United Nations Monetary and Financial Conference. Henry Morgenthau and Harry Dexter White led the American delegation. The conference agreed on the creation of the International Monetary Fund (IMF) and an International Bank for Reconstruction and Development (BRD), which became part of the World Bank. The IMF would monitor exchange rates and lend reserve currencies to indebted countries. The new bank would provide loans to underdeveloped countries. Bretton Woods also gave its name to a new international currency exchange system, where currencies were linked to the US dollar. In exchange the United States agreed to fix the price of gold at $35 an ounce. There would be no more currency warfare or manipulation.

But if there was consensus on the basics, there was none on the future of the BIS. With the IMF at the center of the new international financial system why was the BIS still needed? Henry Morgenthau and Harry White wanted the bank to be abolished. On July 10, 1944, they seemed about to get their wish. Wilhelm Keilhau, of the Norwegian delegation, introduced a motion to liquidate the BIS:

> *Be it resolved that the United Nations Monetary and Financial Conference recommends the liquidation of the Bank for International Settlements at Basel. It is suggested that the liquidation shall begin at the earliest possible date and that the governments of the United Nations now at war with Germany appoint a Commission of Investigation in order to examine the management and the transactions of the Bank during the present war.*

No delegation spoke publicly in defense of the BIS. But behind the scenes its defenders—sections of the State Department, Wall Street, the Bank of England, the British Treasury, and Foreign Office—went into action. Johan Beyen, the hapless Dutch former president of the bank who had handed over the Czechoslovak gold, blamed the US Treasury Department, in particular Harry White for the resolution. White, Beyen claimed, had got the Norwegians to do his "dirty work." White certainly supported the motion, which he believed would force McKittrick to resign, an event he described as "a salutary thing for the world."[15] White's opposition to the BIS—and clear understanding of its wartime role for the Nazis—had long caused alarm at the Bank of England. In December 1943, E. W. Playfair, a senior official at the bank, had written to Otto Niemeyer, the former chairman of the BIS board, drawing his attention to an article in the *New York Times* about White and the BIS. White had "disparaged" the bank and said it had "no significance" in relation to plans for the postwar reconstruction of Europe. Germany, said White, was being nice to the BIS because it hoped to use it to "get back into financial power."[16] White was even more scathing about McKittrick, describing him as "an American president doing business with the Germans while our American boys are fighting Germans." All of which was true and so even more infuriating for the financial mandarins, who preferred to keep their arrangements with the other side out of the public eye.

The Foreign Office advised the British delegation that any resolution dealing with the BIS or its liquidation would be "improper," that most British of sins. Britain, from the start, had been "opposed to doing anything with respect to the BIS," noted Orvis Schmidt, a US Treasury Official.[17] So was Wall Street. Leon Fraser, said Morgenthau, was "one of the spearheads of opposition to what we are doing here and has surrounded himself with a group who are fighting what we are doing here. . . . Now I don't say that Mr. Fraser isn't a very fine American citizen, but he has certain loyalties which run there, just the way Mr. McKittrick has, Mr. Beyen has. . . . " The BIS was a kind of club for central bankers, said Morgenthau and people like Schacht and Funk still hoped that the "same kind of thing would continue after the war."[18] Morgenthau was an implacable opponent not just of the BIS but of any kind of reconstruction that would allow Germany to dominate Europe. His plan for the country called for German heavy industry to be dismantled or destroyed, for Germany's industrial areas to be internationalized or ceded to neighboring countries, for complete demilitarization, and for the country to be reduced to a pastoral or agricultural economy.

Harry White saw the BIS clearest. The bank's emphasis on its supposed neutrality was an alibi for its future role in reconstructing Europe, he argued:

> *They hope to be a moderating influence in the treatment of Germany during the peace conference. That is why Germany has treated it with the greatest of care. She has permitted her to pay dividends; she has let the people in BIS come and go across enemy territory; she has been extremely careful and well-disposed to the BIS, because she nursed that baby along in the hope that that would be a useful agency that would protect her interests beyond those that any other institution around the peace table would.[19]*

On July 18, Ansel Luxford, a member of the US delegation, proposed a new resolution, that no country could join the IMF unless it had "taken the necessary steps to foster the liquidation of the BIS." John Maynard Keynes, the influential economist who was part of the British delegation, was furious. Keynes, who was also close to John Foster Dulles, suffered from angina and became so agitated by the affair that there were rumors he had suffered a heart attack. He demanded that the resolution be withdrawn or he would quit the conference. There could be no linkage between dissolving the BIS and joining the IMF, Keynes wrote to Morgenthau, or Britain would not participate in either the IMF or the new bank for an "indefinite period."[20] Morgenthau backed down.

Eventually, a new Norwegian-Dutch resolution calling for the liquidation of the bank at the "earliest possible moment" was finally agreed. It was a perfect compromise: critics were satisfied that the principle was now established that the BIS must be closed down, while the bank's supporters noted that the resolution set out no date or conditions for this eventuality. Beyen, the former BIS president, distanced himself from the bank, rapidly remodeling himself as a pillar of the postwar democratic order. The BIS was incompatible with the IMF, and its statutes and banking operations would be obsolete after an Allied victory, he now argued. Little wonder that Beyen was described by Orvis Schmidt as a "very shifty fellow" who had "demonstrated his ability to forget what he said five minutes earlier."[21]

The Bretton Woods conference was watched with intense interest in Berlin. Puhl and the Nazi bankers understood that whatever was agreed upon by the fractious delegates, the BIS, or something like it, would survive. There were too many vested interests, on both sides of the conflict, to allow the world's most important channel of transnational finance to be closed down—especially when it had consistently proved its worth under the most arduous of conditions. An article in the Berlin newspaper *Das Reich*, published in September 1944, argued that the global economy was now so complex that an international clearinghouse would be needed once the war was over. The new IMF and IBRD would not be able to perform these functions. Even if the Allies were unwilling to hear "the unspeakable name of the BIS" they would need something like it.[22] *Das Reich* was correct.

IN BASEL, MCKITTRICK was enraged by the attacks on the bank. He wrote to the Bank of England and demanded a full investigation into the BIS's wartime record, which he apparently believed would exonerate him. The prospect of that set off alarms from Whitehall, the British government quarter, to Threadneedle Street, where Lord Catto, the new governor of the Bank of England had taken over from Montagu Norman. McKittrick, noted a Foreign Office memo, had gone native in neutral Switzerland and was "thoroughly out of touch with the way people are thinking nowadays."[23]

The end of the war did not seem to bring McKittrick any closer to reality. In March 1945 Orvis Schmidt, the US Treasury official who had attended the Bretton Woods conference, met with McKittrick in Switzerland. Schmidt, like his boss Henry Morgenthau, was not a fan of either McKittrick or the BIS, and McKittrick knew it. "It was clear that Mr. McKittrick was fully aware of the manner in which he and the BIS are regarded by the Treasury Department," Schmidt wrote.[24] McKittrick tried his best to persuade Schmidt otherwise—if only the Treasury Department understood "the real role that he and the BIS had played" all that would change, the BIS president ardently believed. This seemed unlikely, considering what followed.

Schmidt continued, "The BIS, McKittrick said, had been 'strictly neutral' during the war. The bank was a 'sort of club' for the world's central bankers, a 'little group of like-minded-men who understood and trusted one another.'" This trust was unimpaired by issues such as national, political, or governmental interests. Rather it was a kind of celestial understanding. It would continue "regardless of the condition of the world or of the constantly changing political relations between their respective countries." Unimpressed by McKittrick's eulogy, Schmidt asked McKittrick why the Germans had allowed him to run the BIS in this manner—what was in it for them? In response, McKittrick claimed that, "In order to understand the conduct of the Germans toward the BIS, one must first understand the strength of the confidence and trust that the central bankers had in each other and the strength of their determination to play the game squarely." McKittrick then said that the German members of this elite could positively influence the German government's conduct. These financiers, said McKittrick, were not Nazis but were needed by the Nazis because of their technical skills. "The existence of this little group is the keystone in the explanation of Germany's conduct with respect to the BIS," he explained.[25]

Schmidt asked McKittrick if he could name any members of this group. Only one name was forthcoming: Emil Puhl—the vice president of the Reichsbank, BIS director and guardian of looted gold, for which he would soon be put on trial at Nuremberg. McKittrick admitted that the BIS had accepted payment in gold from the Germans during the war. It had all been kept separately so that it could be checked easily to see if any was looted. McKittrick justified this on the grounds that "he thought it would be better to take the gold and hold it in this fashion rather than refuse it and let the Germans use it for other purposes." [26] The conversation then took a surreal turn. Puhl, McKittrick continued, knew where the looted Belgian gold was: in the vaults of the Reichsbank, where Puhl was holding it "for return to the Belgians after the war," rather as a fence might justify his possession of stolen goods to police investigating a robbery. McKittrick also admitted that the BIS had supplied the Third Reich with foreign exchange. But by doing so, he suggested, the BIS had actually weakened the Nazi economy, as Germany had paid more into the BIS in foreign exchange than it had received. Schmidt was incredulous. "I was surprised that a voluntary recital intended as a defense of the BIS could be such an indictment of that institution," he wrote to Henry Morgenthau.

An American intelligence report on the bank's wartime activities, prepared in December 1945, was even more damning. Much of the report was based on interrogation reports of Emil Puhl, who was singing like the proverbial canary in an effort to save himself from a lengthy prison sentence. Puhl revealed how the Reichsbank had used the BIS to pull out its money from neutral countries before it was blocked and then traded the rescued funds with the BIS. He said that German officials had wanted McKittrick to be re-elected as his opinions were "safely known" and that the BIS was also of great value to the Reichsbank as an "open window to financial information about the outside world." Much of this information, it seems, was provided personally by McKittrick in his conversations with Emil Puhl. Perhaps the most shocking revelation is that McKittrick, after his return from the United States in May 1943, reported to Puhl directly on "the general picture of the current opinions and financial problems in the United States." McKittrick, the report notes, also provided Puhl with advance information about the Allied Tripartite Mission to Switzerland in February 1945, when the Allies pushed Swiss officials to freeze Nazi assets and stop trading with Germany.[27]

McKittrick was not the only BIS manager providing Puhl with intelligence and acting as a go-between for both sides. When Allen Dulles arrived in Bern, one of the first people he met was Per Jacobssen, the BIS's economic adviser. The spymaster and the economist were introduced at a charity party hosted by the wives of the American and British ambassadors. Bern, like Lisbon, Madrid, and Stockholm, was crowded with legions of spies, informers, and secret agents, trading in information, gossip, and intrigue. Dulles and Jacobssen had much to discuss.

As a Swedish national and high-ranking BIS official, Jacobssen was of extreme interest to both the Allied and Axis intelligence services. Jacobssen could freely travel to and from Allied and Axis territory. Jacobssen, like his compatriots the Wallenberg brothers, played both sides. When Jacobssen returned from the United States in the spring of 1942, he discussed American attitudes toward Germany with Emil Puhl, the vice president of the Reichsbank.[28]

Jacobssen also relayed valuable information about the British General Staff to Puhl. In the summer of 1942, Jacobssen asked Paul Hechler, the head of the BIS's banking department, who was also a Nazi party member, to pass some news on to Puhl when Puhl next visited Basel: Jacobssen's

British brother-in-law, General Sir Archibald Nye, had been appointed vice chief of the General Staff. This was valuable intelligence. Both sides carefully watched staff movements among their enemies' military leadership. The arrival or departure of senior officers could herald new strategies or fresh thinking and herald the rise or decline of a particular commander. Aware that he was breaking a confidence, Jacobssen recorded in his diary that Nye's promotion should be kept from the press: "Puhl said he was glad to be told. We might make a gentleman's agreement between Hechler, himself and me not to mention it further. . . . I pointed out that when it was said in London that what I wrote was too friendly to Germany, these journalists obviously did not know who my relatives were."[29] Thankfully for Jacobssen, "these journalists" also did not know that he was passing valuable military information to the Reichsbank.

Jacobssen, accompanied by Hechler, met Puhl in Zürich on May 1, 1943. Puhl and the Reichsbank wanted information about the different plans circulating in Washington for postwar currencies and trade. Forward-thinking Nazi officials were already planning ahead for the postwar era. They needed to know what the Allies were thinking. As ever, Jacobssen was ready to help. The meeting must be discreet, Hechler emphasized to Jacobssen. "Puhl would of course be suspect if people in Germany heard that he had been in Switzerland to discuss these plans, but Puhl hoped, of course, that still one day it would be possible to come to an arrangement with the enemy," Jacobssen recorded in his diary.[30] "Arrangements with the enemy" were why the BIS existed. Puhl's wish was granted. The following month Jacobssen made a speech in Berlin to German commercial bankers, entitled "The Anglo-American Currency Plans," where he shared his thoughts on Allied postwar economic planning, based on what he had learned in the United States.

Thanks to the BIS's economic adviser, Allied postwar economic plans were now public knowledge in Nazi Germany. Yet it seems unlikely that Jacobssen gave this speech without the permission of the United States authorities. As the OSS documents on the Harvard Plan reveal, the US government ensured that the channels to Nazi industrialists and businessmen remained open, even as American and British soldiers walked into a hail of machine-gun bullets on the beaches of Normany. Jacobssen's speech, delivered in German, was translated by the American Legation in Bern and wired to Washington.[31] Jacobssen also passed information on to his brother-in-law Archibald Nye that was useful to the Allies. In 1940, after visiting Berlin, Jacobssen wrote to "Arch," advising Britain and France not to aid Finland in its war with the Soviet Union, as they might soon be on the same side as Russia, fighting the Germans. The letter, said Nye, had been of great value, and he had passed it on to the Foreign Office and intelligence services.[32] Jacobssen, like McKittrick, considered himself above national loyalties, but his heart at least seemed to be with the Allies. He listened to the nine o'clock news from London every night. When the national anthem was played at the end, he rose and stood at attention.

Meanwhile, German anti-Nazi émigrés believed that Georg von Schnitzler, a board member of IG Farben, used the BIS to communicate with the Allies. Von Schnitzler was certainly well placed to send messages to London and Washington. As the sales and commercial chief of the chemical conglomerate, he was one of the Third Reich's most powerful businessmen. Von Schnitzler's boss, Hermann Schmitz, sat on the BIS board. Before von Schnitzler joined IG Farben, he had worked for J. H. Stein, the Cologne bank where Kurt von Schröder was a director, and which ran Special Account "S," Himmler's private slush fund. By 1943, like most German industrialists, von Schnitzler understood that the war was lost. Germany would soon fall under international control, hopefully under the Western Allies. The priority was to preserve IG Farben's factories, sites, and offices so that the chemical conglomerate could quickly resume its dominance after the hostilities were ended.

Von Schnitzler used the BIS to send a message to the Allies that the bombing of German industry had to stop, according to Heinz Pol, who was a former associate editor of the *Vossische Zeitung*, Germany's paper of record until it was dissolved in 1934. Pol had excellent sources among German émigrés and in neutral countries. He wrote,

> *According to information emanating from Lisbon, Schnitzler is said to have drawn up a memorandum, which he has sent to the board of directors of the Bank for International Settlements at Basel, Switzerland. It is not known whether the memorandum arrived in Basel in time for the general meeting, which took place at the beginning of June (the American Mr. McKittrick presiding as usual), but several points raised in the memorandum are known. Schnitzler, the Lisbon sources say, stresses the fact that the term "unconditional surrender" implies that the Germans will still have something to surrender. But if the war of destruction, especially the bombing of the industrial centers in Germany, goes on, then there will be nothing left in the end but ruins and ashes.[33]*

Schnitzler's terms were clear, wrote Pol: "Collaboration on condition that German industry survives." If the bombs stopped falling, the German industrialists would cooperate with the forthcoming occupation. As none of the IG Farben main sites had been much damaged by bombing so far, von Schnitzler's offer "might not sound too unreasonable to other industrialists on the side of the United Nations."[34]

THE BIS WAS used by Japan as a channel to try and negotiate a peace treaty. Japan was a founding member of the bank and kept its links with Basel during the war. In July 1945 two Japanese bankers, Kojiro Kitamura, a board member of the BIS, and Kan Yoshimura, the head of the BIS's Exchange Section, asked Per Jacobssen if he would act as an intermediary to arrange a peace accord. The Allies demanded unconditional surrender, but the crucial point for Tokyo, the bankers said, was that Japan would retain the royal family, and ideally, the country's constitution.[35] Jacobssen, naturally, passed the information to his close friend, Allen Dulles, who took the Japanese proposal to Henry Stimson, the secretary for war. They discussed it in Potsdam on July 20, 1945, but events soon overtook the slow pace of the backdoor diplomacy. On August 6 Hiroshima was destroyed by an atomic bomb, followed by a second one in Nagasaki on August 9. Six days later Japan surrendered.

Jacobssen at least had the excuse that he was a citizen of neutral Sweden to justify his contacts with the Nazi bankers. McKittrick, whose homeland was at war with the Third Reich, did not. Cocooned in Basel, the BIS president seemed to have lost touch with reality, let alone morality. McKittrick had spent the war years in a parallel universe, one in which neutrality meant that the Reichsbank—the financial motor of war, plunder, and genocide—was judged equal to those banks whose assets it had stolen. A place where Puhl, the Reichsbank's vice president and receiver of stolen goods, was actually helping the victims by keeping their goods in a safe place, and where Puhl—and doubtless Hjalmar Schacht as well—were not the builders and managers of the Nazi economy. Instead they were merely technocratic bankers, who only wanted to "play the game squarely."

It is hard to judge which is worse: that McKittrick really believed these arguments, or they were a cynical lawyer's ploy to ward off difficult consequences. McKittrick was certainly nervous about possible consequences of his entanglements with Nazi bankers, especially with Paul Hechler, the head of the banking department, who continued to sign his correspondence "Heil Hitler" throughout the war. Fate came to McKittrick's rescue when Hechler died in 1945. His death "raises a serious administration problem while solving a political one," wrote McKittrick to Roger Auboin.[36] But with Allen Dulles covering his back, McKittrick had nothing to worry about. McKittrick traveled to Germany at least twice in 1945 and in September stayed at Allen Dulles's house in Dahlem, in Berlin. Although McKittrick was still president of the BIS, his laisser-passer was organized by the OSS and numerous senior American officials received him.

Not everybody shared Dulles's enthusiasm for the BIS's president. There was a nasty surprise waiting for McKittrick on his return to Basel. The October 11 edition of the *New York Herald Tribune* carried a scathing attack on the BIS, and the article was reprinted in the *Tribune de Lausanne*, a Swiss newspaper. The article reported that the American occupation authorities in Germany were investigating whether the BIS had supported Germany's gold operations and helped finance Nazi rule in other countries. McKittrick's activities during the war were criticized. The bank may be called to give evidence on its gold transactions with Germany during WWII, it added. Hypersensitive as ever to press criticism, and doubtless mindful of his need to find a new job in the United States, McKittrick asked Allen Dulles to take action. The source of the leaks, he suspected, was an American official named Fox, whom McKittrick had met in Frankfurt. Fox was a colleague of Harry White. "White and his associates have taken consistently an extremely unfriendly attitude toward the BIS and the attacks on the bank at the Bretton Woods conference originated with White," complained McKittrick.[37]

Despite the bad publicity and attacks on McKittrick, the bankers at Basel got on with what they knew best: keeping the money moving. Quietly, carefully, barely noticed by the outside world, the BIS returned to business as usual. In December 1946 the bank held its first postwar directors' meeting. Maurice Frere, the governor of the National Bank of Belgium and BIS board member, traveled to Washington, DC, to lobby US policymakers to free the BIS's blocked assets and to try to defuse the media attacks. He found a sympathetic hearing. The turning point came in May 1948 when the BIS agreed to return 3.74 metric tons of looted gold to Belgium and the Netherlands. In exchange, the Allied Tripartite Commission, which dealt with Nazi plunder, agreed to drop all future claims against the bank. The US Treasury freed all BIS assets. Frere was elected president of the BIS, the bank's first since Thomas McKittrick's term had come to an end in June 1946. The Bretton Woods resolution calling for the BIS to be liquidated quietly faded away.

MEANWHILE, THOMAS MCKITTRICK had a lucrative new job. Soon after he stepped down as BIS president in 1946, he was appointed a vice president of Chase National in New York, in charge of foreign loans. McKittrick was even lauded by those whose stolen goods he had purveyed. He was invited to Brussels and decorated with the royal Order of the Crown of Belgium. The honor, noted a press release, was "in recognition of his friendly attitude to Belgium and his services as President of the Bank for International Settlements during World War II."

PART TWO: **BUNDESREICH**

CHAPTER NINE

UNITED STATES TO EUROPE: UNITE, OR ELSE

*Our whole concept of the unification of Europe was
that it would first contribute to economic unification.
Then we hoped to secure an economic-military unity
and finally a political unity.*[1]

— Averell Harriman, US Special Envoy for the Marshall Plan for
the postwar reconstruction of Europe

Thomas McKittrick opened his hotel door to find fifteen slips of paper on the floor. It was the spring of 1947, and McKittrick, vice president at Chase National Bank, was passing through London. The messages from the switchboard indicated that someone in Washington, DC, was urgently trying to get in touch. McKittrick asked the operator to phone the number, and the call went through soon afterward. A voice said, "Is that you, Tom? This is Averell Harriman. You're coming to work for me for six months. I talked to Winthrop this morning, and he said you could."[2]

"Winthrop" was Winthrop Aldrich, the chairman of the board of Chase National Bank. Aldrich, who had run the bank since 1934, was one of the best-connected financiers in the United States. His father, Nelson Aldrich, had given his name to the plan, which had eventually resulted in the creation of the Federal Reserve system. Winthrop Aldrich was now an outspoken advocate of economic aid to Western Europe. Aldrich and McKittrick were old friends. In December 1945, at the height of the political attacks against McKittrick and the BIS over their acceptance of Nazi gold, McKittrick had written to Aldrich, complaining about "the people in Washington who seem to dislike us so heartily." McKittrick explained, "The situation will need to be handled skillfully." And indeed, it was, at least from the point of view of the BIS, which survived, and its former president, who was now working for Aldrich.[3] Harriman, the man at the other end of the line, was also a prominent banker and a diplomat who had served as US ambassador to London and Moscow. Harriman was now one of the most powerful men in the world, in charge of the Marshall Plan, the $12 billion American aid program to reconstruct postwar Europe. Harriman asked McKittrick if he could be in Paris to start work on June 2. Yes, gladly, replied McKittrick.

TWO MILLENNIA AGO, the Roman philosopher Cicero observed, "The sinews of war are infinite money." An updated version of his epithet would note that "the sinews of war are the transnational flow of infinite money," which will find its way around any obstacle. When the Allied leaders met at Potsdam in August 1945, they agreed that the German economy would be decentralized and the power of the cartels broken up. But the Nazi industrialists had no fear of such threats—Thomas McKittrick, as the OSS Harvard Plan documents show, had already reassured them that even if decartelization took place, the Allies would still guarantee their profits.

By the time Harriman summoned McKittrick to Paris, it had long been decided in Washington that the German business elites would not be punished. The Morgenthau Plan, which called for Germany to be stripped of its industrial might and turned into a pastoral state, had been so watered down by General Lucius Clay, the American commander of occupation forces, that it was meaningless. (Clay had set up shop in Frankfurt at the former headquarters of IG Farben, whose buildings had mysteriously escaped Allied bombing.) Washington's JSC Directive 1779, passed in the summer of 1947, institutionalized this change in policy. German industry would be rebuilt; its steel mills and forges would once again be the powerhouse of Europe.

What would be the role of the BIS in the German renaissance? After 1945, the bank had no reason to exist. The BIS had been founded to manage German reparations payments, and none had been paid since the early 1930s. The BIS claimed it was needed as a meeting place where central bankers could gather to coordinate monetary policy. But as commercial airlines expanded their networks across the world, the BIS's lush hospitality could easily be replicated in a hotel or conference room in London, Paris, Wall Street, or anywhere else the bankers wished to gather. The BIS said it was needed to help coordinate the postwar global economy. The new institutions of the IMF and the World Bank had been founded for precisely this reason. Unlike the BIS, the IMF and World Bank were not Nazi collaborators.

The Basel bankers had also lost their golden touch. For the first time, in 1946, the BIS registered a loss. The founders could not help. Montagu Norman, now in his midseventies, had retired from the Bank of England. Raised to the peerage as Baron Norman of St. Clere, his legacy endured, and he remained influential, but he could no longer move markets with a sentence or two. Nor could Hjalmar Schacht provide assistance to the bank he had once proudly called his own. Schacht had been arrested after the July 1944 plot against Hitler and sent to Dachau concentration camp. He survived and was liberated by the US Army. He was then arrested and put on trial at Nuremberg and charged with organizing Germany for war, which is precisely what he had done. Unbowed by the weight of the proceedings, Shacht and his lawyers were putting up a spirited defense, aided by his sporadic instances of public opposition to the Nazis during the 1930s.

Yet, ultimately, no matter how tainted its reputation, Norman and Schacht's creation would prove as durable as they had hoped. Throughout the war, the repeated arguments of BIS officials that the bank must keep working so that it could play a central role in the reconstruction of postwar Europe had found a ready audience among both the Allied and Axis leadership. Bureaucratic inertia also helped the BIS. The general sentiment in both Washington, DC, and London was that the bank could be useful and was too complicated to dismantle. The BIS was "built to last," argued British Treasury officials. It was both a Swiss corporation and an international organization protected by its own treaty. Britain had just won a war, and there were other priorities for scarce resources. Lord Catto, the new governor of the Bank of England, also came to the BIS's defense: The IMF was completely new, and who knew how effective it would be? The BIS, in contrast had existed for fifteen years and was staffed by experts. Postwar Europe, like prewar Europe, still needed a place for pan-European meetings of central bankers. Basel remained the ideal venue.

BUT BEFORE A cent of Marshall aid could be sent to Europe, the plan had to be approved by the US Congress. Harriman set up a bipartisan committee of political, labor, and business leaders to steer the plan through the US government and persuade American public opinion that it was in their best interest to send tax dollars to the war-ravaged continent. The committee's members included Owen Young, the architect of the last German reparations program, whose own eponymous plan had set up the BIS, and, of course, Allen Dulles, who saw the Marshall Plan as a means of dealing the death blow to the spread of Communism in western Europe. Barely a few months after the war ended, Allen Dulles was already demanding imports of food and raw material to rebuild German industry. He condemned the arrest and detention of one hundred thousand Nazis. "We find ourselves in the concentration camp business on a large scale," he told the Foreign Policy Association in January 1946, as though the German detainees who were fed, clothed, and received medical treatment from the Allies were about to dispatched to the gas chambers.[4]

In July 1947, soon after General Marshall announced his plan, the Conference for European Economic Cooperation (CEEC) met in Paris to work out how it would be implemented. The State Department made it clear to its European allies that American aid would come at a price: financial and economic cooperation between the recipient countries with a view toward eventual European union. The first step was to replace bilateral trade deals and exchange controls with multilateral policies. The following year, the CEEC was institutionalized as the Organization for European Economic Cooperation (OEEC), which still exists today as the Organization for Economic Cooperation and Development (OECD).

The OEEC's mandate was, essentially, to ensure that the State Department's plan for Europe, and, especially Germany, was implemented. It was charged with promoting economic and political cooperation between its members; developing intra-European trade by removing barriers and tariffs and studying the feasibility of customs unions, free trade, and multilateral payments.[5] The Marshall Plan was administered by another new agency, the European Cooperation Administration (ECA), which is where Thomas McKittrick worked. McKittrick arrived in Paris for the first ECA meeting on June 2, 1947. Conditions did not meet the standards of the BIS, he recalled. "The American embassy let us have a room and secretary. But the room didn't have any carpet on the floor and [only] the barest of bare furniture and we sat there."[6] There were twelve people present, and Harriman instructed each as to his responsibilities. McKittrick's was "Trade and payments." The dozen officials had no office, no organization, and no support staff. But they did have $5 billion in the bank, which they had to distribute quickly—and McKittrick no longer had to worry about Henry Morgenthau and Harry Dexter White.

Morgenthau had stepped down as Treasury secretary in 1945 and was now largely retired from public life. He devoted himself to Jewish causes and helping the new state of Israel. White left government and joined the IMF as its first US executive director. He was an idealist as well as a realist. He saw the IMF as a means to promote economic growth through trade and financial stability. White, like the BIS, believed in global financial cooperation as the path to prosperity—but crucially, a cooperation coordinated among governments rather than unelected central bankers and technocrats.

After 1945 White was subjected to sustained attacks on his patriotism, attacks that James M. Boughton, the IMF's official historian, has described as ranging from "the questionable to the bizarre."[7] White's failed attempt to bring the Soviet Union into the IMF in 1944 (when the country was an ally of the United States) and his meetings with Soviet officials were recast as support for Communism. So was his support for the Morgenthau Plan to de-industrialize Germany. White's request to the nationalist government in China to account for how it had spent hundreds of millions of dollars in American aid was respun as sympathy for Mao Tse-Tung's Communist forces. In August 1948, White was called to testify before the House of Representatives Committee on Un-American Activities to be questioned about his relations with the Soviets. Historians continue to investigate these.

There is evidence that White passed sensitive information to Moscow. Decrypted Soviet diplomatic cables from the 1940s detail White's discussions of American foreign policy with a Soviet official. But an authoritative biography of White by Bruce Craig argues that White was regarded by Moscow as a "trusted individual" rather than an active agent.[8] Certainly White's influence on policy making and access to high-level governmental decision making made him a person of great interest to the Soviets. Whether White was an agent or an asset, he was passing sensitive information to a hostile foreign power. Craig argues that White was a Rooseveltian internationalist, who believed in the need for cooperation with the Soviets, rather than a Communist.[9] Either way, such views were no longer acceptable in Washington in the late 1940s.

White suffered from heart trouble. His appearance before the committee was highly stressful. Three days later, he died.

MEANWHILE, THE BIS was swiftly building itself into the new global financial architecture. That September 1947 bank officials in charge of protocol and hospitality were in overdrive. The BIS was preparing for the two most important VIPs it had received since the end of the war: John McCloy, the president of the new World Bank, and Eugene Black, its executive director. There was little danger of discord: McCloy was one of the most influential advocates of normalization with Germany. Black was a former vice president of Chase National—the new employers of Thomas McKittrick. McCloy had deliberately sabotaged the Morgenthau Plan and steered President Roosevelt away from punishing Germany in favor of rebuilding German industry. As the website of the United States embassy in Germany notes, "He was instrumental in undermining the proposed 'Morgenthau Plan' for Germany which would have reduced the country to a land of forests and farms."[10]

The Marshall Plan was certainly a triumph for the prewar Wall Street–Berlin financiers. McCloy, Black, and Harriman all had extensive prewar financial interests in Nazi Germany, as McKittrick had. McCloy had been a partner in Cravath, a powerful New York law firm, which represented General Aniline and Film,

IG Farben's American subsidiary.[11] Like his friend Allen Dulles, McCloy had been based in Paris in the prewar years where he ran the law firm's office. McCloy left Cravath in 1940 to serve as assistant secretary for war. This prevented a potentially ugly conflict of interest, for Cravath's clients also included the United States Alkali Export Association (Alkasso), which had intentionally deprived the United States of vital chemicals during the war.[12]

Alkasso was composed of the eleven most important alkali producers in the United States and handled their foreign trade. In 1936 Alkasso entered into a cartel agreement with Solvay & Cie, the Belgian chemicals company represented by John Foster Dulles, and Imperial Chemical Industries, a British combine. The cartel continued during the war, and in 1942 the Department of Justice launched an investigation into Alkasso, just as it had with Standard Oil. Standard Oil had restricted the United States' ability to produce artificial rubber. Alkasso prevented free trade in soda ash, a basic ingredient in vital war materials such as glass, textiles, and numerous chemicals.

In 1944 the Justice Department launched a civil lawsuit against Alkasso and ICI for breaching the Sherman Anti-Trust Act. Also named as co-conspirators were Solvay & Cie and IG Farben. Alkasso was charged with restricting exports and prohibiting imports, eliminating competition, and price-fixing. Cravath and Alkasso lost the case. The sixty-page decision, delivered by federal judge Samuel Kaufman, was blistering. It found that Alkasso had near total control of alkali imports and exports. Alkasso even ran its own network of inspectors at docks to examine materials leaving the United States. It compiled a blacklist of all competitive exporters and instructed its members not to sell to those on it. It forced its customers to give written assurances that they would not sell their products outside the United States. The cartel had continued during the war years, the decision, delivered in 1949, noted.[13]

McCloy was a ruthless, self-made man who was not known for his humanitarianism. On the contrary—the president of the World Bank had been instrumental in the internment of some 120,000 American citizens and residents of Japanese ancestry, causing an enormous amount of human suffering—a bitter legacy that still lingers today. Arguably, he had blood on his hands. McCloy used his office and influence over Henry Stimson, the secretary for war, to repeatedly block attempts by Jewish organizations to have the US Air Force bomb Auschwitz. By 1944 numerous testimonies of escapees and witnesses had reached Western capitals.[14] It was widely known among both governments and Jewish organizations that the camp was an industrial death factory. Allied bombers regularly overflew the complex and occasionally bombed the outlying IG Farben Buna factory at Auschwitz III and other buildings. It would have been comparatively simple to destroy the key railway junctions and gas chambers. In August 1944, soon after 430,000 Hungarian Jews had been deported to Auschwitz, where most were gassed on arrival, A. Leon Kubowitzki of the World Jewish Congress wrote to McCloy asking that Auschwitz be bombed. McCloy refused. He replied that such an operation would demand diversion of resources being used elsewhere and would be of "doubtful efficacy," an argument also echoed by British officials. McCloy also made the macabre claim that bombing Auschwitz might "provoke even more vindictive action by the Germans," although it is hard to imagine what could be more vindictive than the industrialized extermination of thousands of people per day.[15]

Eugene Black, McCloy's colleague at the World Bank, had joined Chase National in 1933 as vice president. He was promoted to senior vice president in charge of the bank's investment portfolio. This was substantial: at that time, Chase National was the world's largest bank in terms of assets, which is why it was so appreciated by Nazi Germany.

Averell Harriman's financial links with Germany also stretched back decades. Soon after the end of the First World War he had set up his own bank, W. A. Harriman, which carried out extensive business in Germany. Together with Lee, Higginson—the former employers of McKittrick—W. A. Harriman bank lent $20 million to the Berlin City Electric Company, with legal work provided by John Foster Dulles. Harriman was a board member of the International Chamber of Commerce (ICC), as was Thomas

McKittrick. The chamber's president, after 1937, was Thomas Watson, the boss of IBM who had traveled to Berlin to be awarded the Merit Cross of the German Eagle by Hjalmar Schacht and whose Hollerith machine was used by the Nazis to speed up the organization of the Holocaust.

Harriman was an early enthusiast for transnational finance. During the mid-1920s he attended an ICC meeting in Paris, the only American of any prominence present. He later recalled,

> *One evening I remember that I met with the leading bankers and industrialists of the principal countries. I remember the British and German, the French—I can't remember who else was there. It was quite a small dinner—it was a private dinner. Yet, they took the International Chamber of Commerce more seriously than we did and there were some important men present. I asked them why they thought that the United States was moving ahead as we were in the mid-twenties, you remember, whereas Europe was stagnant with built-in unemployment. They said it was because we had a continent of free trade.*[16]

Sometime in the early 1920s, Harriman had traveled to Berlin and met Fritz Thyssen, the powerful German industrialist, according to declassified US documents. Thyssen became one of Hitler's most influential backers and persuaded many of his fellow businessmen to support the Nazis, until he fell out with Hitler after Kristallnacht and fled Germany. Thyssen told Harriman that he wanted to set up a bank in New York to look after his interests in the United States. In 1924, W. A. Harriman duly set up a new bank for Thyssen called the Union Banking Corporation (UBC). UBC had seven directors, including E. Roland Harriman, his brother, and Prescott Bush, the grandfather of President George H. W. Bush, and great-grandfather of George W. Bush. But UBC was not a bank in the normal sense of the word. It was a front for Bank Voor Handel en Scheepvaart, based in Rotterdam in the Netherlands.

Bank Voor Handel en Scheepvaart was wholly owned or controlled by the Thyssen family, US investigators believed.

In 1931 W. A. Harriman merged with Brown Brothers & Co., to form Brown Brothers Harriman (BBH) with offices at 59 Wall Street, a few doors from Sullivan and Cromwell, which was at number 48. The UBC was highly successful. US investigators believed that between 1931 and 1933 UBC bought more than $8 million worth of gold, of which $5 million was sent abroad, probably to Germany.[17] This is why, on November 6, 1942, the US Alien Property Custodian issued vesting order 248 and seized all four thousand shares of UBC and its assets.[18] Harriman, who was traveling the world as President Roosevelt's special envoy to meet with Churchill and Stalin, continued his diplomatic career unhindered. The month after UBC was vested, Joseph Ripley, one of Harriman's oldest and closest business associates, represented Brown Brothers Harriman at McKittrick's dinner at the New York University Club.

WITH CREDENTIALS SUCH as these, McCloy's and Black's visit to the BIS could only be a success. The BIS, its officials pointed out, had much to offer. It was the world's oldest global financial institution. It had unrivaled experience in gold and currency swaps and superb technical expertise. Its annual reports were universally regarded as the single most useful source of financial and economic information. The BIS agreed to host the World Bank's European mission and to provide it with technical support. Soon after, when the World Bank issued its first non-dollar bond, the BIS negotiated the bond's sale to Swiss banks and bought a substantial share for its own account.

It seemed only natural that when the CEEC, the committee in charge of Marshall Plan payments, formed a subcommittee to manage multilateral payments between France, Italy, Luxembourg, the Netherlands, and Belgium, the BIS would be at the center of the new system. Frederick Connolly, a veteran BIS official who had formerly worked at the Bank of England with Montagu Norman, drafted an agreement on multilateral payments, which was signed in Paris in November 1947. The BIS was appointed agent in charge of executing the transfers. The bank hosted a conference for the five signatories and observers from Switzerland, Britain, and the US Treasury and State Departments. A resolution was passed encouraging central banks to use the BIS to settle their payments, rather than doing so directly between creditor and debtor. It also requested that the BIS be informed of any direct transactions.

At first glance, the Paris accord on multilateral payments seems an obscure footnote to postwar economic history. Monetarily, it was almost irrelevant. By the end of 1947, only $1.7 million of $762.1 million outstanding balances between the five signatories had been settled. But this little-known accord was, in fact, highly significant. An important precedent had been set: transactions between central banks would now go through Basel, rather than between national treasuries. Only the BIS had the staff and the expertise, dating back to its experience managing reparations payments in the 1930s, to manage an effective system for intra-European payments. The BIS had effectively reasserted itself as an international clearinghouse for Europe's central banks.

Emboldened by the new payments system, the technocrats and Euro-federalists were now on the rise. Belgium called for a customs union between the Benelux countries and France and Italy. Italy went one better and proposed a customs union between all countries receiving aid under the Marshall Plan, as a step toward European Union.

The postwar blip in the BIS finances was short and temporary. By 1951, the BIS was once again paying dividends to its shareholders. BIS observers attended IMF and World Bank meetings. The bank enjoyed a cordial relationship with the New York Federal Reserve, thanks in part to the legacy of Leon Fraser, the former BIS president who had also served as a director of the New York Fed. (Despite his successful career, Fraser suffered from severe depression. In April 1945 he shot himself in the head with a revolver and died on the way to the hospital.)

THE BRETTON WOODS motion calling for the dissolution of the BIS, and the campaign against the bank led by Henry Morgenthau and Harry White had been the most serious threat yet to the BIS's existence. Although the full details of the bank's role as a channel between the Allies and the Axis were not yet public in the immediate postwar years, the BIS was thoroughly tainted by its acceptance of Nazi gold and its cozy relationship with the Reichsbank. But the bank proved more nimble and agile than its foes. Its managers deftly immediately built the BIS into the new global financial architecture. The BIS did not seek to compete with the IMF and offer loans to indebted countries (although it would later arrange international credits to troubled economies). Nor did it try and compete with the World Bank and fund development projects. Rather, the BIS stuck to what it knew best: offering discreet services, financial coordination, and a confidential venue to central bankers, all of which were in great demand in postwar Europe.

The bank's excellent connections with American policymakers such as Allen Dulles and John McCloy brought an early understanding of Washington's commitment to a new, united Europe. The drive was now unstoppable, with wide political support across European capitals. Such a project, the BIS managers understood, would offer immense new opportunities for the bank over the coming decades. The new Europe would need swift, international payment mechanisms, more harmonized exchange rates, and perhaps eventually a new single currency. There was nobody better placed to offer these services than the technocrats of the BIS.

CHAPTER TEN

ALL IS FORGIVEN

When detained in Dustbin, among a number of references to the financially great he pointed out that the President of the BIS, Mr. McKittrick of the United States, would be able to speak favourably of him.

— British intelligence report on Hermann Schmitz, CEO of IG Farben, while held prisoner at Kransberg Castle, aka "Dustbin," December 1945[1]

While Hermann Schmitz was dropping Thomas McKittrick's name in the hope that the BIS president might somehow spring him from prison, Rudolf Brinckmann was also plotting how to keep his wartime profits. The German banker, who would soon be appointed a director of the BIS, was locked in a bitter dispute with the Warburgs over the ownership of Brinckmann, Wirtz and Company, in Hamburg, the successor to M. M. Warburg bank, which had been Aryanized by the Nazis.

Brinckmann had joined M. M. Warburg in 1920 and worked as the office manager. He spoke six languages and was seen as loyal, dependable, and trustworthy. The Warburgs joked that Brinckmann was their "in-house Aryan," even though he was actually Mediterranean looking, because of his Greek-Turkish background. M. M. Warburg was then one of the world's most influential banks, the centerpiece of a financial dynasty whose name was a byword for stability and prudence. The family trusted Brinckmann absolutely, so when the Nazis took power in 1933, he was granted full power of attorney and took the place of the members of the Warburg family on other company boards. Five years later, when the bank was Aryanized, Brinckmann, together with Paul Wirtz, was made a director, on the understanding that he would look after the Warburgs' interests.

Brinckmann's wartime record was ambiguous. He had hired Nazi party loyalists and purged the last remaining Jewish employees. Staff began to wear Nazi party insignia. Brinckmann wrote letters to former clients, pointing out that now that the bank had been Aryanized there was no reason not to come back, the letter usually ending with "Heil Hitler."[2] He traveled to Essen to win back the account of the Krupp family of industrialists, who were one of Hitler's most important backers. Brinckmann renamed the bank after himself, and he also negotiated the release of fourteen members of the Warburg family and employees from Nazi-occupied Amsterdam, who eventually reached the United States.

After the war numerous German bankers, including Brinckmann, were placed under house arrest. But the Warburgs, grateful that their bank still existed, albeit in another form and under another name, helped Brinckmann as much as they could. They provided a supply of food. His house arrest was lifted. They got him a place on a de-Nazification tribunal—an immensely influential position. Brinckmann initially offered to return the bank to the family, but as the full horror of the Holocaust became public, the Warburgs declined, ambivalent about their return to Germany.

Brinckmann was soon glad that his offer was refused, because the bank was profitable. Soon after, some of the Warburgs, including Eric, decided to settle in Germany and asked for their bank to be returned. Brinckmann refused. Like many German owners of formerly Jewish concerns, he rewrote history. The 1938 transfer into his name was not an Aryanization, he claimed. Rather, he had saved the remnants of a collapsed bank. The Warburgs should be grateful to him, rather than vice versa. He offered the family a ten percent ownership stake. That was unacceptable, said the family. If it had not been for M. M. Warburg, Brinckmann, Wirtz and Company would not exist. It was built on the ruins of the Warburg empire and even operated out of the same building. The two sides finally agreed that the family would take 25 percent, with a five-year option on 50 percent.

Brinckmann joined the BIS board of directors in 1950, after the Warburgs put his name forward. But if the Warburgs hoped that trips to Switzerland, the BIS's famed hospitality, and the inside information gleaned at the bank's lunches and dinners would mollify Brinckmann, they were quickly disappointed. The BIS, it seemed, had gone to Brinckmann's head, and he remained as stubborn as ever. Eric Warburg, a prominent member of the Jewish banking dynasty, dubbed the new BIS board member "John Foster Brinckmann," after John Foster Dulles, the ruthless lawyer turned Cold War warrior who was soon to be appointed secretary of state. Sigmund Warburg wrote to Eric in 1950, "During the last few years I've found Brinckmann extraordinarily arrogant and egotistical, but during my last discussion in Hamburg I found that his arrogance and his egotism had gradually reached a point where they are scarcely bearable any longer."[3] There seemed no end in sight to the dispute.

DESPITE THE MARSHALL Plan, postwar Germany was devastated, its population barely scraping a living. A fifth of all housing stocks had been destroyed, food production was about half of its prewar levels, and industrial output in 1947 was one-third of its 1938 level.[4] Basic goods were rationed, and wages and prices were controlled. The black market was thriving, and there was no properly functioning central bank. Officially, the Reichsbank had ceased to exist. The Reichsmark staggered on, still in circulation, although the main unit of currency was American cigarettes.

In 1948, everything changed. The Reichsbank was abolished completely and replaced by the Bank deutscher Länder (BdL). The deutschmark replaced the Reichsmark. The BdL was a national clearinghouse for the banks of the German regional states in the western occupation zone, modeled broadly on the US Federal Reserve. Unlike the Reichsbank, which had been brought under government control, the BdL, which would now represent Germany at the BIS in Basel, had its independence constitutionally guaranteed.

Hjalmar Schacht was not impressed with the deutschmark. It was backed neither by gold nor by foreign currency reserves. It was a fiat currency, imposed by the Western authorities. Schacht told Wilhelm Vocke, the president of the new German national bank, that the deutschmark would collapse in six weeks. But Schacht was wrong. The deutschmark was backed, and by assets even more powerful than gold or foreign exchange: public confidence and postwar planning by the Nazi leadership.

At the same time, Ludwig Erhard, the economic director of the British and American occupation zones, lifted price restrictions and controls. The results were spectacular. Employment soared, inflation plummeted, the economy boomed. The deutschmark was stable and enjoyed the public's full confidence. The western powers and their German subordinates proclaimed the dawn of a new era.

But the new central bank, currency, and Germany's economic recovery were all deeply rooted in the Third Reich. Because German companies, especially armaments firms, had reinvested their massive profits, despite the Allied bombing campaign and reparations, Germany's capital stock—its productive equipment, buildings, infrastructure, and other assets—was actually greater in 1948 than in 1936.[5]

The lines of financial continuity between the Third Reich and postwar Germany reached right to the top. The BdL's first president, Vocke, was a Reichsbank veteran and ally of Hjalmar Schacht. Wilhelm Vocke had sat on the Reichsbank board from 1919 to 1939 and was Germany's alternate member on the BIS board from 1930 to 1938. He would now return to Basel for the governors' meetings. Vocke remained loyal to his former boss and testified at Schacht's trial at Nuremberg. He made the unlikely claim that Schacht had believed Germany's weapons buildup was intended to support a policy of armed neutrality and to reduce unemployment.[6] Vocke, however, had not joined the Nazi party, unlike many of his colleagues at the BdL. Every state institution in postwar Germany—the police, judiciary, civil servants, teachers, doctors, and the intelligence services—relied on former Nazis to function. But the continuity among the bankers was striking. Between 1948 and 1980, 39 percent of officials on the executive and governing boards of either the BdL, the central banks of the regional states, or the Bündesbank (the BdL's successor) were former Nazis.[7]

Some, such as Fritz Paersch, had been important figures in Hitler's economic empire. Paersch was the mastermind of the Nazi plunder and despoliation of Poland. As president of the central bank in German-occupied Poland, he reorganized the currency. Without his work, the Nazi occupation would not have been able to function economically. Hans Frank, the governor general of Poland who oversaw the murder, enslavement, and deportation of millions of Poles and Polish Jews was a great admirer of Paersch. Frank was found guilty of war crimes at Nuremberg and executed. And Paersch should have been put on trial as well, but instead he lived freely and applied for a senior position at the BdL. He was rejected because of his wartime past but was compensated with a position as vice president of the Hesse state central bank, where he worked until 1957. Paersch then found a new sinecure: as official liquidator of the Reichsbank, whose legal affairs still stuttered on.[8]

Like Schacht during the 1930s, Ludwig Erhard, the economic director of the western occupation zones, was hailed as a miracle maker. The truth was more prosaic. Erhard, a future chancellor of West Germany, was an ambiguous figure. He had refused to join any Nazi party organizations and was connected to the German resistance. But Erhard had accepted funds from the Reichsgruppe Industrie, the organization of German industrialists, including IG Farben, that supported Hitler. He was awarded the war service cross for his work on economics. By 1943 Erhard's work had come to the attention of the German bankers and industrialists who realized that the war was lost. They formed two groups to prepare for the future and ensure their continuing economic power in the postwar world: the Committee for Foreign Economic Affairs, composed of financiers and industrialists, and the Small Working Group, composed solely of industrialists, including Hermann Schmitz, the CEO of IG Farben and BIS director.[9] Erhard was the connection between the two groups.

The members of the Committee for Foreign Economic Affairs included Hermann Abs of Deutsche Bank, the most powerful commercial banker in the Third Reich. The dapper, elegant Abs was an old friend of the BIS. He had been sent there by Schacht during the 1930s to try and stall demands for repayments of the loans that financed Germany after 1918.[10] In Basel, Abs frequently met with a British banker called Charles Gunston, who was a protégé of Montagu Norman. Gunston managed the Bank of England's German desk, which made him immensely important during the 1930s. Gunston was so keen on the new Germany that he spent his 1934 summer holidays at a work camp for enthusiastic Nazi party members.[11] He also admired Abs and later described him as "Very urbane. Always a velvet glove around an iron fist." Abs did not join the Nazi party, but he was so essential for the functioning of the Third Reich's economy that he did not need to. As the head of Deutsche Bank's foreign department during the war, Abs was the lynchpin of the continent-wide plunder, directing the absorption of Aryanized banks and companies across the Third Reich. During the twelve years of the Third Reich, the bank's wealth quadrupled. Abs sat on the board of dozens of companies, including, naturally, IG Farben.[12]

In 1943 the Nazi industrialists asked Erhard to write a paper on how German industry could be converted back to peacetime production. Erhard argued for a free and competitive market with a gradual elimination of state controls. German industry would be redirected, as quickly as possible, to producing consumer goods.[13] Erhard was taking a substantial risk by putting his name to such thoughts: any postwar planning that assumed that Germany might lose the war was enough to send the author to a concentration camp.

But Erhard had protection at the highest levels of the Nazi state: Otto Ohlendorf, the chief of the SS internal security service. The SS was a business as well as a killing machine, the state engine of looting, plunder, and despoliation, from the gold extracted from the teeth of concentration camp victims to the banks, steelworks, factories, and chemical plants of Nazi-occupied countries. Ohlendorf had extensive first-hand experience of the SS's methods. Between 1941 and 1942, Ohlendorf had commanded Einsatzgruppe D, the extermination squad operating in southern Ukraine, which had murdered ninety thousand men, women, and children. Ohlendorf, an intelligent and educated man, showed great concern for the psychological welfare of his squad's gunmen. He ordered that they should all fire at the same time at their victims, so as to avoid any feelings of personal responsibility.

Ohlendorf also held a senior position at the Ministry of Economics, supposedly focusing on Nazi Germany's foreign trade. By 1943, after the Russian victory at Stalingrad, Ohlendorf also understood that the Third Reich would eventually lose the war. His real job was to plan how the SS would keep its financial empire so that Germany would reassert its economic dominance over Europe after the inevitable defeat. The postwar priority was rapid monetary stabilization, to preserve economic stability and avoid Weimar-style hyperinflation. Germany would need a new currency, which would have to be imposed by the occupying powers, as well as a mixed economy of state and private sectors. There was an obvious overlap with Erhard's ideas. Ohlendorf came to hear of Erhard's work, and Erhard was persuaded to send him a copy of his memo.

As the Allies advanced on Germany, the Nazis stepped up their plans for the postwar era. On August 10, 1944, an elite group of industrialists gathered at the Maison Rouge Hotel in Strasbourg, including representatives of Krupp, Messerschmitt, Volkswagen, and officials from several ministries. Also in attendance was a French spy, whose report reached the headquarters of the Allied invasion force, from where it was forwarded to the State Department and the Treasury. The account of the meeting is known as the Red House Report.

Germany had lost the war, the Nazi industrialists agreed, but the struggle would continue along new lines. The Fourth Reich would be a financial, rather than a military imperium. The industrialists were to plan for a "postwar commercial campaign." They should make "contacts and alliances" with foreign firms but ensure this was done without "attracting any suspicion." Large sums would have to be borrowed from foreign countries. Just as in the prewar era, the US connection and links to chemical firms, such as the American Chemical Foundation, were essential to expanding German interests. The Zeiss lens company, the Leica camera firm, and the Hamburg-American line had been "especially effective in protecting German interests abroad." The firms' New York addresses were passed around the meeting.

A smaller group attended a second, select meeting. There the industrialists were instructed to "prepare themselves to finance the Nazi party, which would be forced to go underground." The prohibition against exporting capital had been lifted, and the government would help the industrialists to send as much money to neutral countries as possible, through two Swiss banks. The Nazi party recognized that after the defeat, its best-known leaders would be "condemned as war criminals," the intelligence report concluded. However, the party and the industrialists were cooperating in placing the most important figures in positions at German factories as research or technical experts.[14]

US Treasury officials were closely watching this massive export of German capital, much of which was going to South America. Funds were pouring out of Germany and other Nazi-controlled territories, Harry Dexter White told a meeting of Treasury officials in July 1944 during the Bretton Woods conference. Nazi leaders were preparing to flee the country or have their property confiscated. "They bought estates and industries and corporations, and there is evidence that the German corporations have been buying into South American corporations in the expectation of being able to re-establish themselves there after the war."[15] The cloaking operation was extremely complex, said White. "They are working through first, second and third fronts, so it is pretty hard to trace it without having all the data available." The Treasury officials also discussed the BIS at the same meeting, noting that out of twenty-one board members and senior officials, sixteen were "representatives of countries that are either now our enemies, or are occupied," including Walther Funk and Hermann Schmitz.[16]

Emil Puhl discussed the Nazi leadership's postwar strategy with McKittrick at the BIS in March 1945, during the last few weeks of the war. The information he passed to McKittrick echoes that included in the Red House Report and Harry Dexter White's discussion at Bretton Woods. Military defeat was merely a temporary setback. The Nazis were fanatics and would never give up their ideals, Puhl explained. Instead they would go underground. McKittrick immediately informed Dulles of the conversation. Dulles sent the information on to London, Paris, and Washington on March 21, 1945. His telegram noted that Puhl had "just arrived" in Basel:

> *He said that the jig was up but that Nazis had made careful plans to go underground, that every essential figure had his designated place, that Nazism would not end with military defeat as Hitler and his fanatical followers would no more change their philosophy than would Socrates or Mohammed, that these men were just as convinced of their cause as ever and carried a great body of people with them. He emphasized that Nazism was like a religion, not merely a political regime.*[17]

After the Allied victory, Donald MacLaren, the British intelligence agent who had brought down GAF, IG Farben's US subsidiary, was sent to Berlin to investigate the chemicals conglomerate. MacLaren wrote an extensive dossier on IG Farben, its history and key personnel, and its central role in preparing and waging war. MacLaren laid out in detail how IG Farben's trading partners in New York and London, such as Standard Oil, had willingly entered into cartel arrangements with the chemical conglomerate, thus ceding control to Germany and helping it to re-arm.

SO WHAT THEN should be the fate of the Nazi industrialists such as Hermann Schmitz? For MacLaren, the answer was clear. Schmitz had murdered, enslaved, and plundered from behind his desk, rather than on the battlefield. He was a war criminal as much as the leaders of the SS and should face the same punishment. But not all Allied officials agreed. When MacLaren asked his superiors if the industrialists were to be included with the Nazi military leadership as war criminals, he was told, "The term 'industrialists' raises a point on which no definite line has been laid down."[18] Schmitz, as MacLaren noted, certainly believed himself to be protected by his connection to the BIS and to Thomas McKittrick.

At one stage it seemed justice might be done. In 1947, twenty-four IG Farben executives, including Schmitz, were put on trial at Nuremberg. Twelve were found guilty. The sentences were derisory. Schmitz was sentenced to four years. Georg von Schnitzler, the commercial chief, who had apparently used the BIS to contact the Allies, received five years. Otto Ambros, a senior manager of IG Auschwitz, received eight years. Ambrus testified that the prisoners at IG Auschwitz were fortunate to "have been spared all that which happened" in the main concentration camp. The IG managers had also saved them a commute. The slave laborers could live on-site and no longer had to march fourteen kilometers a day to and from the main camp. "There was no stinting when Monowitz was built. It was heated and hygienic," Ambrus explained, although Rudy Kennedy, who worked as a slave laborer for IG Farben when he was a teenage boy, remembered conditions rather differently. The slave laborers were served soup at lunchtime, soup with a "higher calorific content" than most Germans enjoyed in the immediate postwar years. "I believe that IG Farben and its officials deserve not a reproach, but due recognition," Ambrus later wrote, and they would soon get it.[19]

IG Farben was broken up into four successor companies: BASF, Bayer, Hoechst, and Cassella. The dismantling was no punishment. The shareholders asked the occupation authorities to transfer the conglomerate's assets to the successor firms, and they agreed. BASF, Bayer and Hoechst immediately reconstituted themselves, with the same staff working in the same offices and factories. A new holding company was created to deal with the legal fallout and consequences of the breakup. The legacy firms said they had no obligations for IG Farben's sins, as they had not legally existed during the war. It was a shameless and completely successful legal maneuver.

In 1949 John McCloy left the World Bank and started work as US High Commissioner for West Germany. McCloy, the former partner in the Cravath law firm that had represented GAF, the American wing of IG Farben, did not forget his former business partners. Hermann Schmitz was released from prison in 1950, and by February 1951 all of the IG Farben executives were free. McCloy also freed Alfried Krupp. The Krupp industrial empire had worked about eighty thousand slave laborers to death in a network of fifty-seven labor camps guarded by the SS. Krupp was sentenced to twelve years imprisonment, but he served less than three.

Otto Ohlendorf, the former commander of Einsatzgruppe D and protector of Ludwig Erhard, was an exception. He was hanged. But McCloy ordered that Nazi camp doctors who had conducted experiments on inmates, Nazi judges who had dispensed Gestapo justice, and SS officers who had organized mass killings be freed or have their sentences drastically reduced.[20] Seventy-four of the 104 defendants convicted at Nuremberg had their sentences substantially reduced, and ten death sentences were commuted.[21] Heinz Hermann Schubert, Ohlendorf's adjutant, who had personally supervised a mass execution of seven hundred people at Simferopol, had his death sentence commuted and was sentenced to ten years in prison.

The IG Farben managers were swiftly welcomed back into the German business community. Hermann Schmitz joined the supervisory board of the Deutsche Bank. Otto Ambros, provider of soup to slave laborers, joined numerous company boards and set up as an economic consultant. His clients included Konrad Adenauer, the federal chancellor. Kurt von Schröder, the banker and BIS director who had brokered Hitler's rise to power, was found disguised as an SS corporal in a POW camp in France. He was tried by a German court for crimes against humanity and was sentenced to three months in prison. Walther Funk, the dissolute Reichsbank president and BIS director, was found guilty of war crimes and sentenced to life imprisonment. The trial established how Funk had worked with Himmler, the SS chief, to ensure that gold and valuables from camp victims were credited to a special account at the Reichsbank in the name of "Max Heiliger" for the SS. Funk was released from Spandau prison for health reasons in 1957 and died three years later. Emil Puhl, Funk's deputy, BIS director, and friend of Thomas McKittrick, was also convicted of war crimes. Sentenced to five years, he was released in 1949.

Ironically, it seems the Warburgs were also instrumental in the reconstruction of German industry, thanks to the family's friendship with McCloy. Freddie Warburg had persuaded McCloy to take the position of president of the World Bank. The two men had known each other since the 1920s when McCloy had done legal work for Kuhn, Loeb, a branch of the Warburg empire. When Eric Warburg and McCloy dined together in August 1949, Warburg pleaded with McCloy to stop the dismantling and destruction of German industrial plants. Soon after, Warburg gave McCloy a list of ten steel, gas, and synthetic rubber concerns, including the Thyssen steel works and the Krupp gas works, to be saved. All were spared.[22] McCloy occasionally took a moral stand—he repeatedly told Germany to return Jewish property. When he was informed that Germans who served on de-Nazification boards were being shunned as traitors, he ordered state governments to guarantee such people civil service jobs.

As for Schacht, charged with organizing Germany for war, he still had powerful friends in London and Washington. Green Hackworth, the legal adviser to the State Department, was working behind the scenes to help the former Reichsbank president. During the war, Hackworth had repeatedly sabotaged attempts to publicize Nazi war crimes and bring their perpetrators to justice, arguing that such moves would endanger American POWs.[23] Breckinridge Long, the assistant secretary of state, who had once praised Mussolini, supported Hackworth. Long and his aides had prevented Jewish refugees from obtaining visas, suppressed news of the Holocaust, and derailed attempts to document Nazi war crimes. In 1944 Henry Morgenthau's staff wrote a detailed paper that documented the State Department's wartime record. Its title was "Report to the Secretary on the Acquiescence of this Government in the Murder of Jews."[24]

Once again the Dulles connection came to the fore. In late 1945 Schacht requested that Hans Bernd Gisevius be summoned as a defense witness to testify on his behalf. Gisevius, the wartime German consul in Zürich, was also an officer in the Abwehr, German military intelligence, a member of the anti-Hitler resistance, and one of Allen Dulles's most important agents, known as OSS source 512. Declassified US intelligence documents show that Gisevius was expected to testify that Schacht had attempted to overthrow Hitler in 1938 and to talk about Schacht's difficult relationship with the Nazi party, so that Schacht could present himself as a member of the resistance.

The documents reveal how much effort the State Department made to get Gisevius, who was living near Geneva in Switzerland, to Nuremberg to aid Schacht. A telegram from US diplomats in Berlin to the State Department, on December 10, 1945, requests that the "necessary arrangements be made to bring him to Nuremberg on ten days' notice and that Tribunal be kept fully advised through this office."[25] Three days later, Leland Harrison, the US ambassador to Switzerland, cabled Washington that Gisevius was willing to appear as a defense witness for Schacht and could depart for Nuremberg any time in January on forty-eight hours' notice. Harrison asked the State Department to alert him when Gisevius should arrive in Nuremberg.[26] The US government, was, in effect, acting as an aide to Schacht's defense lawyer, arranging for Gisevius's transport and logistics, and coordinating his appearance with the Nuremberg Tribunal.

The US team at Nuremberg was split over Schacht. Robert Jackson, the chief US prosecutor, wanted to prosecute him. But his deputy, William Donovan, the former OSS chief, was opposed. Donovan argued that Schacht had been sympathetic to the Allies in the early years of the war. And there was the postwar German economy to consider, always a crucial factor in US policy calculations. A harsh cross-examination of Schacht would alienate the important German businessmen and financiers who favored good relations with the United States.[27] There was consternation in Washington when Schacht's lawyer told the press that Sam Woods, the US Consul General in

Zürich, had offered the Reichsbank president a deal in 1939—that if he resigned from Hitler's government, he would be returned to power after the war. Considering all we now know about the secret back channels between the United States and Nazi businessmen, this seems highly plausible. Woods had long been a conduit between the US government and the Axis powers. After Admiral Horthy, Hungary's wartime leader who had permitted 430,000 of his own citizens to be deported to Auschwitz, was released from custody in 1946, Woods invited him to his wedding.[28]

The State Department's efforts on Schacht's behalf worked. He was initially found guilty but was then acquitted, to the fury of the Soviet judge. There were also suspicions that Montagu Norman had somehow managed to influence the proceedings through Sir Geoffrey Lawrence, the British judge. The British obsession with class seemed to play a part. Francis Biddle, the American judge, recorded in his diary that Lawrence had claimed Schacht was a "man of character" while other defendants were "ruffians."[29] Norman was immensely relieved when Schacht was not hanged at Nuremberg, recalled his stepson, the writer Peregrine Worsthorne. "He did not think Schacht was guilty for the crimes of the war, but obviously being on speaking terms with any prominent Nazi made you a pariah after the war. He had made his mind up about Schacht before the war and the horrors." (In later years Priscilla Norman angrily denied that her husband had tried to influence the outcome of Schacht's trial.)[30]

Intriguingly, Worsthorne believes that Norman and Schacht managed to stay in communication during the war—if they did, the BIS would have been the natural channel. "Norman kept up this strange relationship that he had with Schacht, even during the war. Both during the First and Second World Wars the capitalist world was not at war. The bankers kept the system in cold storage. I am sure that there would have been absolutely no record of their contacts and that Norman kept in touch with him without the government knowing."[31]

After several more years of legal travails with the German authorities, Schacht was finally cleared of all charges. He started a lucrative second career as an investment adviser to countries in the developing world and set up his own bank, Schacht & Co. Schacht even visited Israel, albeit inadvertently when his airplane stopped briefly at Lydda airport in 1951. Schacht and his second wife, Manci, wanted to stay on board but were taken to the airport cafeteria to have breakfast. The Schachts handed their passports to the Israeli police and were photographed by reporters. His wife was too nervous to eat, so Schacht ate her breakfast as well. A waiter asked in German how "Herr President" had enjoyed his breakfast, using Schacht's Reichsbank honorific. The waiter told Schacht that he was from Frankfurt and missed his hometown. He asked for Schacht's autograph, which Schacht provided. The Schachts left Israel with no problems, although a furor erupted in the Knesset, the Israeli parliament, when the news broke that Hitler's banker had passed through the Jewish state without being arrested.[32]

CHAPTER ELEVEN

THE GERMAN PHOENIX ARISES

"I say no permanent solution of the German problem seems possible without an effective European union.[1]"

— John McCloy, US High Commissioner for Germany, speaking in London in 1950

With the United States supplying the money through the Marshall Plan and the BIS providing the financial and technical expertise, the drive toward a united Europe was unstoppable. In October 1949, Paul Hoffman, the head of the ECA, which administered the plan, gave a definitive speech in Paris. He called for the expanding western European economies to integrate economically, set up a continent-wide free market, and to coordinate their "national, fiscal, and monetary policies."[2] This meant that governments should harmonize their spending and taxation as well as national interest rates: in other words, to move toward a United States of Europe.

Per Jacobssen, the BIS's influential economic adviser, agreed. Jacobssen believed the new European economies should be based on the free market. The era of autarky, state controls, and price restrictions was over. The ideal mix was an economy with about 80 percent in the private sector. The priority should be financial reconstruction and rebuilding trade and payments systems. Political and economic freedom would ensure prosperity, and welfare provision had to be made compatible with the market economy.[3]

Jacobssen also favored a federal solution for postwar Europe. During the war he had often met with Allen Dulles and British diplomats to persuade them of the merits of supra-nationalism, albeit with a maximum of power left at state level.

In 1946 he went public with his idea. Jacobssen gave a talk at Gettysburg College in Pennsylvania with the grandiose title of "The Re-Education of Europe." The German problem could be solved only as part of the European problem. Postwar Europe would flourish through diversity, but a new loyalty was needed, one which superseded mere national fidelity.[4] Just as in the 1930s, the technocrats believed they knew best, although their ambitions were far more grandiose: the imposition of a new transnational financial, economic, and political structure, whether the people of Europe wanted it or not.

Marshall aid came at a price: remodeling European societies on the American model of consumerism and consumption. Hoffman's propaganda arm produced pamphlets, posters, leaflets, radio programs, and even traveling puppet shows that extolled the American lifestyle. The American dream—a house in the suburbs, a car, and numerous household appliances—was projected as a near-guaranteed benefit of American-style freedom.[5] The key to this was increased productivity on American-style production lines in a transnational free market.

For that to happen, and for the money to flow freely, new mechanisms of international payment had to be constructed, with the BIS at the center. This had started in 1947, when France, Italy, Belgium, the Netherlands, and Luxembourg had signed the Paris accord on multilateral payments, which was managed by the BIS. That was followed a year later by the Agreement for Intra-European Payments and Compensation, signed by sixteen European governments, the representatives of the French and British-American occupation zones of Germany, and the short-lived Free Territory of Trieste, which soon became part of Italy. The United States wanted the process to be speeded up. Washington pushed the European central banks to construct a comprehensive, multilateral payments system, recalled Alexandre Lamfalussy, the BIS general manager between 1985 and 1993, demanding, "For the love of God stop being bilateral and start being multilateral."[6] Europe obeyed, swayed in part by a dedicated grant of $350 million of Marshall Plan funds to set up the European Payments Union. Established in 1950, at a single stroke the EPU removed the thicket of regulations governing European trade. EPU member states all agreed to accept each other's currencies for export payments. Bilateral balances were offset against a central fund, so all debts and credits were owed or received from the EPU. Eighteen countries signed up: all of Western Europe (excluding Scandinavia), Greece, Iceland, Switzerland, Britain, and Turkey. The BIS was appointed agent to the EPU. It managed its banking, kept its accounts, and controlled its funds.[7] The EPU "was the European Union of payments," said Lamfalussy. (The EPU applied to non-residents. Currency controls remained in place for residents.)

During the early 1950s Richard Hall worked at the Bank of England, helping to compose the briefing documents for the governor on his regular visits to the BIS. In 1955 Hall was seconded to the BIS to work on the EPU's monthly settlements and reports. There was no discussion about the BIS's wartime record, he recalled. "One of the BIS's finest achievements, for which it deserves no credit, was surviving the war. That was thanks to Maurice Frere, the Belgian banker who had lobbied hard for the BIS in Washington. He said that the BIS should not be got rid of because it might come in handy some time. Nobody in Basel was bothering their consciences about what the bank did during the war. It was the most sensible thing to do at the time. It was not a question of covering things up, it was really not high on anyone's list of priorities. They were trying to get on with the business of reconstruction and restoring the conditions so that trade and payments could now take place."[8]

The BIS itself remained ambiguous about the EPU. It regarded the multilateral payment mechanisms as slow and unwieldy.[9] The bank preferred free trade and currency convertibility. But, politically, the EPU was invaluable for the BIS. Thanks in large part to the EPU, the bank's future was assured. The BIS and the European integration project were locked into each other. The BIS was the only institution capable of handling the complicated technical processes demanded by economic integration. At each step on the road to a united Europe, the BIS would be there.

In 1951, France, West Germany, Italy, and the Benelux states signed the Treaty of Paris, establishing the European Coal and Steel Community (ECSC). The ECSC created a common market for coal and steel. This dry-sounding construct was, in fact, a profoundly significant development. The coal and steel market was now regulated by the ECSC's governing authority, which meant that the ECSC was a supranational institution, with regulatory powers over its members. For Jean Monnet, the architect and president of the ECSC, the new institution had transcended the old idea of the nation-state. The establishment of the ECSC set a pattern that would be followed for decades, one which still continues today. The removal of national sovereignty was always presented as an economic or technical measure, rather than the profoundly political process that it actually was.

Monnet was an early adopter of the idea of rule by technocrats. The French economist and diplomat was a veteran of the era that had brought forth the BIS: the post-1918 settlement. Born in 1888 to a family of Cognac merchants, Monnet worked for a while for the family firm, spending time in the City of London. During the war he coordinated British and French shipping to maximize their efficiency. In 1919 Monnet attended the Paris Peace Conference as an assistant to the French commerce minister. The carnage of the First World War had turned Monnet, like many of his generation, into a convinced internationalist. Monnet helped found the League of Nations and was appointed deputy secretary-general. But the League's slow and cumbersome decision making and the need to help his family business, which was in difficulties, pushed Monnet back to commerce.

Nowadays, Monnet is spoken of in reverential terms as the "Father of the Europe Union." Monnet's ideas, which for many in Europe are now regarded as near-holy, have shaped our world and look set to do so for generations. His memory endures in buildings, scholarships, awards, and fellowships, including the Jean Monnet Center for International and Regional Economic Law and Justice at the New York University School of Law. Monnet's ideas have generated a whole new academic discipline: European integration studies. More than 785 universities in 72 countries offer the Jean Monnet Program, taught by 1,650 professors to 25,000 students a year.[10] But who were the formative influences on Monnet's thinking? The answer lies not in Paris, Brussels, or war-ravaged Europe, but in Wall Street, where Monnet worked during the 1920s and '30s.

Monnet's hidden history brings us back to some familiar and powerful names. Curiously—or perhaps not, considering the small world of the global financiers in the early twentieth century—Monnet was connected to John Foster Dulles and Sullivan and Cromwell; to John McCloy, then a partner in the Cravath law firm, which represented General Aniline and Film, IG Farben's American subsidiary, and even to Ivar Kreuger, the Swedish match king and con man.

Monnet met John Foster Dulles at the 1919 Paris Peace Conference, and the two men became close friends. They shared a similarly elitist view of the world, a disdain for democratic accountability, and an enthusiasm for making money. Dulles's extensive network of high-level contacts would prove extremely useful to Monnet over the next decades. During the 1920s, Monnet managed Blair & Company, an American finance house. Blair & Co. was represented by the Cravath law firm where John McCloy was a partner, and Monnet and McCloy became close friends. Blair & Co., like many investment houses of the time, was thoroughly corrupt and routinely carried out insider trading operations. Under Monnet's leadership, it kept a preferred list of fifty-eight clients who were brought in on profitable deals.[11] Monnet also worked with Dulles and several American banks, including Chase, on the stabilization of the Polish economy, which gave him an early understanding of the power of transitional finance to make or break a country's economy. When Blair & Co. was incorporated into the Bank of America, Monnet moved to San Francisco to run the new subsidiary. The firm's shares plummeted in the crash of 1929, and Monnet returned to Europe.[12]

After Kreuger, the Swedish match king and con man, went bust, John Foster Dulles sent Monnet to Stockholm to protect the interests of Kreuger's American creditors. In 1933, bored with Sweden, Monnet moved to China to help the government set up the Chinese Development Corporation, to develop communications and infrastructure. Monnet then returned to the United States and moved into a large apartment at Fifth Avenue and 92nd Street.[13] John Foster Dulles then suggested that Monnet—whom he described as "one of the most brilliant men I know" and "an intimate friend"[14]—go into business with another close friend of his, a banker called George Murnane.

In fact Monnet and Murnane had known each other since the First World War, when Murnane had worked for the American Red Cross in France. Murnane was a partner in Lee, Higginson—the Boston investment firm that had financed Kreuger and for whose London branch Thomas McKittrick worked. "I have long felt that they would make an ideal combination," Dulles wrote of Monnet and Murnane. The two men agreed to set up a new international finance house, using Dulles's legal services. At this time Sullivan and Cromwell was making so much money, especially from its business in Germany, that Dulles suggested the law firm invest in his friends' new company, Monnet, Murnane & Company. Sullivan and Cromwell put up $25,000, and Dulles invested another $25,000 of his own money.[15] Monnet focused on business in France and China, and Murnane looked after Solvay & Cie, the Belgium chemical firm that was a partner of IG Farben. Dulles was the lawyer for Solvay & Cie's American subsidiary.

When the Second World War broke out, Monnet put his contacts and belief in international cooperation to good use. He was sent to London to oversee British and French arms production. From there he went to the United States, where he co-ordinated arms and aircraft purchases and encouraged American manufacturers to boost their output. Monnet met his "intimate friend" John Foster Dulles whenever he could. The two men shared a common vision for postwar Europe, one now being articulated by decision makers from Basel to Berlin and Washington, DC. There could be no return to the prewar system of nation-states, Dulles wrote in 1941:

> *We should seek the political reorganization of continental Europe as a federated commonwealth. There must be a large measure of local self-government along ethnic lines. This can be assured through federal principles, which in this respect are very flexible. But the reestablishment of some twenty-five wholly independent sovereign states in Europe would be political folly.*[16]

National sovereignty led inevitably to war, Dulles argued in 1942. "The fact of the matter is that economic unity in Europe has primarily been held back by a small group of self-seeking politicians in every nation. . . . Because a lot of politicians want to hold on to the trappings of sovereignty, are we to allow a condition to persist which makes recurrent war inevitable and which now, apparently, also inevitably involves our being drawn into such wars?"[17] Dulles's arguments for a federal Europe were rooted not in hazy idealism about a Europe living in peace and security for its own sake, but hard-headed realism: the preservation of American military and geopolitical interests, building a bulwark against the Soviets, and the preservation of the links between the prewar transnational financial elites in Wall Street and Germany. A united Europe was simply the best means to achieve these ends.

MONNET RETURNED TO Paris after the war's end and began to plan the supranational project that he had drawn up with John Foster Dulles. The ECSC was the first step on the road to today's European Union. The European federal project, like its financial agent the BIS, operated by stealth. The stated reason for the creation of the ECSC was to harmonize coal and steel production and sales in postwar Europe and usher a new spirit of economic cooperation and harmony between Germany and its neighbors that would prevent future wars. The real reason was to ensure the continuing dominance of the German steel and cartels and the power of men such as Alfried Krupp, whose industrial empire had worked eighty thousand slave laborers to death, and who was about to be released from prison by Monnet's close friend John McCloy.

The coal and steel barons intimidated even Ludwig Erhard, the architect of the German economic miracle, recalled Dutch politician Jelle Zijlstra, who had briefly served as prime minister from 1966 to 1967, before being appointed president and chairman of the board of the BIS, where he remained until 1981. Eight years after his retirement, as Europe prepared for the introduction of a single currency, Zijlstra gave a lengthy interview, where he spoke freely about the secret history of the European unity project.[18] The ECSC was a "political exercise" and fundamentally, was "an impossibility," Zijlstra said. The Germans "without any doubt" regarded it as a *dachorganisation* (umbrella organization) for their steel and coal cartels.

Zijlstra served as Dutch minister for economics for most of the 1950s. After a few months in office he went to visit one of Holland's largest coal and steel traders. His host warned him that the German coal and steel barons were so powerful that they were virtually a state within a state. Do not, he advised Zijlstra, upset them. Two months later, Zijlstra received an invitation to the Ruhr, Germany's industrial heartland, to meet the barons himself. He was wined and dined and received the same warning. Zijlstra, then still in his mid-thirties, was not cowed. He thanked the coal and steel barons for their time and returned to Holland.

Zijlstra saw the ECSC for what it was: a cartel for the German steel and coal producers that fixed prices in their favor, while removing its members states' power to run two crucial strategic industries. He soon clashed with Ludwig Erhard. The German economist's commitment to free trade was less ardent when the country's own interests and those of the coal and steel barons were involved. Zijlstra berated Erhard and told him, "You are not true to your own faith." Erhard did not deny the accusation. He shrugged and told Zijlstra, *"Lieber Kollege, wir sind doch alle Sünder!"* (Dear Colleague, we are all sinners). "In that debate," recalled Zijlstra, "the coal and steel industrialists, the people from the Ruhr, saw the community as a possibility of extending their structures to the European system. And they were not, and they never have been free traders."

Back in 1944, as we have seen, McKittrick, the BIS president, was cutting deals with German industrialists with the support of the OSS and the State Department, as outlined in the Harvard Plan documents. The industrialists' postwar cooperation, McKittrick promised, would preserve their industries and even bring a guarantee of continued profits. The ECSC fit perfectly into that framework.

Zijlstra knew Monnet well. The French technocrat was an unelected bureaucrat, but he still had the power to instruct governments, including the West German government, said Zijlstra. If a problem arose, "Monnet went to see the governments and told them what they had to do. Monnet had an enormous authority over the national governments . . . he certainly visited from time to time the minister of foreign affairs and even prime ministers. He was very powerful."[19] Monnet's power had multiple roots. He was immensely charismatic and persuasive, with a sharp, precise intellect. But more than that, Monnet had John Foster Dulles, Allen Dulles, John McCloy, and the American government behind him.

Much of the United States political and intelligence establishment believed, like Jean Monnet, and indeed Winston Churchill, the wartime British prime minister, that a unified Europe would never go to war again, which meant that the United States would never have to go to war again in Europe. Germany needed to be locked into the unification project, both as a bulwark of stability, and as a counterpoint to rising Soviet power on the other side of the Iron Curtain. With Marshall Plan aid dependent on progress toward a federal Europe, the United States could, and did, wield enormous influence on the political structures of the postwar continent.

In May 1948, eight hundred delegates met at The Hague, under the chairmanship of Sir Winston Churchill, to create the European Movement, with the ultimate aim of a federal union. The movement's secretary-general was Joseph Retinger, a former adviser to the Polish government-in-exile during the war. At the same time, Allen Dulles and William Donovan were using their OSS contacts and expertise to set up the American Committee for a United Europe (ACUE). The ACUE's role was to channel funds to the European federalists and to use the new techniques of psychological warfare, such as the Harvard Plan, which had been honed during the war, to push for a united Europe.

Donovan was appointed chairman of the ACUE and Allen Dulles his deputy. Walter Bedell Smith, the director of the CIA, the successor to the OSS, also sat on the board. Between 1949 and 1960, the ACUE injected more than $3 million into the European Movement, always at least half of its budget and often more. As Professor Richard Aldrich, an intelligence historian, notes, the European Movement's officers and directors included at least four CIA officers. Donovan pushed hard for the creation of the ECSC. He gathered petitions from American and European politicians and released them to the press and directed a stream of federalist propaganda at members of Congress."[20] The message from Washington was consistent: Europe must unite. In April 1950,

John McCloy gave a widely quoted speech in London, saying that the German problem could be solved only by a combination of economic and political factors, echoing the arguments of Per Jacobssen in 1946. "The fact is, we cannot solve the German problem without fitting it into the larger context of a united Europe. . . . These economic factors lead directly to the political. To insure the freer flow of trade and the development of European markets will require effective political machinery." McCloy concluded, "I say no permanent solution of the German problem seems possible without an effective European union."[21]

From Paris to Washington, DC, the postwar committees and movements pushing for European federalism presented themselves as new and innovative, offering a fresh approach for a new era. But they were deeply rooted in the old ways of doing business—of powerful men gathering over lunch or dinner to reshape the world as they saw fit. During the war Allen Dulles had met with Thomas McKittrick and Per Jacobssen to plan the postwar European economic order. Jean Monnet had honed his thoughts on European unity with John Foster Dulles. Per Jacobssen had traveled to Berlin to share American plans for the postwar European economy with Emil Puhl, the BIS director, war criminal, and Reichsbank vice president. None of these discussions were made public, even though the plans hatched there would shape the modern world. The United States' involvement in the European project continued the tradition of secrecy and covert action well into the 1960s. A State Department memo, dated June 11, 1965, to Robert Marjolin, the French president of the European Economic Community, recommends that he pursue monetary union without public discussion. The memo advises him to suppress debate until the "adoption of such proposals would become virtually inescapable."[22]

THE NEW TRANSNATIONAL ECSC naturally needed a transnational bank. In 1954 the ECSC was negotiating with United States for $100 million loan. The monies were to be spent investing in coal and steel projects. The US government had pushed hard for the creation of the ECSC but was reluctant to lend it such a large sum. The ECSC was a new organization. Who knew if it would even exist in a few years? The BIS came to the rescue. The bank would act as the middleman between the ECSC and the United States and manage the loan. If the ECSC no longer existed when the $100 million was due to be repaid, the BIS would collect the money and would then repay the United States. The involvement of the BIS reassured the US Treasury. The loan was agreed. With the BIS's imprimatur the ECSC could now obtain credit on the international market.

The following year the BIS celebrated its twenty-fifth birthday. The bank's swift engineering of itself into the postwar global financial system was proving extremely profitable. Between 1950 and 1959 the bank's assets and liabilities increased 4.7 times, while gold deposits, mainly from central banks, increased by 14 times, and currency deposits increased more than fourfold. The bank was as discreet as ever. Compared to the complications of the war years, the new era of peace was far simpler to navigate. In 1955 the Bank deutscher Länder was prepared to lend $100 million to the Bank of France but feared domestic criticism during an election year. The BIS offered to hold the monies on deposit for the BdL while it was understood, although certainly not mentioned in the contract, that it would make an advance of the same sum to France. That France, a victor of the war, needed to borrow such a substantial sum from Germany, a defeated country, was testimony to the effectiveness of the Marshall Plan.

Newly confident of its future, the BIS had started to issue stern policy prescriptions to the world's governments. Jacobssen was still fulminating against the curse of rising prices. "The inflation mentality," demanded the 1956 annual report, "must be extirpated."[23] The BIS also criticized the cost of the substantial programs of public works launched by postwar European governments to raise standards of living, housing, and public services. "With regard to all these activities, the governments should, in the first place, abstain from inflationary methods of financing," warned Jacobssen in the 1956 annual report. "But usually that is not enough; if the private economy is to develop and maintain a high level of investment for productive purposes—as would certainly be advantageous for a number of countries—other claims on resources must be kept within reasonable limits and in a great many cases this means that public expenditure should be curtailed."[24] An unelected, unaccountable, and secretive financial institution was issuing policy prescriptions for democratic governments.

This was Jacobssen's last report. He left the BIS in 1956 to run the IMF. Many of his colleagues were amazed at his decision. It was clear that the political dynamic was toward ever more financial and political European integration, all of which would need the BIS. And the project was working. Europe was stable and at peace. Trade and industrial production were breaking records. The BIS's future was assured. The European Payments Union, managed by the BIS, was so successful that by 1959 western European currencies became freely convertible into each other and into the US dollar.

The IMF was new and still defining its role. Sir Otto Niemeyer, the veteran British banker and former chairman of the BIS board, told Jacobssen that the IMF had no future and that he would be wasting his time there. But Jacobssen felt that after twenty-five years at BIS it was time to move on.

JACOBSSEN WAS NOT the only international banker on the move. In 1956 Eric Warburg joined Brinckmann, Wirtz & Company as a partner. Rudolf Brinckmann, the bank's owner and BIS director, ungraciously told Warburg that he should be grateful to be allowed to return to the successor bank to the House of Warburg. The dispute between the Warburgs and their former employee remained as rancorous as ever. Brinckmann still refused to change the bank's name back to Warburg, or even include the family name in the bank's title as it might mean a loss of Arab business.

Emil Puhl, the former vice president of the Reichsbank and BIS board member, also had travel plans. In 1954 Puhl applied for a US visa, despite his conviction for war crimes, which would under normal circumstances immediately disqualify such a request. But it seemed there were special rules for valued international bankers, even for Nazi financiers. Puhl gave the Chase National Bank, the employers of his old friend McKittrick, as his reference. During the trial of Walther Funk, Puhl's former boss, Thomas Dodd, an American war crimes prosecutor, told the court that Chase National had once offered Puhl a job in New York.[25] Perhaps the bank wanted to make this offer again. The US Consul General in Berlin wrote of Puhl's application, "It should be noted that the Consulate General has in the course of its examination found no other grounds that would prevent Mr. Puhl from receiving a non-immigrant visa. Mr. Puhl is one of the outstanding bankers in Germany and wishes to proceed to the United States on the invitation of several well-known American bankers to participate in discussions of some importance."[26] It is not publicly known if Puhl traveled to the United States, and if he did, with whom he met.

Donald MacLaren, the British spy who brought down IG Farben's American operation and who investigated IG Farben's postwar empire, returned home from Berlin to civilian life. MacLaren's analysis of IG Farben remains as incisive as ever. "It has been called a State within a State; in the end it almost became the State itself."[27] The defeat of Hitler was merely a temporary setback, MacLaren warned. His conclusions echoed the Red House Report on the Nazi industrialists' postwar plans and Puhl's conversations with McKittrick: "Men who built such an elaborate structure and who thought so thoroughly of every contingency in the past are not likely to disappear from the scene without leaving a group of younger men who wait for the day when our backs are turned and our interest wanes to gather again their scattered resources of money and men to engage once more in an attempt of economic domination of the world."[28]

MacLaren was correct. The key man was indeed younger, born nineteen years after Hermann Schmitz. A BIS veteran who had worked in Basel during the early 1930s, he would be fulsomely welcomed onto the bank's board.

CHAPTER TWELVE

THE RISE OF THE DESK-MURDERERS

"What a Blessing we have a Blessing."

— The American view of Karl Blessing, appointed the first president
of the Bundesbank in 1958[1]

A fter fifteen years at the New York Federal Reserve, Charles Coombs was not easily awed. But even he was impressed at the financial firepower present at the BIS governors' meeting in December 1960. Gathered in one room, sipping their coffee in an anonymous former hotel near Basel railway station, were the governors of the banks of England, France, Germany, Italy, Sweden, Belgium, and the Netherlands. But despite their urbane appearance and easy familiarity with each other, the governors were worried men—as was Coombs himself.

The combined dollar holdings of their banks totaled $6 billion. Under the Bretton Woods system the dollar-to-gold exchange rate was fixed at $35 an ounce. As long as the London gold market stayed around that price, the value of their dollar reserves was stable. But earlier that year the price of gold had jumped to $40 an ounce. The dollar was a victim of its own success. There were too many dollars in circulation or held by national banks as part of their reserves to be redeemable for gold at $35 an ounce. Thus the dollar's value against gold was declining. The central bankers could sell their reserves, but such a move would certainly crash the dollar and fuel global instability.

The central bankers wanted to ask Coombs about the financial plans of the new Kennedy administration, which would take office in January 1961, he recalled in his memoirs.[2] Coombs's book provides a rare and fascinating glimpse into the secret deals reached at the Basel governors' meetings. The central bankers "were very worried men that day, genuinely distressed by the impending clash between their sworn duty to protect the value of their countries' international reserves and their fear of precipitating a dollar crisis by cashing in dollars for gold."[3] Much was riding on Coombs's answers. If he could reassure the other bankers, the dollar would retain their confidence. If not, he might trigger a worldwide financial crisis.

The bankers were reassured. The new US government would firmly maintain gold parity at $35 an ounce and would work to reduce the balance of payments deficit, Coombs promised. The governors welcomed his assurances and requested that he, or a representative of the Federal Reserve, attend every Basel meeting from now on, even if only as an observer. Thirty years after the founding of the BIS, the United States officially still kept itself at a distance. Three of the BIS's presidents had been American—Gates McGarrah, Leon Fraser, and Thomas McKittrick—but the Federal Reserve had never taken up the stock allocated to it at the bank's founding. Coombs was honored to be invited to the Sunday evening dinner, the "inner sanctum from which all lower ranking officials were normally excluded."

Coombs regularly attended the governors' meetings from 1960 until his retirement in 1975. He relished his time at the BIS. He usually left New York on Thursday afternoon, after the meeting of the directors of the New York Federal Reserve, and went straight to Idlewild Airport to fly to Zürich, arriving on Friday. From there he traveled to Basel and his usual room at the Schweizerhof Hotel, near the BIS. It was exhausting but exhilarating, with meetings and discussions on Friday night and all through the weekend until Monday morning when he flew back to New York. But his jet lag soon evaporated. "As the central bankers converged on Basel from all the European capitals and from Ottawa, New York, and Tokyo, the fatigue of our journey seemed to vanish as we greeted old friends and listened to the inside story of what was really going on in the financial markets of the world."

Basel was the "ideal meeting place for central bankers seeking a refuge for quiet and confidential discussion of highly charged financial issues." In between the formal meetings, the bankers drifted down the corridors between their private offices, "always stopping to shake hands in the continental fashion with any colleague going in the opposite direction." The meetings were worth the trip in themselves, wrote Coombs, providing "not only a quiet testing ground for new ideas and approaches but also an early warning system when things were beginning to go wrong." The dinners, especially, gave "priceless access." "I could generally tell from those dinner discussions which birds would fly and which would not," he recalled.

Like couples who had been married for years, the bankers could read each other's minds. "There is something deeply satisfying in dealing with fellow professionals in any technical field. Never any speeches, everyone focusing clearly on the issue at hand, sentences frequently left unfinished because everyone instinctively knew the rest and in an almost uncanny way, a simultaneous realization of the appropriate technical solution. None of us were romantic internationalists, but where we could see a clear overlapping of national interests our minds instinctively reached out to one another in a true camaraderie of professional cooperation."

Coombs was especially impressed with Karl Blessing, the president of the Bundesbank, the new West German national bank, who "played a towering role":

> *As a young man he had worked on the staff of the BIS and once recounted to me his anguished memories of those days as he watched from Basel the breakdown of international financial co-operation in the early thirties. Now as President of the Bundesbank with the mark entrusted to his care, he wielded his enormous authority with courage and sensitive discernment of his world financial responsibilities. A cheerfully resolute man, Blessing was an unfailing source of strength and morale in all of our Basel meetings. I thought of him as truly a great man of his times.*

Blessing was indeed a man of his times, although not in the way that Coombs believed. The Bundesbank president embodied the new class of rulers in West

Germany, many of whom were the same people who had managed Nazi Germany. Former Nazis ran or held senior positions in the banking and finance sectors, the military, the intelligence service, and government administration. Hans Globke, the national security adviser to Chancellor Konrad Adenauer, had helped write the Nuremberg anti-Jewish laws. Richard Gehlen, the head of West Germany's intelligence service, was the wartime chief of military intelligence on the Eastern Front, where the German army and SS troops had slaughtered hundreds of thousands of civilians. The directors of IG Farben, as we have seen, swiftly returned to lucrative business careers.

The unfortunate past of these men was rarely discussed. And Blessing, too, was adept at rewriting history, none more than his own. He had worked at the BIS during the 1930s, although his claim of "anguished memories" is risible. He had joined the BIS under instructions from his employers at the Reichsbank, with the express purpose of not facilitating, but wrecking international financial cooperation. Blessing's 1930 memorandum, "Opinion on How the Reichsbank Should Conduct Itself in the BIS," called for German officials to argue that reparations were "completely utopian," to make impossible demands, and to undermine the BIS's legitimacy in order to derail the Young Plan.

Blessing had returned to Germany in 1934 to work as an adviser at the Ministry of Economics. His patron, Hjalmar Schacht, then brought him back to the Reichsbank and appointed him its youngest director. Blessing loudly proclaimed his loyalty, declaring, "National Socialist economic and financial policy, like National Socialist policy for freedom and equality, has taken upon itself the law of action. We will allow no one in the future to strike this from our hand."[4] Blessing joined the Nazi party, and after the 1938 Anschluss—the absorption of Austria—he was rewarded with the job of absorbing the Austrian National Bank. It was joyous work for a true believer: "Just three months separate us from the memorable day, which will remain unforgettable for us. And yet in this short period, all the measures have been put into place with the goal of forging together the two economies into an unbreakable whole."[5]

Blessing was also forward thinking. When Germany's Jews were fined one million Reichmarks for the cost of the Kristallnacht pogrom in November 1938, he worried that Jews would sell their government bonds to raise the cash, which would drive down the market. The answer was for the Reichsbank to limit sales of Jewish-owned securities to one thousand Reichmarks.

The following year Blessing, together with Schacht, left the Reichsbank. Blessing had also signed the directors' memorandum criticizing Hitler's armaments spending. But the former BIS official was a canny survivor. He swiftly courted Walther Funk, Schacht's successor as president. With Funk's imprimatur, Blessing returned to the Reichsbank as a member of its advisory board. Blessing moved in the highest circles of the Third Reich. He attended thirty-eight meetings of the Himmlerkreis, the circle of Nazi industrialists who channeled funds to the SS chief through Special Account "S" at Kurt von Schröder's J. H. Stein bank. Blessing went on two trips with the group to visit concentration camps, guided by Himmler himself. Blessing later said of the Himmlerkreis, "I thought it was just for beer evenings."[6]

Blessing's importance went far beyond the monies he donated to the SS. He embodied the kind of intelligent, sophisticated technocrat who was essential both for the Nazi regime and for the perpetuation of German economic interests after the war ended. Hannah Arendt, the German-Jewish writer and philosopher, described the bureaucrats who organized the Holocaust as "desk-murderers." They did not raise a gun to the naked victims standing over the death-pit or pull the lever to release the gas. They merely stamped and moved pieces of paper from one government department to another and kept the money moving. But without them the Third Reich could not function. Blessing, too, was a desk-murderer.

In April 1939 Blessing joined the board of the German subsidiary of Unilever, a giant Anglo-Dutch company that manufactured fats and oils. The following year Germany invaded the Netherlands, and Blessing was appointed one of three administrators looking after Unilever's interests across the Reich. Meanwhile, Hermann Goering—the chief of the Luftwaffe, the German air force, and the minister in charge of the four-year plan—set up Kontinental-Öl to exploit the oil reserves of central Europe and the Balkans. This was a project after Blessing's own heart. He recognized the importance of Germany's allies in the east and south—Croatia, Hungary, Romania, and Bulgaria—as a means of ensuring Nazi economic hegemony and supplies of raw material. The Danube, he said, was the "river of the future," and petrol and grain would flow up it to Germany.[7]

Together with Walther Funk, the president of the Reichsbank, and Heinrich Bütefisch of IG Farben, Blessing was appointed to the board of Kontinental-Öl. As Christopher Simpson notes, the establishment of the Reich's oil company represented a triumph for the businessmen and bankers. The hardline Nazi ideologues around the SS wanted state control, government ownership, and centralized planning of the economy, especially of vital strategic industries. However the business elite, such as Schacht and Blessing, favored a more commercial approach.[8] Germany should dominate world markets, they believed, but there was no need to control every aspect of them. Kontinental-Öl was the answer: a government-supported monopoly to take over the oil industries of eastern Europe, with financial services provided by Hermann Abs at Deutsche Bank.

Kontinental-Öl, like IG Farben, was built on plunder, exploitation, slavery, and murder. As the Nazi oil empire expanded eastward, Kontinental became one of the Third Reich's largest users of concentration camp inmates, ghetto workers, and prisoners. The firm ran at least ten concentration camps in Poland alone, where the workers were leased from the SS. In Ukraine, for example, Kontinental paid the SS and the German police administration five zlotys a day for a man, and four for a woman. The average life expectancy of a slave laborer was between three and six months. When Kontinental's camps were shut down, many of the inmates were shot. The Borisow camp was closed in March 1943 with about eight hundred prisoners still alive. According to Red Cross records, about eighty men and twenty women were evacuated to Smolensk, and the rest were executed.[9]

As the financial director of Kontinental-Öl, Blessing was at the epicenter of this nexus of death and profit. He oversaw its acquisition of new firms in the east. He managed the company "payroll," much of which was concerned with payments to the SS for the concentration camp labor the firm used—labor that was also used to build the new company headquarters in Berlin. Unfortunately for Blessing and his managers, the half-starved, traumatized labor force was not very productive. As late as March 1945, one of Blessing's underlings complained that work in Upper Silesia was being held up by the "use of concentration camp prisoners of low performance."

Blessing was arrested and imprisoned at the war's end, while the Allies considered whether to charge him with war crimes, as he certainly deserved. But behind the scenes, Blessing had powerful allies: Allen Dulles and Thomas McKittrick. The Nazi bankers and industrialists were correct in their belief that the western powers would need them to rebuild the German economy. In the contest between justice and realpolitik, Dulles would make sure that the latter would triumph.

In July 1945 the US occupation authorities asked Dulles to furnish a list of Germans "eligible on the basis of ability and political record for posts in a reconstituted German administration." The first set of lists was quickly submitted. But by autumn, Dulles, now running the OSS station in Berlin, had more detailed information about suitable German bankers. Much of this would have come from McKittrick.

In September 1945 Dulles submitted his new white list. It was divided into two categories: A and B. On the A list were three names judged suitable for "higher posts in a ministry." The B list contained five names that were suggested for "lesser posts such as Bureau head or division chief." [10] Among the names in group A was that of Ernst Hülse, the former head of the BIS banking department. Hülse, said Dulles, enjoyed "excellent connections with banking circles abroad," had a Jewish wife, and was definitely anti-Nazi. Hülse was appointed to the Reichsbank in the British zone and was named president of the central bank for the federal state of Nordheim-Westfalen.

The first name on the B list was that of Karl Blessing, whom Dulles described as a "prominent businessman and financial expert" with "considerable experience in international trade."[11] Dulles was well informed about Blessing's central role at Kontinental-Öl, which the American spymaster described as a "government-owned holding company organized to coordinate German-controlled oil properties throughout Europe." Dulles hedged his bets. Blessing's relationship with Kontinental-Öl might, he wrote, disqualify him for a "high government position." However Blessing had accepted the job "under pressure" and had been in touch with the German resistance. In addition, Dulles added, Blessing had not been a member of the Nazi Party. In fact Blessing had joined in 1937. And Blessing's party records were held by the US authorities, had Dulles bothered to check. Blessing's main claim to anti-Nazi activity was being included on the list of the July 1944 anti-Hitler plotters as a potential minister for economics. When the conspirators were arrested, Blessing was protected by Walther Funk, who told the Gestapo that Blessing had not known anything about the plot.

The whitewashing of Blessing was not the exception, but the rule. Declassified telegrams revealed that Dulles had long planned to rescue important German industrialists and scientists. In January 1945, Dulles wrote to William Casey, who was running operations inside Germany and who later served as CIA director in the 1980s:

> *My project contemplates that in normal course of events and without any prior contact with us but merely to escape impending chaos, important German industrialists, scientists, etc., will desire to find some haven, preferably Switzerland. If Switzerland is closed to them, these men might possibly turn to Russia as their only alternative. . . . Discreet preliminary conversations indicate some hope of securing Swiss cooperation."[12]*

Not everyone in Washington approved. The following month First Lady Eleanor Roosevelt wrote to her husband, "Memo for the President. Allen Dulles who is in charge of Bill Donovan's outfit in Paris has been counsel, closely tied up with the Schroeder Bank. That is likely to be the representative of the underground Nazi interests after the war. There seems to be in Paris a great many people who are pretty close to the big business side!"[13]

The president's wife was certainly well informed about the importance of the Schröder bank network, which reached from Germany to London and New York, and to the BIS via Kurt von Schröder. But by summer 1945, after the death of her husband, Mrs. Roosevelt's opinions counted for little in Washington.

Blessing was not charged with war crimes. Instead, with Allen Dulles's help, he was freed and returned to his old job at Unilever. He became one of the highest paid executives in Europe, earning $75,000 a year. Blessing took a pay cut to $50,000 a year when he joined the Bundesbank in 1958, but the power and prestige was ample compensation. By the early 1960s, when Blessing was a regular attender at the Basel governor meetings, he had transformed himself into a former member of the resistance.

Hermann Abs, of Deutsche Bank, was the most powerful commercial banker in the Third Reich, and he was not on Dulles's A list. Rather, he was high on an Allied blacklist of important Nazi officials to be arrested. In the American zone Colonel Bernard Bernstein, the head of the Finance division, had Abs, indeed all the Nazi financiers in his sights. Bernstein ordered that every banker and industrialist be detained as a suspected war criminal.

Luckily for Abs, he was living in the British zone. There he met his old friend, Charles Gunston of the Bank of England, whom he used to see in Basel during the 1930s at BIS meetings. Gunston was a senior official in the British occupation authority. Gunston had no interest in the Nazi atrocities. All he cared about was getting the banks working again. Gunston asked Abs to help rebuild the banking system in the British zone. Abs was more than happy to oblige. Bernstein was enraged and demanded that Abs be extradited to the American zone. Gunston refused, but in early January 1946 he returned to England. Abs was then finally arrested as a suspected war criminal, and he spent three months in prison before being released and was never charged. Instead Abs went to work, fulfilling his promise to his old friend Charles Gunston.

KARL BLESSING, LIKE Hermann Abs, certainly understood when to be helpful. In 1960 the gold spike threatened to undermine the stability of the postwar financial system. The United States and Britain proposed joint operations on the London market to protect the value of both countries' reserves. Blessing quickly offered to make some of West Germany's reserves available to the Bank of England. But any coordinated international action would need bilateral agreements, which would necessitate lengthy negotiations with governments. Britain persuaded the United States that there was a much simpler approach to organizing multilateral interventions: through the governors' meetings at BIS. Between them the countries represented there, as well as the United States, accounted for about 80 percent of the world's reserves. The BIS staff was not enthusiastic about the idea. As the world pioneer in transnational finance, the BIS was a firm believer in the primacy of market forces. The market was now being shunted aside, wrote one official, "so that the inconvenience of certain financial policies can be avoided."[14]

Any such doubts were ignored by the governors. In November 1961 the London Gold Pool (LGP) was set up. The United States, West Germany, France, Italy, Britain, Belgium, the Netherlands, and Switzerland contributed a total of $270 million to the pool. The funds would be used to maintain dollar parity at $35 an ounce, in line with the Bretton Woods agreements. The banks would keep the gold price stable, by buying and selling when necessary. All of the participating banks agreed not to buy gold themselves on the London market while the pool was in existence. The BIS gold cartel was constructed on conditions of complete secrecy. There was not even a formal written agreement. The bankers' word, and a handshake, was enough to seal the deal. As Coombs noted of the governors' meetings, "However much money was involved, no agreements were ever signed nor memoranda of understanding ever initialized. The word of each official was sufficient, and there were never any disappointments."[15]

The Bank of England carried out the LGP's monetary transactions, but the BIS was essential to its operations. Every month the Bank of England reported to an experts' group of officials from BIS member banks and the BIS itself, which met at the BIS.

Eventually, word got out. The story was picked up by *The Times* (of London), then by *The Economist*. The LGP was forced to release detailed accounts, which were published in the Bank of England's quarterly bulletin. For the first five years, the LGP worked. The price in London stayed between $35.04 and $35.20 per ounce. The group of gold experts expanded their briefs to cover the foreign exchange market. The gold pool became the Committee on Gold and Foreign Exchange. It still exists today and is known as the BIS Markets Committee. The committee's agenda and deliberations remain secret.

THERE WERE TIMES, especially during crises, that the mutual trust engendered over the lunches and dinners in Basel proved crucial in stabilizing the global financial system.

November 23, 1963, was such a day. The assassination of President John F. Kennedy triggered panic selling on the stock market. Coombs was at work at the New York Fed when the news came through. He put aside his shock and horror and focused on the task at hand: the immediate defense of the dollar. Coombs considered banning foreign exchange transactions to prevent panic selling, but such a decision would be slow to implement and would need political support. Immediate action was needed, though, and he decided that closing the foreign exchange market was anyway not feasible. It would send a signal of panic and desperation. There would be a frenzy of selling of both dollars and gold.

The answer, Coombs decided, was for the United States to sell massive amounts of foreign currency to defend the dollar. The question was where could Coombs get it? He had access to only $16 million worth and held none at all of several major European currencies. He could sell gold to cover the purchases. But once news got out that the United States was selling its gold reserves after its president had been assassinated, the dollar would immediately plunge.

The best option was to borrow and sell foreign currency by drawing on the Federal Reserve's currency swap network. Currency swaps allowed Central Bank A to hold reserves in Central Bank B's currency (or a third currency), which Central Bank A could draw on, without having to purchase the foreign currency from Central Bank B. This was an excellent solution apart from one small problem: the time difference. No bank could draw on currency swaps without the approval of the partner bank. The president had been shot at 1:30 p.m. Eastern Standard Time, six hours behind Europe. The European governors that Coombs urgently needed to contact had left their offices and were on their way to dinner or home. There were no mobile telephones or Internet. The governors were unreachable.

Coombs now faced the most important decision—or rather, gamble—of his life. If he bet wrong, not just his career would end. He would be remembered as the man who wrecked the dollar at a time of a national crisis. There was no time to consult or get the support of his superiors. A run on the dollar could start at any moment. Could he count on the governors of Europe's central banks to underwrite the sale by the Federal Reserve of hundreds of millions of dollars' worth of their currencies without their prior consent or knowledge? For if the sales went ahead, and the governors protested, or refused to authorize the transactions, both he, and the dollar, would be finished. The governors, he decided, would back him.

At 2 p.m., Coombs instructed the foreign exchange desk to offer 10 million deutschmarks for sale and to inform the bank acting as the Fed's agent that more such offerings would follow. Eight minutes later the Fed offered substantial amounts of sterling, followed by large holding of Dutch guilders and Swiss francs. Meanwhile, the Bank of Canada had stabilized the US-Canadian dollar exchange rate, and the Fed reciprocated.

At 2:30 p.m. Coombs ordered his officials to inform the market that the Federal Reserve would supply foreign exchange in unlimited amounts to defend the dollar and would call in its entire $2 billion of available credit swaps if necessary. Only then did Coombs report to Alfred Hayes, the president of the New York Fed. Meanwhile, the New York Fed's telephone operators were searching for the other central bankers. They reached Roy Bridge, of the Bank of England, first. He immediately agreed to help. Bridge told Coombs he could ask for "all that he wanted." The Bundesbank was equally cooperative. As soon as the Frankfurt foreign exchange market opened on the following Monday, the Bundesbank made sure to show itself as a buyer of dollars. In Bern the Swiss bankers agreed to enlarge the Fed's credit facility by another $100 million. Coombs's strategy worked. The stock market recovered. When the markets opened on Monday, the dollar remained stable.

THE BIS WAS going from strength to strength. In 1961 the ten key industrial IMF member states, known as the G10 (which largely overlapped with the membership of the BIS) set up the General Agreement to Borrow (GAB). The G10, plus Switzerland (which did not join the IMF until 1992) put aside $6 billion as a stand-by credit for the IMF. The GAB funds were to be made available if an IMF member was suddenly threatened by short-term capital flight. Two years later, the IMF began a detailed study of the international monetary system. It asked the BIS to provide information on the gold and Eurocurrency markets and central banks' short-term credit arrangements.[16] When the IMF report was published in 1964 it recommended that all G10 central banks send the BIS confidential statistics about their monetary reserves. The BIS, as the depository of this data, could then act as an early warning system if a country's reserves were being depleted and might need to draw on the GAB. So it seemed only natural that the Sunday evening governors' dinners at the BIS should be expanded to include Canada and Japan. (The two countries were members of the GAB but did not join the BIS until 1970.) The BIS had effectively relocated one of the most important international meetings of the key IMF members from Washington to Basel.

When in 1964 the central bankers of the European Economic Community set up their Governors' Committee to coordinate monetary policy, the committee was located not in Brussels, the home of the European project, or Frankfurt, the site of the Bundesbank, but at the BIS headquarters. The BIS helpfully provided the Governors' Committee with the necessary secretarial and administrative support. The following year, in 1965, the BIS even reached agreement on its 1930s investments in Germany—the Young Plan loans. The Reichsbank had serviced the loans and paid interest until the end of the war in April 1945. After a twenty-year break, Germany agreed to resume paying interest on the loans but deferred the capital repayment until 1996.

The deal was brokered by Hermann Abs, who had returned to Deutsche Bank. Like Karl Blessing, Abs had expertly whitewashed his Nazi past. There was no mention of Abs's role at the bank that organized the plunder of Nazi-occupied countries, or his former position on the board of IG Farben. Abs had been the most powerful commercial banker in the Third Reich and now enjoyed similar status and acclaim in the new West Germany. He was also a welcome guest in the world's treasuries and chancelleries. Abs sat on the board of so many companies, including Daimler Benz, the Federal Railways, and Lufthansa, that a law, known as "Lex Abs," was passed limiting the number of positions an individual could hold to ten.

When Per Jacobssen died in 1963 after just seven years at the IMF, Abs became a founding sponsor of the Per Jacobssen Foundation. The list of his cosponsors reads like a roll call of the transnational financial elite and includes some familiar names, such as Eugene Black, the former president of the World Bank; Marcus Wallenberg, tutor to Thomas McKittrick and vice chairman of Enskilda Bank; Roger Auboin, the former general manager of the BIS; Rudolf Brinckmann, the veteran BIS director; Jean Monnet, the architect of European unity; and Marius Holthrop, the BIS president. Abs died in 1994 at the age of ninety-two, garlanded with honors and acclaim. A gushing obituary in the *Independent* newspaper, a normally skeptical

British publication, acclaimed him as the "outstanding German banker" of his time. Which was true enough, as Abs had embodied a century of German banking, although not in the adulatory sense that the writer had envisaged.[17]

ALWAYS QUICK TO adapt to changing circumstances, the BIS spotted a new opportunity during the 1960s. The continuing drain on Britain's economy of its empire and the country's general economic malaise made sterling increasingly vulnerable. But sterling was also a reserve currency, especially across Britain's current and former dominions. Thus sterling, like the price of gold, had to be stabilized. The BIS was not a lender of last resort, but it could arrange loans to troubled central banks. In June 1966 a group of European central banks, the New York Federal Reserve, and the BIS agreed to make around $1 billion available to the Bank of England to defend sterling. This was significant, not just because of the sums involved, but because the BIS was its center. All the monies involved, apart from French and American funds, would be paid through a single account at the BIS. The bank was now coordinating a long-term strategic rescue of one of the world's reserve currencies.

However opaque the governors' meetings were, they were a more edifying spectacle than the farcical and very public scenes at the November 1968 G10 conference in Bonn. With the franc and sterling under pressure, and German reserves up by $4 billion, the conference was always going to be difficult.

This time the finance ministers were in charge. The bankers were banished to the lounges and corridors. Paris and London pressed for a devaluation of the mark, but Germany resisted. Roy Jenkins, the British finance minister, mentioned that the governors' meeting at Basel had favored revaluation of the mark. Karl Schiller, the German economics minister, rounded on Karl Blessing, the president of the Bundesbank. He demanded to know on what authority Blessing had discussed the national currency value with foreign officials, as though unaware that such discussions had been taking place at Basel since the BIS was established in 1930, and indeed were one of the main reasons for its existence. Schiller demanded that Jelle Zijlstra, the BIS president, provide him with a full report on the Basel governors' meeting. Zijlstra politely told him to "go to hell."

Excluded from the discussions, the governors spent their time playing Ping-Pong, drinking champagne and hunting down an ever-shrinking supply of canapés, all of which were encased in aspic. At one stage Charles Coombs and the governor of the Bank of France eyed a single frankfurter on a waiter's tray. They agreed to divide it. Outside the conference center, hordes of television crews and reporters were besieging the building, while German protestors angrily demanded that those inside "save the mark." In fact, it was the French franc that needed to be saved, and the general consensus was that the currency would need to be devalued by around 11 percent.

Zijlstra went into action. He convened an emergency governors' meeting over lunch on Friday to see what support could be raised for the franc. It was an impressive performance. Zijlstra secured a pledge of $2 billion within half an hour. In the event, Charles de Gaulle, the president of France, decided that the franc would not be devalued. He introduced stringent exchange controls and other monetary restrictions. They worked until spring 1969, when French reserves began to drain away once more. Fresh attacks followed. The franc was finally devalued in August 1969, by 11.1 percent, just as had been discussed in Bonn.

IN DECEMBER 1969, Karl Blessing retired. His friends and admirers held a gala dinner in his honor. Blessing told those assembled—many of whom, like him, had airbrushed their past of inconvenient episodes—that "monetary discipline" had always been the center-point of his banking career. The Nazi regime, which he had loyally and enthusiastically served for all of its twelve years of existence, was smoothly dismissed. "We lived until 1945, or, rather, until 1948, with this many-headed, never-loved monster of the Reichsmark, going downhill all the time."[18] Blessing planned, he said, to spend much of his retirement in the south of France.

The following year, in 1970, McKittrick passed away at a nursing home in New Jersey at the age of eighty-one. The *New York Times* ran a glowing story about the "world financier," as it described him. McKittrick had stayed at the Chase National Bank until he retired in 1954. He later headed a World Bank mission to India. The former BIS president had been decorated by Belgium, Italy, and Romania, the article noted. McKittrick's secret deals with Nazi industrialists, his friendship with Emil Puhl and the BIS's acceptance of looted Nazi gold were not mentioned.

Montagu Norman had died in 1950, but Hjalmar Schacht continued roaming the world. Asian and Arab countries had no interest in his tainted history and welcomed his expertise. But others remembered. Around 1960 Schacht met with Sigmund Warburg because Schacht wanted Warburg to take a stake in a banking operation in the Philippines. The encounter was heavy with things unsaid. Schacht was unusually nervous, and his speech was repeatedly punctuated with the phrase "in short." Warburg listened politely and promised to think over Schacht's idea, but he never followed up.[19] Schacht finally retired in 1963 and lived in Munich with his second wife, Manci. He died in 1970 after he slipped and badly hurt himself while trying to put on his formal dinner trousers.

Blessing's retirement was short. In April 1971, at the age of seventy-one, he suffered a heart attack while on holiday in Orange, in France. Even in death, the myths and lies endured. The *New York Times* marked Blessing's passing with an article as laudatory as its summary of McKittrick's career. After Blessing left Unilever, the Times noted, he had "held various less exposed positions in the mineral oil industry."[20] As for the slave laborers, leased for a few zlotys a day from the SS before being worked to death or executed at Kontinental-Öl's network of concentration camps, it was as if they had never existed.

CHAPTER THIRTEEN

THE TOWER ARISES

"To be frank, I have no use for politicians. They lack the judgment of central bankers."

— Fritz Leutwiler, BIS president and chairman of the board, 1982–1984[1]

By 1970 Rudolf Brinckmann had served on the BIS board for almost two decades. But his membership in the world's most exclusive club had not made the German banker any more amenable to settling the bitter dispute with the Warburgs over the name and ownership of the bank they both claimed. Eric Warburg, now seventy years old, remained a partner in Brinckmann, Wirtz & Co. He still went to work each morning to the building, which had once belonged to his family and which he felt was rightly theirs. Warburg and Brinckmann both attended the bank's morning meeting, then ignored each other for the rest of the day. The whole situation, Warburg said, was "unbearable."

The Warburgs suggested that the bank be renamed M. M. Warburg, Brinckmann & Co. The BIS director offered Brinckman, Wirtz–M. M. Warburg & Co., and so it went on. But Brinckmann could feel that Germany's bankers were turning against him. Hermann Abs described the imbroglio as a scandal. But it may have been Jacob Wallenberg, of the Swedish banking dynasty, who finally forced Brinckmann to change his mind. On a visit to the bank's Hamburg headquarters, Wallenberg told Brinckmann that when he had first come to the building, in 1913, the name of the firm was "M. M. Warburg & Co, and not, as today, Brinckmann, Wirtz & Co."

Brinckmann finally surrendered in 1969, and the bank was renamed M. M. Warburg–Brinckmann, Wirtz & Co. The following year, he stepped down from the board of the BIS. Brinckmann retired from his, that is, the Warburgs', newly renamed bank on the last day of December 1973, at the age of eighty-four. Their battle won, the Warburgs proposed that the bank hold a farewell reception for Brinckmann at the Hamburg branch of the Bundesbank. The gala event was planned for January 2 the following year. The two sides planned a gracious closure, both of Brinckmann's career and of a long and often turbulent relationship that had spanned five decades. But it was not to be. As Eric Warburg and Rudolf Brinckmann walked toward the Bundesbank building, Brinckmann suddenly gasped for air, collapsed, and died.[2]

THE PASSING OF Brinckmann, like that of Hjalmar Schacht and Karl Blessing, marked the end of the postwar era, the transition to the modern, globalized, economy and the rise of the new generation of central bankers. Money moved faster, markets reacted quicker, and countries were now interconnected in ways that would have seemed inconceivable when the BIS was founded in 1930. Its headquarters, at the former Grand Hôtel et Savoy Hôtel Univers, at Centralbahnstrasse 7, had served the central bankers well for several decades. But it had been built as a hotel, not as the headquarters of an international bank that was rapidly growing in power and influence and which stood at the heart of the European integration project. In 1958 the BIS employed 158 staff. By 1971 that number had grown to 237. The bank's membership was steadily expanding, as was the bank's growing global reach. The national banks of Spain, Portugal, Iceland, South Africa, Turkey, Canada, Australia, and Japan had all joined. BIS membership was now a point of pride for the newly emerging economies. The monthly governors' meetings needed to cater not just to the central bankers, but to the legions of assistants, staff, and junior officials who invariably accompanied the governors.

Richard Hall returned to the BIS in 1972, rising to become assistant general manager (the equivalent of deputy manager) before his retirement in 1992. Hall had first spent eighteen months at the bank in 1955 and 1956, seconded from the Bank of England to work on the European Payments Union. That era now seemed something from the pages of a dusty history book. "Things like exchange controls and the gold standard had occupied a lot of people's time then. But the world had changed tremendously between 1956 and 1972, and the BIS had changed with it," he recalled. The BIS had survived, evolved, and was now certain of its place in the world. "The bank felt more confident. Not only had it survived the immediate postwar problems, but it had gone on to demonstrate its usefulness to central bank governors as a place for coordinating, consultation, and even weeping on each other's shoulders sometimes about how dreadful these governments are. The central bankers would share their worries and responsibilities and someone else would say, 'Yes, I have one of those as well, do you have any good ideas for dealing with this?'"[3]

The BIS commissioned Martin Burckhardt, a local architect, to design a new, custom-built headquarters. Burckhardt drew up a plan for an ultramodern circular tower block with twenty-four floors. The first version was rejected as too high. Even after the tower was shortened, some local residents objected. A city-wide referendum was held, and the building's supporters won an overwhelming majority—32,000 in favor, while 14,000 voted against.[4] The foundation stone was laid in 1973, and the bank moved into its new offices in 1977. The move was essential, said Richard Hall. "Some of the staff had regrets, but others thought it was about time. The old building had its limitations, and we had burst out of it. We needed more space for more people."

For a staid and secretive organization, the BIS had chosen a surprisingly high-profile headquarters. Where once the entrance to the BIS had been tucked away next to a chocolate shop, the new building, at Centralbahnplatz 2, was eighteen stories high. It loomed almost menacingly over downtown Basel, like a rocket about to take off and launch itself into space. The sunlight glinted off the rows of opaque, bronze-tinted windows. The national flags of member banks stood in a row by the entrance, like a miniature United Nations. The bank's circular corridors and globular 1970s furniture were very stylish, if not daring, for staid central bankers. Even now, the building, which is still in use, appears to have been transplanted from a 1970s James Bond film, as though a steely eyed villain might suddenly stride down its long, looping corridors and frog-march an unwary visitor into a secret annex.

The veterans of the bank grumbled about the "Tower of Basel" as it soon became known. The BIS was no longer invisible. Tourists gawped, and locals took pride that the world's most influential bank was now on display for all to see. Fritz Leutwiler, the president of the Swiss National Bank as well as the BIS, did not approve at all. In the old building, Leutwiler knew when the governor of the Bank of England was in the neighboring office, because he could hear him walking down the corridors and opening his door. The building's prominence infuriated Leutwiler, who like many bankers of his generation believed that the BIS's affairs were best conducted with as low a profile as possible. "That was the last thing we wanted. If it was up to me, it would never have been built," he said of the new headquarters.[5]

The new headquarters were not just stylish, but enjoyed state-of-the-art technology. The BIS managers had realized early on the importance of computers for international finance. They understood that the rapidly globalizing economy would demand ever faster and more secure means of transmitting and storing data. The bank would play a central role in collating, analyzing, and cross-border banking transactions. It provided the secretariat for the G10's group of computer experts who were developing electronic systems for messaging and automated international payments. The BIS also operated an experimental data bank, which provided macroeconomic data for central banks. All this demanded high levels of security.

The BIS's safety and security features are now standard on government and corporate headquarters, but in 1977 they were ahead of their time. The bank, still protected by international treaty, guards its sovereignty as keenly as its secrecy. Thus the architects, and the bankers, tried to plan for every conceivable eventuality. That meant making the building as self-contained as possible. The Swiss authorities need the permission of the management to enter the premises. By far the best thing was to ensure that there would never be a reason to summon them.

The Tower of Basel boasts its own bomb shelter in the basement, a sprinkler system with two backup levels, in-house medical facilities, and lengthy underground corridors to house its archive. Most visitors—apart from central bankers—may not walk anywhere unattended and must call for an escort to walk from room to room. They are not allowed into the staff canteen, which serves lunch every day from 12:30 to 2 p.m, and they must leave the bank at this time. The security guards, who keep a close watch on the building through an extensive CCTV system, will quickly terminate any unauthorized wanderings, and the errant stroller will likely be escorted from the premises. The top floor, which hosts a superb restaurant, is certainly out of bounds, for that is where the governors gather for dinner on Sunday evenings. The aim, said Gunther Schleminger, the bank's general manager under President Leutwiler, was to provide "a complete clubhouse for central bankers." The BIS staff also have their own luxurious country club just outside Basel, with tennis courts and a swimming pool.

It takes a certain verve to build an eighteen-story circular block in the middle of one of Switzerland's most important and historic cities, especially when the organization housed inside is not subject to Swiss jurisdiction. But the BIS has always been a survivor, swiftly adapting to changing circumstances and decisively building itself into the evolving global economy. The new headquarters was a statement—in concrete and tinted glass—that, at the age of thirty-seven, the BIS had come of age. The Tower of Basel, like the bank itself, was nearly invulnerable. Naturally, the high-profile building did not bring any relaxation of the bank's obsessive secrecy. Passers-by could stare at the building but still had no idea what went on inside. The details of the BIS's transactions for the central banks, the deliberations of the governors' meetings, and the bank's powerful committees remained confidential.

The rapidly globalizing economy, argued the governors, made that confidentiality and trust between the central bankers and the BIS even more crucial. During the Second World War, the BIS had acted as an information channel between the Allies and the Axis. It served the same purpose during the Cold War, as a neutral and extremely comfortable meeting point for the Communist and capitalist worlds. Central bankers from behind the Iron Curtain regularly visited the BIS, not just to obtain credit, but also to draw on the bank's expertise in the gold and foreign exchange markets. The BIS was always generous to its visitors from behind the Iron Curtain. It covered their travel costs and paid them a per diem in hard currency. Once in Basel, plied with fine food and wine, with some Swiss francs in their pockets, the Eastern Bloc bankers were friendly, loquacious, and a most useful source of economic intelligence.

This worked so well that by 1976 the central bankers of the Eastern Bloc countries even had their own biannual governors' meetings at Basel, hosted by the BIS. The more the Communists adapted to capitalism, the sooner their system would collapse, the BIS managers believed—correctly as it turned out. Senior BIS officials also regularly visited East European capitals to meet with central bankers. Budapest, where life was much more pleasant than in Warsaw or Bucharest was a favorite. Hungary was often at the center of the BIS's Cold War intrigue. As the BIS annual report for 1982–1983 primly notes, the BIS and the National Bank of Hungary had a "long-standing business relationship."

The central European nation was one of the BIS's earliest members. One of the bank's first acts was to extend credit to Hungary and several of its neighbors, in 1931. The relationship had endured through the Cold War and by the early 1980s was about to flower. János Kádár, the Hungarian leader, was tentatively experimenting with limited private enterprise. Kádár's "Goulash Communism," as it was dubbed, was being watched with great interest in the West. Hungary's economy was the most liberal in the region, and the country applied to join the IMF in 1980. Frigyes Hárshegyi, a veteran Hungarian banker, first visited the BIS in 1978. Hárshegyi was then the Hungarian delegate to the International Investment Bank in Moscow, which served the Soviet Union and its socialist allies. At this time Western commercial banks were lending to the socialist countries, but capitalist banking mechanisms demanded a steep learning curve from the East European financiers who were used to operating in a state-controlled economy. The meetings at Basel helped Hárshegyi and his colleagues to understand how a free market banking system worked, he recalled. "The BIS was like a stock exchange of information. The atmosphere was always friendly, avoiding political statements and concentrating on financial and professional questions."[6]

But Hungary had a problem. Foreign borrowing had financed Goulash Communism, which had brought social peace by providing work, housing, holidays, and limited travel to the West. By 1982 Hungary owed more than $10 billion in foreign debt, much of it short-term.[7] The imposition of martial law in Poland and the subsequent debt crisis together with the parlous state of the neighboring Romanian economy had alarmed investors and the international markets. Even though Hungary was in a completely different situation, with a far more liberal regime and some promising economic indicators, the "regionalization" factor meant that Hungary's creditors were rushing for the exit. Money was flooding out.

János Fekete, a senior official of the Hungarian National Bank, was charged with persuading the BIS to help. He had excellent contacts at the BIS and regularly attended meetings there. Fekete was optimistic that Hungary would be allowed to join the IMF, and indeed the country would not have applied without positive signals from the fund's Washington headquarters. IMF membership would anchor Hungary firmly in the global financial system, instead of the Soviet make-believe equivalent. But the fund moved slowly, and Hungary's creditors were pressing hard. The legendary ingenuity of Hungarians was being tested to the limit. The Hungarians have brought the world numerous inventions, from the ballpoint pen to nuclear weapons. Indeed they are famed for being so wily that the old joke defines a Magyar as "someone who enters a revolving door behind you but comes out in front." Fekete proved similarly inventive.

Hungary desperately needed funds, Fekete explained to Fritz Leutwiler, but lacked sufficient foreign exchange or gold reserves. The Hungarian banker suggested that the BIS organize a bridging loan, until Hungary could join the IMF and apply for financial assistance. The BIS loan would be returned as soon as Hungary was in the IMF and received its first credit. Leutwiler was minded to look sympathetically on Fekete's request. Leutwiler understood that the regionalization approach, which equated comparatively liberal and forward-looking Hungary with totalitarian Romania or Poland, languishing under the rule of the generals, showed poor judgment. Hungary, and Fekete, were old friends of the BIS. The BIS was always very helpful, says Hárshegyi, Fekete's former colleague. "They saw that this was a short-term crisis and that Hungary's economic philosophy was always to service its debts."[8]

Once again, the personal connection proved crucial. Leutwiler called Jacques de la Rosière, the managing director of the IMF, in Washington. The BIS president wanted to know two things. How was Hungary's membership application progressing? And would Budapest be likely to receive IMF assistance?

With hindsight, a lot was riding on this telephone call, probably more than either Fekete or Leutwiler realized. Had de la Rosière signaled that Hungary's IMF membership application was not likely to be approved, or even just that it was stalling, Leutwiler would likely have politely ushered Fekete from his office with no firm commitment to help. The capital exodus from Budapest would have continued, the economy would have faced collapse, and the country's tentative experiments with the free market would doubtless have ended. The reformers within the Hungarian politburo would have been weakened and the hard-liners, who opposed what they saw as dangerous capitalist experiments, been greatly strengthened.

Such a course of events would certainly have been "regionalized." The defeat of the Hungarian liberals would likely have been mirrored across the Soviet bloc, perhaps even in Moscow, where Hungary was regarded as a licensed wild card, able to test the capitalist waters in ways the Soviet Union could not. De la Larosière was able to reassure Leutwiler: Hungary would soon be a member and qualify for financial assistance. Thus reassured, Leutwiler agreed to Fekete's request for a bridging loan. In March and May 1982 the BIS arranged two loans to Hungary for a total of $210 million, and a further $300 million followed in September. By the end of the year, Hungary had joined the IMF. The fund's board approved a credit line of $520 million. Hungary repaid its debt to BIS.

Unbeknown to him, Leutwiler had set in motion a series of events that would soon help to redraw the map of Europe. The backing of the BIS and the IMF sent a powerful signal that the Fund, and the BIS and its shareholders—other central banks—had faith in the Hungarian leadership's plans for reform. The Hungarian reformers further liberalized the country's economy. Private entrepreneurs began to push the limits of freedom, and foreign investors looked at Hungary with renewed interest. Hungary's international bankers, like Hárshegyi and Fekete, already saw the deficits of the socialist system. Their visits to Basel only reinforced their understanding of its profound inefficiencies and stultifying effect on business. The central banks in the socialist bloc had very different functions to their capitalist counterparts. The Hungarian National Bank was a state commercial bank, supplying credit and financing foreign trade. The Basel meetings were also valuable tutorials in how to turn a socialist state bank into a traditional central bank, responsible for controlling the money supply and controlling interest rates.

By the late 1980s, even the old guard realized that the one-party state did not work. The Hungarian leader Kádár resigned, and negotiations began for a peaceful transition to democracy. The Iron Curtain was first opened in Hungary, three months before the Berlin Wall was breached. One day in August 1989 tens of thousands of East German refugees gathered on the Hungarian-Austrian frontier. By then it was clear that Communism was dying. As they surged forward, the border guards stood by and let them through. By the end of the year the entire Soviet bloc had collapsed. The BIS had played an important role in this process. The bank's bridging loan had reinforced international confidence in the Hungarian reformers, which in turn had boosted their political standing at home, which had weakened the grip of the Communist party and allowed the opening of the Iron Curtain. That in turn triggered a domino effect across the region and accelerated the collapse of the one-party system.

The Soviet Union itself was less welcome in Basel. Part of the problem was that Moscow still claimed ownership of the gold holdings of the Baltic States—Latvia, Lithuania and Estonia—which Thomas McKittrick had refused to hand to the Soviets back in 1940. By 1980 the three states no longer existed and had been absorbed into the Soviet Union. But the gold did exist, and the Russians wanted it. The Soviet Union continued to inquire about membership possibilities during the 1960s, but the bank remained steadfast. The BIS continued, correctly, to keep possession of the Baltic reserves—and was duly vindicated when the three Baltic States regained their independence in 1991 and the Soviet Union collapsed. The Bank of Russia was finally admitted in 1996.

Mexico too was on the brink of going bust in 1982—and taking the international banking system down with it. Mexico was saddled with an $80 billion external debt. In order to meet its obligations, Mexico had been borrowing overnight funds in New York to pay the interest. But the loans were eating themselves: each day Mexico had to borrow more to pay the interest on the previous day's loans. The Mexican economy was in danger of entering a death spiral. The IMF was prepared to loan Mexico $4.5 billion, but the fund moved slowly, and the paperwork might take months to be approved. Here, too, the BIS connection helped save the country. Paul Volcker, the chairman of the US Federal Reserve, and Fritz Leutwiler, the BIS president, organized a rescue package.[9]

Back in 1968 when Jelle Zijlstra, the BIS president, had sought to secure the French franc at the Bonn IMF conference, he managed to secure pledges of $2 billion over lunch. Volcker and Leutwiler took slightly longer, although their mission was slowed by the fact that the bankers were not gathered around a single table, as they had been in 1968. As with Hungary, the BIS financing was not intended as a substitute for the IMF rescue package but would be a temporary stopgap, until the IMF loans were authorized.

Volcker's initial suggestion of $1.5 billion was bumped up to $1.85 billion, with $925 million from the Federal Reserve, and the remainder to come from the central banks would be channeled through the BIS. Similar arrangements soon followed for Brazil, Argentina, and Yugoslavia. These arrangements suited everyone involved. The rescue packages were presented as BIS-led. The bank had arranged the loans, but the United States and the other G10 countries made the actual funds available. The rescue packages carried substantial political risks for the participating central banks, especially the Federal Reserve. But the central role of the BIS internationalized the bailout.

BY THE MID-1980s, the controversy over the Tower of Basel had faded away. The sleek, modernist building, looming over Centralbahnplatz, had become part of the Swiss city's urban skyline. The circular tower block, pointing skyward, symbolized the bank's new reach and ever more ambitious aspirations. The bank had shown a protean ability not just to survive but to flourish in rapidly changing circumstances. The ostensible reason for the BIS's foundation—the management of German reparations payments for the First World War—was now a fading memory. So was the Bretton Woods conference, where Henry Morgenthau and Harry Dexter

White had tried to have the bank closed down. The financial system designed there, which fixed the price of gold at $35 an ounce was also gone, ended by President Nixon in 1971.

But the BIS now stood at the center of the global financial system. Leutwiler, the BIS president, had saved the Hungarian economy with a telephone call and accelerated the process of political reform that would eventually bring down Communism. The bank was managing multiple bailout packages that were easing the Latin American debt crisis and so preventing a potential catastrophic run on American banks. Some banks however, could not be rescued. There, too, the BIS positioned itself at the center of events. In 1974 the Franklin National Bank in New York and the Bankhaus Herstatt in Germany went bust after overextending themselves. At the time, Franklin was the biggest American bank in history to fail. Herstatt was a much smaller private bank but did substantial foreign exchange business in the United States. In response the BIS and the G10 governors set up the Basel Committee on Banking Supervision to begin the long, complicated, and still ongoing process of regulating commercial banks. The committee, naturally, was based at the BIS, from where it operates to this day. By hosting and providing secretarial and administrative services to new transnational financial groupings, such as the EEC Governors' Committee and the Basel Committee on Banking Supervision, the bank was steadily making itself indispensable for the functioning of the global economy. The committees' location in the Tower of Basel brought prestige, a stream of admiring visitors and dignitaries, and a new sense of permanence. There were no modern equivalents of Henry Morgenthau or Harry Dexter White, demanding that the BIS be closed down.

The BIS was also surprisingly nimble. The bank had been an early adopter of computer technology and its ultrasecure databases, which were hosted in the tower, were fast becoming the essential reference store for information on central banks and cross-border banking transactions. Some of that information was collated in the bank's annual reports that were ever more informative and had become required reading in the world's treasuries, finance ministries, and trading houses. The *58th Annual Report*, published in June 1988, was 223 pages long. Its eight lengthy, detailed sections included the bank's analyses of general economic developments, international trade and payments, domestic and international financial markets, monetary policy, the international monetary system, and the BIS's own banking activities. These were increasingly lucrative. The accounts for the year ending March 31, 1988, showed a net tax-free profit of almost 96 million Swiss gold francs, an increase of almost five million more than the previous year.

Tucked away on pages 197 and 198, under the report of the bank's functions as agent, trustee, and depositary, and written in a banker's dry prose, were telling details that highlighted the BIS's central and vital role in the European integration project. Behind the scenes, the BIS continued to provide the financial expertise and technical assistance for the most significant economic development in postwar history: the drive toward European union. From the secret wartime discussions between Per Jacobssen, the bank's economic adviser, and Emil Puhl, the BIS director and Reichsbank vice president, to the detailed plans for the implementation of European Monetary Union in the late 1980s, the BIS played a driving role at every stage.

The BIS managed the 1947 Paris agreement on multilateral payments. Three years later the accord grew into the European Payments Union and the BIS was appointed the new system's agent. When European currencies became convertible, the EPU became the European Monetary Agreement that was managed, naturally, by the BIS. The BIS was deeply entwined with the European Coal and Steel Community, the first supranational European organization. It had signed an Act of Pledge with the ECSC in 1954 and subsequently handled all the loans issued by the ECSC. The BIS imprimatur gave the fledging organization vital credibility on international markets. The last ECSC loan had been redeemed in 1985–1986, and all unused funds had been returned to the European Commission in Luxembourg, the bank's 1988 annual report noted.

The BIS had hosted the Committee of Governors of European Economic Community Central Banks since it first met in 1964 and provided its secretariat. The EEC Governors' Committee coordinated and integrated the monetary policies of its members, a precursor to eventual European economic union. The committee was independent of the BIS, but its members later included Alexandre Lamfalussy, the bank's general manager from 1985 to 1993. The committee managed the first limits on exchange rate fluctuations within European currencies, a mechanism known as the "Snake in the Tunnel," which was an important step toward European monetary union.

The EEC Governors' Committee was significant, said Richard Hall, the former assistant general manager of the BIS. "The discussions in the European Economic Community were intergovernmental and central bankers were always number two to ministers. But the central bankers had been coming to Basel for many years, before monetary union was discussed. They were accustomed to talking together and doing things together and they did not want to be upstaged by finance ministers. They were already in Basel once a month for the BIS meetings, so they set up the committee there and the bank was very happy for them to do that."[10]

The BIS was the agent for the European Monetary Cooperation Fund, which had been set up by the Committee of Governors to manage short-term credit arrangements for members of the European Economic Community, the predecessor of the European Union. The bank was also the agent for the clearing and settlement system for the European Currency Unit (ECU) that was the precursor of the euro.

The establishment of the European Coal and Steel Community and its evolution into the European Economic Community were presented as an unmitigated boon for the countries concerned. But the most dramatic and far-reaching peaceful re-ordering of Europe in modern times—the steady and relentless erosion of national sovereignty—was implemented by sleight of hand. The key, for both the European project and the ever-broader mandate of the BIS, was to present decisions, policies, and actions as "technical" and "apolitical," of no concern to the average informed citizen. In fact, the opposite was true. There could hardly be anything more political than the handing over of national powers to unelected supranational bodies, while the necessary financial mechanisms were arranged and managed by a secretive and completely unaccountable bank in Basel.

By the late 1980s this process was effectively unstoppable. In the summer of 1988 the EEC central bank governors were asked to serve, in their personal capacity (so that they would not be seen as representing their national banks), on the Committee for the Study of Economic and Monetary Union (EMU), which prepared for the adoption of a single European currency, the euro. The committee was better known by the name of its chairman, Jacques Delors, a French civil servant and politician.[11] Delors was president of the European Commission, which oversees the implementation of European laws and policies.

The Delors Committee had seventeen members, including Karl Otto Pöhl, the president of the Bundesbank; Robin Leigh-Pemberton, the governor of the Bank of England; and Willem Duisenberg, the president of the Netherland National Bank, all of whom were board members of the BIS. The questions of how, when, and even if EMU should be carried out were left to the politicians. The committee was concerned with the technical aspects, rather than the political implications. Once again, the BIS was at the center of events. The Delors Committee did not meet in Brussels, the site of the European Commission, or Strasbourg, the home of the European Parliament, or Frankfurt. It set up shop in Basel. There it enjoyed its own dedicated support staff, supplied by the BIS.

Behind the scenes, one of its most influential members was Alexandre Lamfalussy, the Hungarian-born BIS general manager. Lamfalussy had fled his homeland after the Soviet takeover in the late 1940s. He moved to Belgium and taught at the Catholic University of Louvain and later at Yale. Lamfalussy joined the BIS in 1976 as economic adviser, the post once held by Per Jacobssen. In 1985 he was appointed general manager. Lamfalussy was widely regarded as the intellectual powerhouse behind European economic integration and, from the project's earliest beginnings, had a deep grasp of both its practical operation and theoretical underpinning. When the Snake, the fixed-limit exchange rate mechanism, had run into trouble, for example, the governors had turned to Lamfalussy for advice.

So it was only natural that the Delors Committee would frequently defer to Lamfalussy's opinions, all of which greatly annoyed European officials visiting from Brussels. They could not understand why the great European monetary integration project was being directed from a suite of rooms in a tower block by Basel central railway station, which was out of their political and legal jurisdiction. But Delors's primary concern was not the prickly Eurocrats, but the central bankers. He understood that without them EMU could not take place. "It was the genius of Delors, who was a great manipulator—in the good sense of the term—who realized that he absolutely did not want to and would not hurt the feelings of the governors of the central bank," Lamfalussy recalled.[12] Logistics also played a role. Many of the Delors Committee's most important members, such as Pöhl and Leigh-Pemberton, already came to Basel for the governors' meetings. There, at the Sunday evening G10 governors' dinner, the central bankers decided what Lamfalussy described as the "norms of cooperation," in circumstances as secretive as ever. "This was the dinner where we talked about the most difficult issues, with no notes or anything."[13]

The Delors Committee also had two rapporteurs: Gunter Baer and Tomasso Padoa-Schioppa. Baer had worked as an economist at the BIS. Padoa-Schioppa was an Italian economist who is considered one of the intellectual founding fathers of the euro. The rapporteurs were immensely influential. They prepared the meetings, wrote reports, and "held the fountain pen," as Lamfalussy put it. "It was my officials that prepared the meetings in Basel of a project that was primarily European."[14]

The Delors Committee presented its report on EMU in April 1989. Central banks' reserves would be off limits to governments. Borrowing in non–European Community currencies should be limited. There would be sanctions against countries that exceeded a budget deficit threshold (currently three percent). Crucially, the sanctions would apply not just to members of the future Eurozone, but to all European Union member states. The report called for European countries to take substantial steps toward economic convergence, budgetary discipline, and price stability, before moving decisively toward economic and monetary union.

However it was unclear how this strict, common financial discipline would be imposed. A common monetary policy, based on a shared currency, demanded a common fiscal policy with shared rules for government taxation and spending, Lamfalussy argued in a memo in January 1989, but there were no plans for this:

> *In short, it would seem to me very strange if we did not insist on the need to make appropriate arrangements that would allow the gradual emergence, and the full operation once the EMU is completed, of a Community-wide macroeconomic fiscal policy which would be the natural complement to the common monetary policy of the Community.[15]*

As Harold James notes, Lamfalussy's memo was both "apposite and intellectually compelling."[16] It neatly summarized the contradiction of a transnational currency with no transnational fiscal policy—a contradiction that remains unresolved and has both triggered and fueled the Eurozone crisis. The following month, Lamfalussy, during a discussion of the kind of controlling and supervisory budgetary methods needed for EMU, even suggested adding the word "enforceable" to the final draft. His suggestion was not incorporated into the report. Nonetheless, even without a common fiscal policy, Lamfalussy argued that Europe must press ahead with monetary union, if only because the European Monetary System (EMS), which limited exchange rate variations, had fallen victim to the law of unintended consequences. The system intended to stabilize currencies was having the opposite effect.

Speculators were pouring money into Italy. There inflation in 1988 was around five percent, compared to Germany at 1.3 percent. High inflation meant higher interest rates, but as the lira was locked into the EMS, its value was guaranteed. For investors there was no downside. The liberalization of capital movements had accelerated this process. The EMS was vulnerable, argued Lamfalussy and Europe must move to EMU as soon as possible. "It is for this reason that I would be in favor of a first stage that could be implemented as quickly as possible and not in a two or three year distant future, but starting this autumn or at least at the end of the year."[17]

The Delors Report, as it became known, was forty-three pages long. It was accompanied by a collection of fifteen papers which were written by the members of the committee. The influence of the BIS was clear. Jacques Delors wrote two of the papers, the first with the kind of grandiose title beloved of French politicians: "Economic and Monetary Union and Re-launching the Construction of Europe." Three papers were written by Alexandre Lamfalussy. Lamfalussy's articles dealt with some of the most important technical aspects of the process of monetary and economic union: the macro-coordination of fiscal policies in an economic and monetary union; the European Currency Unit banking market; and a proposal for centralizing monetary policy.

Back in the 1920s, Norman had mused to Benjamin Strong, the chairman of the New York Federal Reserve, about the need for a "private and eclectic Central banks' club, small at first, large in the future." When Norman had summoned Walter Layton, the editor of *The Economist*, to his office to ask him to draft the bank's statutes, he had emphasized that they must, above all, guarantee the BIS's independence. The Delors Report confirmed that crucial principle. Governments would be excluded from monetary policy making. The Delors report called for the creation of a new institution to centrally decide and coordinate member states' monetary policy operations, to be called the European System of Central Banks (ESCB). Montagu Norman may not have approved of a Europe-wide currency, but he would certainly have applauded the report's demand that the ESCB must be completely independent from both national governments and European authorities.

The Delors Report's recommendations that the European Union should adopt a single currency and a unified monetary policy were accepted. The momentum toward monetary, economic, and political union was unstoppable. A new bank, the most powerful institution within the ESCB, would be created to define and implement monetary policy. The European Central Bank's primary task would be to ensure price stability while remaining free of all political pressures. It sounded all too familiar.

PART THREE: **MELTDOWN**

CHAPTER FOURTEEN

THE SECOND TOWER

"European economic unity will come, for its time is here."
— Walther Funk, 1942[1]

The Reichsbank president and BIS director was half right. European economic unity did indeed arrive, but it came sixty years after he predicted. Walther Funk lived to see two of the most important early milestones: the establishment in 1951 of the European Coal and Steel Community, Europe's first supranational institution, whose loans were managed by the BIS, and the signing of the Treaty of Rome in 1957, when the six core countries—Germany, France, Italy, Belgium, Luxembourg, and the Netherlands—established the European Economic Community.

Funk was released from Spandau Prison in Berlin the same year and died in 1960, but his pan-European plan for a continent free of trade and currency restrictions lived on and flourished. A European customs union came into existence in 1968. Just over a decade later, in 1979, Europeans voted in the first elections for the European Parliament. In 1992 twelve European countries signed the Maastricht Treaty, which brought the European Union into existence. On January 1, 1993, the European single market began operating across the twelve member states of the European Union. Its citizens could live and work freely wherever they wanted, companies could sell their products, and currencies and capital flowed unhindered.

Funk would certainly have applauded. The Nazi economics minister had raised the idea of European monetary union as early as 1940, to be introduced incrementally by harmonizing currency fluctuations and constraining exchange rates, as indeed happened.

To point out any similarities between the Nazis' postwar economic plans for Europe and today's European Union is to risk ridicule and invective. The European integration project, has, for many, become an untouchable truth, an article of faith in the world's inexorable progress toward a brighter and more secure future. Certainly, European integration has many achievements to its credit: speeding up reconstruction after 1945; opening the continent for free trade and nurturing a new generation of pan-Europeans who think beyond national borders. By incorporating the shaky democracies of post–Communist Europe the European Union has helped stabilize the eastern half of the continent. The oft-stated values of the European Union: human rights, democracy, and protection of minorities are the very antithesis of the Third's Reich's ideology.

But it is a massive and illogical mental leap to claim, as did Helmut Kohl, the German chancellor, in 1996, "The policy of European integration is in reality a question of war and peace in the twenty-first century."[2] Kohl's statement embodies the technocrats' belief, reaching back to Jean Monnet and Montagu Norman, that the wise guidance of a managerial and financial elite is all that is needed for Europe to prosper—and to prevent its fractious, ungrateful peoples from reverting to their natural warlike state. The historian Antony Beevor makes a more convincing counterclaim: Western Europe has remained free of wars since 1945, not because of the European Union, but because of democracy. "It is simply a question of governance. Democracies do not fight each other."[3]

The uncomfortable, unspoken truth is that the parallels between the plans of the Nazi leadership for the postwar European economy and the subsequent process of European monetary and economic integration are real. The BIS runs like a thread through both. Funk's deputy Emil Puhl described the BIS as the "only real foreign branch" of the Reichsbank, because it was the crucial connection of the Reichsbank to the international network of central bankers.[4] These connections outlived the war. The BIS helped ensure that the postwar successors to the Reichsbank, the Bank deutscher Länder, and the Bundesbank, would continue to dominate the economies of postwar Europe. The BIS provided the BdL and the Bundesbank with both legitimacy and prestige. The BdL, followed by the Bundesbank, took the Reichsbank's former place at the governors' meetings. The BIS gave the Bundesbank an instant network of connections to other central banks and a platform to shape the debate about the postwar European economy. Nor did the personnel change much: Karl Blessing, Schacht's protégé, worked at the BIS during the early 1930s, transferred to the Reichsbank, oversaw an empire of slave laborers during the war, then returned to the BIS in 1958 as the president of the Bundesbank.

During the 1930s and '40s, like the 1980s and '90s, the politicians laid out the general theory of European unification, while the technocrats—such as Funk—outlined the practical steps. As early as 1940, Arthur Seyss-Inquart, the ruler of the Nazi-occupied Netherlands, called for a new European community "above and beyond the concept of the nation-state," which would "transform the living space given us by history into a new spiritual realm."[5] The new Europe would benefit from "the most modern production techniques and a continent-wide system of trade and communications developed on a joint basis." Rapidly increasing prosperity was inevitable "once national barriers are removed."[6]

When Hitler called for the "clutter of small nations" to be removed, Funk readily agreed. "There must be a readiness to subordinate one's own interests in certain cases to that of the European Community."[7] The Reichsbank president laid out his thoughts in a detailed, eight-page memo called "Economic Reorganization of Europe," a copy of which is stored in the BIS archive in Basel. The document was translated by Per Jacobssen's staff and passed to Thomas McKittrick on July 26, 1940.[8]

All sorts of slogans were flying around about the "construction and organization of the German and the European economic system after the war," and the favorite was "European large-unit economy," noted Funk in his 1940 paper. Such a construct did not yet exist, but "the new European economy must be an organic growth" and will result from "close economic collaboration between Germany and European countries." The Reichsmark would be the dominant currency, but the currency basis of postwar Europe was of secondary importance to economic leadership. "Given a healthy European economy and a sensible division of labor between the European economies, the currency problem will solve itself because it will then be merely a question of suitable monetary technique." Here Funk seems to anticipate the arguments of the euro enthusiasts who, fifty years later, claimed that a common currency, if properly constructed in the right economic conditions, could not fail.

Funk's analysis and prediction are unsettlingly prescient of the subsequent course of postwar European economic and political history. The Reichsmark would be the dominant currency, and once it had been freed of foreign debt, its currency area must "continue to widen." Bilateral payments must be transformed into multilateral economic transactions and clearing arrangements, "so that the various countries may enter into properly regulated economic relations with one another through the intermediary of clearing arrangements of this kind"—just as happened with the 1947 Paris agreement on multilateral payments and its successor mechanisms, such as the European Payments Union (EPU).

Foreign exchange controls could not be abolished in one move or monetary union quickly introduced. The process must be incremental, Funk argued, anticipating the need for a halfway system like the EPU, which liberated non-residents from exchange controls, although they remained in place for citizens. "The problem is not one of free exchange or European monetary union, but in the first place, of a further development of clearing techniques for the purpose of ensuring a smooth course for payments within the countries participating in the clearing." The conversion rates must be controlled and kept stable. This was also the aim of the Snake in the Tunnel and the European Monetary System, which were, like the EPU, managed or serviced which were, like the EPU, by the BIS.

An actual monetary union was more complicated, Funk presciently argued, as it demanded "a gradually assimilated standard of living, and even in the future the standard cannot be the same in all the countries participating in the European clearing"—a statement that neatly anticipated the modern disequilibrium between Germany and Greece. But once the European central clearing system was operating, foreign exchange restrictions would be abolished, first for travelers crossing frontiers and then for import trade. There would be a bonfire of regulations that slowed down trade and commerce; Funk wrote, "Meticulous surveillance and all the regulations, which weigh down on the individual business enterprise with a mass of forms, will no longer be necessary."[9]

Funk also predicted, correctly, that the future European currencies would not be linked to gold. The new multilateral monetary system would provide the necessary backing. The deciding factor in trade relations would be the quality of German goods for export, "and in this respect we really need have no anxiety." German needs would be central to the new European economy. Germany would reach long-term economic agreements with European countries so that they would plan their long-term production on the German market, and there would also be "better outlets for German goods on European markets."[10]

The Nazi leadership welcomed Funk's plans. In 1942, The German Foreign Ministry created a "Europe Committee," whose members drafted plans for a German-dominated European confederation. That same year the Berlin Union of Businessmen and Industrialists held a conference at the city's Economic University, entitled "European Economic Community." As the writer John Laughland notes, the titles of the speeches delivered at the conference are "eerily reminiscent of modern pro-European discourse." They include "The Economic Face of the New Europe," "The Development Towards the European Economic Community," "European Currency Matters," and the hardy perennial, still much discussed today: "The Fundamental Question: Is Europe a Geographical Concept or a Political Fact."[11] In June a German official drafted the "Basic Elements of a Plan for the New Europe," which outlined how the new confederation would work. Much of it sounds very familiar. The section entitled "The Economic Organization of Europe" called for a European customs union, a European clearing center that would stabilize currency rates with the eventual objective of European monetary union, and the "harmonization of labor conditions and social welfare."[12]

Germany's postwar remodeling of itself as a penitent bastion of democracy was predicted by Heinz Pol. Pol, a former editor of a Berlin newspaper, had fled from the Nazis to the United States. The BIS, wrote Pol, was a central pillar of this policy of expediency: the recognition that the war was lost, and Germany needed to make a deal with Allies that would preserve its dominance of Europe. During the war, both Hermann Schmitz, the CEO of IG Farben, and Kurt von Schröder, the Nazi banker, used their positions as BIS directors to keep channels open to the Allies, wrote Pol in his book, *The Hidden Enemy*, which was published in 1943. "Since the beginning of this war, both have maintained contacts, through go-betweens, with their business friends in all the countries of the United Nations."[13]

The OSS Harvard Plan documents detailing Thomas McKittrick's role in negotiating deals with German industrialists confirm Pol's assertion that the BIS was a contact point for negotiations about Germany's plans to dominate postwar Europe. Pol's predictions of how postwar German leaders would rapidly abandon the outward trappings of Nazism still make unsettling reading:

> To obtain a peace, which would leave them in power, they will suddenly flaunt "European spirit" and offer worldwide "co-operation." They will chatter about liberty, equality, and fraternity. They will, all of a sudden, make up to the Jews. They will swear to live up to the demands of the Atlantic Charter and any other charter. They will share power with everybody and they will even let others rule for a while. They will do all this and more, if only they are allowed to keep some positions of power and control, that is, the only positions that count: in the army—were it even reduced to a few thousand men; in the key economic organizations; in the courts; in the universities; in the schools.[14]

Which is precisely what happened, when, after 1945 former Nazis took many of the key positions of "power and control" in the new Germany. Their legacy has proved extremely profitable. Germany now has the largest economy in the European Union and the fourth largest in the world. Greece faces collapse, and Spain is mired in recession, but Germany is booming, with growth rates of 3.7 percent in 2010 and 3 percent in 2011. Much of this success is based, as Funk predicted, on the high quality of German exports. Germany's total share of world trade is about 9 percent. The country is especially strong in the biotechnology, genetic engineering, and pharmaceutical sectors.

BASF and Bayer, two of IG Farben's successor companies, are dominant in their fields. BASF is the world's largest chemicals company with annual sales of 73.5 billion euros. Bayer, which makes aspirin, employs 112,000 people. Bayer felt no shame about its roots in IG Farben. In 1964 Bayer set up a foundation to honor Fritz ter Meer on his eightieth birthday with a donation of 2 million deutschmarks. Ter Meer had handled IG Farben's negotiations with Standard Oil and oversaw the building of IG Auschwitz. Found guilty of war crimes, ter Meer was sentenced to seven years imprisonment in 1948. He was freed in 1950 and later joined the supervisory board of Bayer. Bayer's foundation honoring him was renamed in 2005 and existed until 2007.

By the early 1990s, Funk's "European Large-Unit Economy," perhaps better known as the Eurozone, was clearly in sight. The technical preparations had been going on for decades—at least since 1964, when the Governors' Committee of European central banks had first met at the BIS to coordinate monetary policy, if not 1947, when the Paris accord on multilateral payments was signed. The positive reception for the 1989 Delors Report, which had been drafted at the BIS and which laid out the plan for EMU, meant that the political momentum was unstoppable.

In December 1993 Alexandre Lamfalussy stepped down as general manager of the BIS to start work as the director of the European Monetary Institute (EMI), the precursor of the European Central Bank. He would be much missed. "Lamfalussy put the BIS on the map. He was superb, very bright," said Geoffrey Bell, the founder of the G30 advisory group, an international think tank. "Lamfalussy was a thinker, especially when the bank started to move into intellectual issues such as bank regulation and the general state of the world."[15]

The EMI opened its doors the following month. Lamfalussy did not have far to go: the institute was based at the BIS. The president was charged with a mammoth task: the construction of the first trans-European monetary institution, in preparation for the introduction of the single currency. Nobody was better qualified for the job. Lamfalussy had been at the center of the drive to European monetary unity almost since its inception. The Hungarian economist had once boasted that it was his subordinates who "held the fountain pen" and "prepared the meetings in Basel of a project that was primarily European."

After eleven months, in November 1994, the EMI had outgrown the BIS and moved to Frankfurt. Its new home was a skyscraper at Willy-Brandt-Platz, known as the "Eurotower." The small number of staff that Lamfalussy brought from the BIS was not sufficient. The EMI president had to recruit 150 people in six months, and the network of contacts he had built up over seventeen years at the BIS was invaluable. "I knew everyone, and when I saw that there was a hole in the organization, or that we needed someone . . . I knew exactly who to ask, and I could ask them for everything. It was a phenomenal advantage." Lamfalussy's network was also an advantage for the EMI's governors, he recalled, "because they also knew each other and the staff too."[16]

The Eurotower was forty stories tall, more than double the BIS's eighteen floors. The size of the Frankfurt skyscraper symbolized its role as the home of an idea that had been nurtured at the BIS but which had now far outgrown its birthplace. Nonetheless, the small, clubbable world of the Tower of Basel was soon replicated there. Back in the 1960s Charles Coombs, of the New York Federal Reserve, recalled that the central bankers at the BIS governors' meetings frequently did not even need to finish their sentences "because everyone instinctively knew the rest and in an almost uncanny way, a simultaneous realization of the appropriate technical solution." The EMI president enjoyed the same kind of telepathy with Hans Tietmeyer, the president of the Bundesbank, and Jacques Delors, the president of the European Commission.

When Europe's most powerful bankers and politicians came to Frankfurt to discuss the single currency project, Lamfalussy sat at the head of the table.

"When Tietmeyer or Delors . . . would put up his hand to ask a question, I would know exactly what he would ask, and he also knew that I would know exactly what he wanted to ask. It was enough just to look at them and I knew what they wanted to talk about because I knew what they thought."[17]

THE DEPARTURE OF the EMI for Frankfurt left a void at the BIS. The long, looping corridors were quieter, the air of excitement that the bank was at the center of the most ambitious monetary project in European history had dissipated, and the chatter in the staff restaurant was more subdued. Even the Governors' Committee, which had met at the BIS since 1964, was gone. The committee's members—the governors of the European Central Banks—now formed the council of the EMI.

Once again, the BIS faced an existential crisis: Did it still need to exist? The bank was certainly still profitable. The accounts for the year ending March 1995 showed a net profit of 162.4 million gold francs. But if the BIS had no international role, it would be increasingly difficult to justify its existence and the extensive legal privileges that helped guarantee those profits. The bank had a new manager, Andrew Crockett, a British economist who had worked for the IMF from 1972 to 1989. Crocket came to the BIS in 1994 from the Bank of England, where he had spent four years as an executive director. There he could observe firsthand the after-effects of the "Big Bang," the 1986 deregulation of the City of the London.

Until the Big Bang, the Square Mile had been still a clubby, comfortable place of old school tie connections and long lunches, where Montagu Norman would have felt at home. That world vanished almost overnight. Wall Street investment banks poured into the Square Mile, bringing aggressive new tactics. The 1933 Glass-Steagall Act, which separated investment banking and deposit taking, was still in force in the United States. London, newly unburdened from cumbersome regulations, offered fabulous opportunities, heightened by the rapid growth of computer technology, which accelerated trading. The BIS gave the Big Bang a cautious welcome. "It was feared that if nothing was done, the

Stock Exchange would be unable to compete with foreign institutions and business would move abroad," the BIS noted in its 1987 Annual Report.[18] The changes had brought a "major inflow" of capital to British and foreign banks, the BIS noted, but had highlighted the importance of Chinese walls within firms to avoid conflicts of interest. The Chinese walls however, soon crumbled under the tsunami of money. The city firms' new American partners often had few qualms about conflicts of interest. They advised a company on a merger, and then sold the new shares.

Some said that the BIS job was Crockett's consolation prize for his failure to get the top job at the IMF. Either way, he had not joined the BIS to see it fade away. Crockett's international background brought valuable perspective to what could still be a cozy and parochial institution. Crockett understood that the establishment of the EMI marked the end of an era for the BIS. The bank was sixty-four years old, of pensionable age. Its original mission, of managing German reparations payments from the First World War, had long faded away, the details of the arcane disputes preserved in dusty files in the bank's archives.

Suddenly the BIS looked like an anachronism, a hangover of the era of credit controls and currency restrictions in a global economy that was ever more interlinked, dynamic, and faster moving. Small, unimportant countries such as Belgium and the Netherlands sat on the board, but where were the central banks of China, Brazil, Saudi Arabia, and Russia? True, Japan, Canada, and Turkey had joined, but many, especially in the United States, regarded the bank as a thoroughly Eurocentric institution. William White, from the Bank of Canada, joined the BIS in May 1995 as head of the Monetary and Economic Department, the bank's research arm. "When I arrived, people were asking what is the BIS going to do after the euro? It was a legitimate question. It was a very heavily European organization. Once the EMI was set up, all the Euro stuff was going to get done somewhere else."[19]

The BIS had to find a new purpose. To Crockett it was clear, White recalled. "Crockett said, we are going to go global." But for that to happen, the United States needed to be on board. More than sixty years after the BIS was founded, the Federal Reserve still kept its distance and had not taken up its tranche of shares, despite the BIS's deep American roots. The United States had always followed what was happening at the bank and the discussions taking place there. But the American Federal Reserve officials who traveled to Basel were there as observers, not as representatives of a member bank. Crockett wanted to end this anomaly. All the countries that took part in the G10 Sunday evening governors' meeting at the BIS should be members of the bank and be represented on the board of the bank, he believed. The Federal Reserve needed first to join the bank, then the board.[20]

During the 1970s and '80s, Washington had not been especially interested in the BIS. The focus then had been primarily on trade, rather than finance, said Karen Johnson, a former Federal Reserve director for International Finance. "Trade behaves in a rather predictable way. It's hard to change, but it's also hard to surprise you. That began to alter in the 1980s and changed hugely in the 1990s." Rapidly increasing globalization, the growing power of international markets and money's ability to flow ever faster around the world highlighted how the United States economy was inextricably linked to the global financial system. "Financial linkages had become vastly more important. The actions occurring in the financial markets were much faster. Crises or unanticipated events were far more likely to occur on the financial side," said Johnson.

Crockett's lobbying worked. In 1994 the Federal Reserve finally took up its shares in the BIS, joined the bank and appointed two directors to the board: the chairman of the Federal Reserve and the president of the New York Federal Reserve. The decision to join the board was made, noted Charles J. Siegman, a senior official in the Federal Reserve's International Finance Division, "in recognition of the increasingly important role of the BIS as the principal forum for consultation, cooperation and information exchange among central bankers and in anticipation of a broadening of that role."[21] The American decision sent a powerful signal to the world suggesting that the BIS was still relevant, necessary and could contribute to international financial stability.

Two years later, in 1996, the central banks or monetary authorities of China, India, Russia, Brazil, Hong Kong, Singapore, and Saudi Arabia joined. The BIS's future was assured.

As director of the Division of International Finance, Karen Johnson attended the governors' meetings for nine years, from 1998 until her retirement in 2007, accompanying either Alan Greenspan, the chairman of the Federal Reserve or his successor, Ben Bernanke, or their deputies. Johnson successfully pushed for the Federal Reserve to pay attention to the BIS. "The American attitude to the BIS changed because the world changed. The BIS was expanding its membership because countries in the rest of the world now mattered in ways they hadn't mattered before. The BIS went from being a Eurocentric thing to which the United States paid little attention, to something global and international. Once we took up our shares the degree to which senior members of the Fed became involved changed completely."[22]

The Federal Reserve and the New York Federal Reserve, like all visiting central banks, opened up a micro-branch in the BIS headquarters during the Basel weekends. Both had their own offices, as well as a shared extra room for staffers or other governors who might also be attending. Johnson enjoyed her trips to Basel. From Stanford University, she had joined the Federal Reserve in 1979—a rare woman in the male-dominated world of central banking. "Going to these international meetings, I was again the only woman in the room, but because I had the Fed on my nametag, that opened every door I wanted."[23]

IN JUNE 1998, four years and five months after Alexandre Lamfalussy left the BIS to set up the EMI, it was closed down—a mark of its success, rather than its failure. The European Central Bank opened for business. Seven months later, on January 1, 1999, eleven countries launched the euro. Technically, the birth of the single currency was an extraordinary achievement, justly earning the former BIS manager the title of "Father of the Euro." The euro finally replaced national currencies in January 2002. The press coverage, much of which was jubilant, focused on the benefits. These were considerable, at least in terms of convenience and ease of monetary transactions, and markedly similar to those predicted by Funk in his 1940 memo. Travelers could use the same currency from Portugal's Atlantic coast to Finland's Arctic border. So could companies trading in the Eurozone. Bank charges for European foreign currency accounts, commission on changing currencies, cumbersome record keeping, all these vanished instantly. The Stability and Growth Pact, signed in 1997, would theoretically ensure budgetary discipline and keep the currency stable. National budget deficits would not be allowed to exceed three percent of GDP.

Among the jubilation, less attention was paid to the political aspects of the single currency. Once again, the creeping removal of national sovereignty was portrayed as a fundamentally technocratic innovation, rather than a political decision—as indeed had been the case since the establishment of the European Coal and Steel Community in 1951.

When a country joined the Eurozone, its central bank automatically became part of the European System of Central Banks, whose centerpiece was the ECB. The member country surrendered control over its monetary policy, although it was represented on the ECB's Governing Council. There was logic to this: a common currency would soon go out of business if each member state were running an independent monetary fiefdom.

In London the idea of surrendering monetary sovereignty was regarded with horror. In Washington, DC, Paul Volcker took a more nuanced view. He supported the idea of a European Central Bank, but still thought, "It was a very peculiar thing to have a central bank without a government."[24] The chairman of the Federal Reserve could see the reasoning behind a single bank and currency but thought that they needed to be properly integrated with fiscal discipline. "There were negative factors as well as positive ones. Someone was always devaluing a currency. Then they would make attempts to stabilize it, and then it would fall apart. So it made sense to me to have a common currency if you are having a lot of problems. But it was too optimistic to think that the mere fact of a common currency would force discipline on individual members because they could no longer devalue their currencies."[25]

For many, it seemed that the introduction of the euro was, in part, a continuation of the Second World War by other means. The real issues were not monetary, but political. French politicians believed that the single currency would solve the German problem forever. Twice in a century Germany had laid waste to Europe. But now that Germany was locked into the European integration project, or even shackled to it, it would neither want, nor be able to go to war again. Germany's future and prosperity would be inexorably linked to that of its most important neighbor and rival: France. Of course, national rivalries would continue, but the Germans would be part of a trans-European currency that would dilute their monetary sovereignty and finally lay the ghosts of the Second World War to rest. The French believed—erroneously as it turned out—that Berlin would no longer be able to dominate the European economy. In fact, for the Bundesbank shaped the design of the ECB, ensuring that it was focused on price stability, and retained enormous influence over the ECB's operations.

The creation of the euro was a political compromise, said Zsigmond Jarai, a former governor of the National Bank of Hungary and minister of finance. "France let Germany unify in 1989. But France was worried that a unified Germany would dominate the whole continent and would be too strong. So Paris said, OK, you can unify but without the deutschmark, and we will have the euro instead. The German accepted and also won a new market in Eastern Europe for their exports." The deutschmark was the basis of the euro, said Jarai. "The aim was to export German economic stability to France and Italy. The deutschmark was always the strong currency, and the Bundesbank was the bank that could control inflation. France and Italy were unable to do that. The aim was to use the ECB to force France and Italy to keep their money under control."[26]

The new currency, intended to symbolize a new era of European cooperation was really a means of settling old scores, said Rupert Pennant-Rea, who served as deputy governor of the Bank of England from 1993 to 1995.

The euro was a monstrous creation. It was driven by the politics of the Franco-German relationship, which had its obvious

*echo in the relationship between the Bundesbank and the Bank of
France, where, on the whole, what the first did the second did immediately afterward. The French political class hated the fact that
they had to dance to the Bundesbank's tunes. You could argue that,
from a French point of view, the euro was little more than a way
out of that continuous insult to their national pride. The French
felt they were more or less equal with the Germans on most sub-
jects, but on monetary issues they were always, always second and
subservient. They hated that.*

AND FOR ALL the technical expertise supplied by Lamfalussy and his
BIS-in-exile in Frankfurt, the project was doomed from the start, the British
former central banker argued. "It was completely misdesigned. You should
not create a monetary union of such disparate economies because it doesn't
work. There were a lot of economists saying that, but the politicians said
we know better, we are creating history. We have an evangelical legitimacy
which you mere mortals don't understand."[27]

Why, then, did the Germans agree? The Bundesbank, said Pennant-Rea,
always hated the idea of the euro, because it clearly saw that monetary union
would dilute German monetary sovereignty. But Chancellor Helmut Kohl,
President François Mitterrand, and Jacques Delors were fixated on their place
in the history books. The loss of monetary sovereignty was a small price to
pay for redesigning a continent—to a plan drawn up in Berlin as much as Paris
and Brussels. "I think it was a matter of great men and their moment. This is
us creating the new Europe, where all that ghastly history of the last century
we can now firmly say is gone and will never return, because we have now
created something utterly different. But that bore no relation to what the great
majority of the German people were thinking or wanted, their leaders never
tested public opinion. It was horrific."[28]

Whatever his inner doubts, Lamfalussy got on with the job of making the
euro happen. The Hungarian economist was a modest and likeable person,

said Pennant-Rea. "He was trying to find the truth in the economics of it. But he was working on the creation of the euro in a highly politicized environment, trying to be faithful to his economic analyses and not let the politics turn his head."

Even those more sympathetic to the project admit it was flawed from the outset. The Eurozone had two inherent flaws. First, it was not a homogeneous currency area. Uniting countries as diverse as Germany and Greece—or Italy or France for that matter—each with different cultures, histories, economic and fiscal policies, and attitudes toward the role of the state and rights to raise taxes was always going to be a hazardous enterprise, as indeed Walter Funk had predicted in 1940. Second, the Eurozone needed a credible transnational fiscal system, with rules and an enforcement mechanism, as Lamfalussy had argued. National governments in the Eurozone retained the rights to raise taxes and control their public spending, even though those decisions ultimately impacted on the other members. Thus all the Eurozone members were, in effect, held hostage to each other—with no means of controlling those outside influences.

The counter argument is that the momentum toward full union was now unstoppable. The euro was a currency whose time had come. Like Hjalmar Schacht's rentenmark that was introduced to wipe out the hyperinflation in the 1920s, or the deutschmark that was brought in to stabilize the postwar economy, the euro would work, or have to work, because enough people, especially among Europe's ruling class, believed that it would. And the euro was always about more than a common currency. The introduction of EMU, the technocrats believed, would somehow force a resolution of the euro's contradictions and then catalyse the process of full European monetary, economic and political union. "The member countries of the Eurozone and the European Union have always used somewhat narrow decisions about economic structure to try to build a broader political economy in Europe," said Malcolm Knight, who served as BIS manager from 2003 to 2008.[29]

In other words, technical decisions about financial and monetary policy have been used to introduce the supranational state by stealth—often via the BIS. The warnings about the single currency's contradictions went unheeded and Europe is now paying the price. Some of the Eurozone's problems should have been foreseen, argued Nathan Sheets, who served as head of the Federal Reserve's division of International Finance from 2008 to 2011. "When they drew up the treaties, they didn't have any B-plans. They made it impossible for somebody to leave or be expelled. There are no clear mechanisms for dealing with a country whose sovereign debt is under stress. There was an insufficient commitment to surveillance and making sure people stayed within the rules."[30] These flaws were exacerbated by the subsequent expansion of the Eurozone to seventeen members. "They started the Eurozone with a very heterogeneous group of countries and then they made it even more so by bringing in those additional countries."[31]

It was obvious from the outset that the euro could not work, said Zsigmond Jarai, who attended numerous meetings at the BIS and was well acquainted with his compatriot, Alexandre Lamfalussy. "Before the crisis, Lamfalussy told me, because it was clear to everybody, that if you have a common currency you have to have a common economic and fiscal policy from the beginning. Lamfalussy told me that the idea was they create the currency first and that will force the creation of a more common economic and fiscal policy."[32] Europe, however, is still waiting.

CHAPTER FIFTEEN

THE ALL-SEEING EYE

"I had a file six inches thick on Freddie Mac and Fannie Mae."

— William White

T he BIS's decision to collect statistics on international banking activity and computerize its data repository had paid handsome dividends. The bank rapidly became one of the best-informed financial institutions in the world, especially about cross-border banking transactions and the flow of international capital. Commercial banks, including some that were domiciled in off-shore financial centers, supplied data on their assets and liabilities and foreign currency and cross-border transactions to a central banking authority—usually the national bank or its equivalent—which aggregated the data and forwarded it to the BIS. The bank then published some of the information in its *Quarterly Review*. The BIS had been designed as a bank for central banks. But agile as ever, it had remodeled itself as an essential point of reference for information on the commercial banking sector and all that flowed from that.

The *65th Annual Report*, covering 1994–1995, was 228 pages long and was a veritable encyclopedia of economic and financial statistics and indicators. It covered international trade in both the Western and developing world: monetary policy, bond markets, exchange rates, capital flows in emerging and Western markets, and developments in international financial markets. It offered summaries, analyses, and guidance, and called for greater cooperation and coordination between banks and regulatory authorities.

When William White arrived in Basel from Ottawa in 1995, he took over a highly regarded economic research department. The bank's prescriptions had remained more or less constant since Per Jacobssen had arrived in 1931 and written the first reports: tight control of credit and the need to control inflation. "If there is one thing that distinguishes the BIS way of looking at things from virtually everybody else," said White, "it is that they do put more emphasis on the bad things that can happen from excessive lending. That goes back to the 1930s and the bank's founding after the hyperinflation in Germany."[1]

The bank had warned about the excessively easy credit that was fueling the Asian economic boom during the 1990s. When the Asian debt crisis exploded in 1997 and the Thai baht collapsed and spread contagion across the region, the BIS was vindicated, although that was meager comfort. "People said the Southeast Asian debt crisis came out of nowhere and was impossible to predict," said White. "This is all nonsense. The BIS banking statistics made it very clear in the 1990s that huge amounts of money were being borrowed in foreign currencies for very short terms, then being lent out in domestic currency at much longer maturities. The Asian debt crisis was an accident waiting to happen."[2]

Knowing there was a problem, however, did not mean the bank could always persuade policymakers to take preventative or remedial measures. Just a few years later, in the early 2000s, the United States was also facing a similar potential financial meltdown. The repeal in 1999 of the Glass-Steagall Act that separated banks' deposit taking and broking activities had helped fuel a credit boom and asset bubble. Glass-Steagall had been passed in 1933 during the Great Depression. The warnings of those who said that repealing the act would trigger another cycle of boom, bust, and depression were ignored.

BIS officials were especially concerned about the Federal National Mortgage Association (FNMA), known colloquially as Fannie Mae, and the Federal Home Loan Mortgage Corporation (FHLMC), known as Freddie Mac. The two institutions were government enterprises that provided liquidity to the mortgage system. They purchased home loans, providing the loans met their criteria, and turned them into mortgage-backed securities. Freddie and

Fannie then sold the securities to outside investors and guaranteed both the principal and the interest payments. Thanks to the government's imprimatur, the system worked and remained stable.

But in the early 2000s, Wall Street worked out how to purchase and securitize mortgages without going through Freddie or Fannie. Finance houses such as Lehman Brothers and Bear Stearns bundled high-risk subprime mortgages—those granted to borrowers with a poor credit rating—into securities. The Wall Street finance houses then sold them to investors, few of whom understood the risks they were buying.

The global credit system was vastly overstretched. The BIS had repeatedly warned that excessive global credit growth, poor lending practices by commercial banks, private sector excesses and global imbalances were fueling a potential crisis. But as rivers of easy money flowed around the world, it seemed nobody was listening. BIS officials did not consider Freddie and Fannie to be a contaminant of global markets. Rather, they were a potential trigger for disaster. The central bankers needed to take notice. The place to discuss Freddie and Fannie was the BIS Committee on the Global Financial System. The committee, composed of deputy governors of central banks and other officials, was charged with analyzing and responding to stress in global financial markets. But it seemed that the central bankers did not want to talk about Freddie and Fannie. The issue was considered politically untouchable.

The United States was not the only country with powerful and risky government-sponsored enterprises—commercial companies backed by the state. France had its Caisse des dépôts et consignations, a state development and investment fund; each German state had its own bank, known as a Landesbank, and Japan offered banking services at its post office. The combination of state guarantees for commercial risks was potentially explosive, whether in Tokyo, Toulouse, or Texas. Attempts were made to get the committee to consider the whole question of government-sponsored enterprises, without focusing attention on any one country. These too, failed.

Long after he left the Bank of England, the BIS annual reports remained essential reading, said Rupert Pennant-Rea.

> *The BIS started warning about the problems with excessive credit growth, excessive interconnectedness and some of the other major frailties in the financial system back in 2003 or 2004. Everybody says nobody foresaw 2007–2008; that's not true. One organisation that did was the BIS. Not in every detail. But in terms of warning, that things were going wrong, that there was far too much debt on every sector's balance sheets, that banks were in a very dangerous interconnected area, with positions against each other and overleveraged, a lot of that is in those rather dull looking annual reports.[3]*

The work of hosting the BIS committees is less glamorous than, for example, preparing for the governors' meetings. But in the long-term the committees are at least as useful for the bank: the BIS has made itself a central, indispensable pillar of the forums dealing with the most important questions about the global financial system. Every year more than five thousand senior executives and officials from central banks and supervisory authorities travel to Basel. The bank organizes specialist gatherings on topics including monetary and financial stability, reserve management, information technology, and internal auditing. Over the years the BIS has made itself the central hub for the world's central bank governors and their staffs.

Among the bank's six committees, only the Basel Committee on Banking Supervision that deals with commercial banking supervision, usually receives media attention, as its work directly affects the public that hold their accounts in commercial banks. The aim of the Basel Committee, as it is usually known, according to the BIS website, is to "enhance understanding of key supervisory issues and improve the quality of banking supervision worldwide."

PARADOXICALLY, THE INCREASE in globalization was highlighting national banking disparities. Not only banking supervision standards varied from country to country, but so did the definitions of capital assets. Some banks counted long-term debts and off-balance sheet items as assets, while others did not. In 1988 the Basel Committee drew up new rules, which said, in essence, that bank capital must equal at least 8 percent of its assets, including its loans and liabilities. If a bank did not have sufficient capital, it must reduce its liabilities and risk exposure. The committee has no powers of enforcement, but it does have enormous moral authority. Any bank wishing to operate on international markets must adhere to the 8 percent rule.

Basel I, as the 1998 accord is known, has continued to evolve. Basel II, published in 2004, further honed and regulated capital requirements, quantified risk, and standardized international regulations, so as not to create competitive inequality, meaning that customers search for banks with looser controls. Regulating capital requirements while leaving banks free to lend is a delicate balancing act, said William McDonough, who served as chairman of the New York Federal Reserve from 1993 to 2003, and chaired the Basel Committee from 2000 to 2003. "One recognizes that there is an inherent conflict. The avoidance of financial crises is the public good, so for that a higher capital requirement is better. On the other hand, the whole capitalist free market system works by the savings of some being transferred and made available for the investment of others. So there has to be a trade where one does the best one can."[4]

Looking back with hindsight at the economic crash of late 2007, it is clear that the capital requirements of Basel II were insufficient, said McDonough. "The aim of Basel II was to bring up capital requirements but to do so in a way that would not stifle the world economy. In the event the rules were not as strong or as fine-tuned as they needed to be when the crisis came."[5] The Basel III accords, which have not yet been implemented, aim to further hone the regulations governing banks' capital requirements.

No matter how dedicated the regulators are, they are always behind the traders. McDonough said, "We did not anticipate the blowing up of the exotic instruments that brought down Lehman Brothers and the spin effect that resulted from that. If it had been, then hopefully somebody would have tried to avoid it."[6] But the regulators, like generals, are inevitably fighting the last battle. Capital moves faster, the global economy is ever more entwined, and financial instruments are more complex. Each time a new set of rules is issued, Wall Street hires the best and brightest financial and legal brains to find a way to push compliance to new limits. Despite its legions of experts, the BIS was unable to predict or prevent the Libor scandal, when commercial banks made vast profits by manipulating interbank lending rates for their own advantage. The Basel banking accords did not deal with Libor.

For all its endorsement of good bank governance, the BIS has been criticized over its own commercial actions. The BIS's main shareholders have always been central banks, but after the bank was founded in 1930 some of the original shareholders—US, French, and Belgian banks—sold part of their holdings. At the end of 2000, almost 14 percent of the BIS's capital, 72,648 shares, was still in private hands and being traded. The BIS announced that it would buy back those shares in a compulsory re-purchase. Thanks to the BIS's legal status, the decision could not be contested. But the price could. The bank offered 16,000 Swiss francs per share.

Three shareholders refused to accept the price. It was around twice the shares' trading price but still less than the shares would be worth if valued as a proportion of the net asset value of the bank, they argued. First Eagle Funds, a New York–based group of mutual funds, and the other two, small private investors, took the case to the Hague Arbitral Tribunal, which governs disputes with the BIS. The tribunal ruled in their favor. It said that the BIS had miscalculated the shares' value. The tribunal awarded the private shareholders an extra 7,977.56 Swiss francs per share, plus 5 percent interest, bringing the total extra to 9,052.90 Swiss francs—over 50 percent more than the original offer.[7] The decision, noted the *Central Banking Journal*, was a "humiliating rebuff" for the board of directors who had signed off on the original price, including Jean-Claude Trichet, chairman of the Federal Reserve Alan Greenspan, and the governor of the Bank of England Sir Eddie George.[8]

The problem was not the compulsory squeeze out of private shareholders, said Charles de Vaulx, then the portfolio manager of First Eagle Funds, and now chief investment officer and portfolio manager at International Value Advisers. "I could understand that it was an accident of history that the shares happened to be listed, and the bank wanted to buy them back. But the price has to be fair. A squeeze-out deal, which is compulsory, has to have higher standards. The supreme irony is that the BIS has always portrayed itself as promoting proper capital adequacy, transparency, corporate governance, all these good things, which make the world a better place. But when it came to buying back their own shares, why aren't they holding themselves up to the same standards?"[9] Andrew Crockett, the BIS's general manager from 1994 to 2003, said at the time that he believed the offer was "fair" based on the valuation by J. P. Morgan.[10]

MEANWHILE, IN FRANKFURT, the European Central Bank flourished. The ECB is now one of the world's most powerful central banks. It manages monetary policy for seventeen Eurozone members, an area that reaches from the Atlantic coast of Portugal to the Turkish frontier, and which is home to more than 330 million people.

The influence of the BIS, the ECB's parent bank, is clear. The ECB is an ultramodern, even a postmodern institution—as Paul Volcker noted—a central bank without a country or national reserves. It is the ultimate financial expression of Jean Monnet's supranational dream. But the ECB's founding ethos is firmly rooted in the Norman-Schacht era. Its structure, modus operandi, and lack of accountability mirror that of the BIS. Like the BIS, the ECB is rigorously protected by international law, in its case the Maastricht Treaty that founded the European Union.

This is partly because the ECB was always a political as much as a monetary construct, rooted in trade-offs and behind-the-scenes deals. As the most powerful central bank in Europe, the Bundesbank was extremely influential in the design of the ECB. The Bundesbank ensured that the ECB's "primary objective," as the ECB notes on its website, is to "maintain price stability" with inflation rates below 2 percent.[11] (The Federal Reserve, in contrast, has a dual mandate of combating unemployment and inflation.) "The Germans take a very narrow view of the proper role of central banks, that it is to do almost exclusively with the preservation of price stability," said William White. "That comes from their history and experience of hyperinflation."[12]

To whom then is the ECB democratically accountable? In effect, nobody. The ECB's Governing Council has direct control over the tools of monetary policy. It is prohibited from taking advice from Eurozone governments.[13] The European Parliament has no meaningful authority over the ECB. "The ECB enjoys an extraordinary amount of independence," wrote Professor Anne Sibert, an expert on bank governance, in a 2009 paper. "It has an unusual amount of target independence; its degree of operational independence is probably unprecedented; it is almost completely financially independent; it is nearly functionally independent," meaning that the ECB has control over most instruments of monetary policy and the freedom to use them as it sees fit.[14]

The ECB does issue a press release after the monetary policy meetings of the Governing Council, detailing any changes in bank rates and the ECB's president holds a press conference. The bank also publishes a monthly bulletin. But this is the bare minimum of reporting requirements – and a long way from proper accountability. Like the BIS, the ECB keeps its inner workings secret. "The ECB lacks transparency, especially procedural transparency," noted Professor Sibert. "We do not know how decisions are reached; it appears that votes are not even taken. Press conferences are no substitute for a failure to publish minutes."[15]

The US Federal Reserve issues a press release after each meeting of the Federal Open Market Committee (FOMC). The release includes the vote of the FOMC and the views of any dissenters. After each meeting of the FOMC, the minutes of the previous meeting are released, with a detailed summary of the reasons for the policy decisions taken. The Federal Reserve is accountable to Congress. The bank's chairman appears twice a year before Congress, and before each appearance the board submits a comprehensive report. It is a meaningful, comprehensive analysis, taking in the interconnections between monetary and fiscal policy and the impact of the Federal Reserve's decisions. The

Bank of England also publishes the minutes of its monetary policy meetings, with a two-week delay.

The European Parliament has passed repeated resolutions demanding that the ECB publish the minutes of the Governing Council meetings and to release a summary of the vote, without naming names. The central bank governors who are members of the ECB's governing Council use the same arguments as to why this should not happen as those advanced by BIS officials for not releasing any minutes of the governors' meetings: that they would limit the free exchange of ideas at the meeting. The minutes of the ECB Governing Council might also reveal, how despite the ECB's claim to be above national politics, the governors of member central banks can still put their home countries' interests before those of the Eurozone as a whole.

ECB officials argue that the European Parliament's lack of power over the ECB does not take into account its specific role as a unique, supranational bank. "This does not imply that the ECB might be less accountable than the other central banks . . . it merely points to specific features of the European way of holding the bank accountable."[16] The ECB says that it enjoys "input legitimacy," as an institution established through the treaty that brought the European Union into existence. However "input legitimacy" is less impressive than it may sound. As the crisis in the Eurozone has worsened the ECB's "input legitimacy" has steadily evaporated.

In a nod to democracy, it was decided that the Maastricht Treaty needed to be ratified by all twelve EU members. But only three of the signatories trusted their citizens sufficiently to hold a referendum. Perhaps the politicians anticipated the results. Denmark narrowly rejected the treaty in 1992, with 50.7 percent voting no. France stunned the federalists when just 51 percent of the population voted in favor. Only Ireland was enthusiastic, with a 68.7 percent vote. The remaining nine members delegated the vote to their parliaments, all of which approved the treaty. Denmark voted again the following year. Copenhagen negotiated four opt-outs from the treaty, including the right not to join the European Union. This time the yes vote won, with 56.7 percent.

The ongoing experience of European union seemed only to dampen its citizens' enthusiasm. In 2005 France and the Netherlands both voted no in referenda on the new European constitution, which would have replaced previous treaties and further accelerated the federalization process. European officials then stepped around this by renaming the constitution as the Lisbon Treaty and arguing that it merely amended previous treaties—thus there was no need for referenda. Only Ireland held a referendum on Lisbon, in June 2008, when 53.4 percent voted no. After sufficient political and pressure was applied, a second referendum was held in October 2009. This time Irish voters voted yes.

The more the European politicians and officials talked of democracy, it seemed, the less the citizens of the continent were able to exercise it. But the course of events in postwar Europe had been decided decades before the ECB opened for business.

Back in October 1941, Thomas McKittrick had received an inquiry from a friend of his living in Louisville, Kentucky, asking about the plans for the postwar financial system. The BIS president replied, "People everywhere are talking about federalisation accompanied by partial abrogation of national sovereignty. . . . The extent to which national sovereignty in this direction is limited must fix the boundaries of international financial authority."[17]

For Europe at least, those bounds were now fixed, permanently, at the ECB's headquarters in the Eurotower at Willy-Brandt-Platz, in downtown Frankfurt. But despite the technocrats' best efforts, real life was proving more complicated than the bank's monetary framework for the new Europe. Germans saved; Greeks spent. Italians did not pay their taxes. The French refused to give up their six-week holidays. Germany and France both broke the Stability and Growth Pact's rules governing public debt. But some things were immutable. The ECB's price obsession, engraved in its statutes, to keep inflation below 2 percent, forced Eurozone governments to slash public services and cut public spending. That in turn reduced consumer demand, stalled economic growth, increased unemployment and triggered a slide into recession that has resulted in Europe's gravest political and economic crisis since 1945.

AS THE GLOBAL financial crisis deepened, the politesse at the BIS governors' meetings began to crack. There is no formal policy coordination at the bimonthly gatherings, but the central bankers try to harmonize their monetary policies for maximum benefit where possible. Yet, paradoxically, as the world's economy has become more globalized, central bankers are turning to local solutions. It has become clear that since the crash of 2007 the governors—who, after all, govern *national* central banks—will work to protect their countries' interests first, even if that has deleterious effects on other nations' economies.

Insiders have said that the divide between those countries that shape the global economy and those that are buffeted by decisions taken in Western capitals is now ever more evident at the Global Economy Meetings. The United States, Japan, and Britain have been injecting trillions of dollars' worth of liquidity into their economies to try and boost growth. The theory is that asset purchases known as "Quantative Easing" will boost commercial banks' balance sheets, increase liquidity, and encourage more lending, which will in turn boost spending, growth, and create jobs. At the same time, the United States, Britain, Japan, and the European Central Bank are implementing a loose monetary policy of ultralow interest rates.

This results in an outflow of hot money, chasing better returns around the world, which causes asset bubbles in the destination economies and distorts exchange rates, making currencies such as the Malaysian ringgit and the Korean won more expensive and thus affecting exports from those countries. "The disagreements on this were more pronounced," said a former central banker, who wished to remain anonymous, of the governors' meetings in late 2012. "Most of the developing countries were saying, 'We don't see that low interest rates are adding to your economic growth and at the same time it causes us problems because of the capital inflows. Our exchange rates go up and we are having real estate bubbles.'" The central bankers remain polite. "Everyone is very careful because you cannot tell other countries what to do. But the developing countries are saying, look, this is what these policies are doing to us. They are causing us problems."[18]

Much of the criticism was directed at the United States, with the main complaints coming from Southeast Asian countries and some Latin American countries. "The more successful they are, the more upset they are. This policy is creating large capital flows into these developing countries, which they don't necessarily need." The governors at the Global Economy Meeting never speak publicly about the discussions that take place inside the BIS, but similar debates are happening in other fora, where they feel less constrained. In December 2012 Glenn Stevens, the governor of the Reserve Bank of Australia, gave a speech in Bangkok that was seen as a barely veiled attack on the Federal Reserve, the Bank of Japan, and the European Central Bank. Stevens even accused the three of "exporting their weaknesses" in language unlikely to be used at a governors' dinner.[19]

But there was more optimism about the euro. "Everyone was waiting for Mario Draghi's magic touch," said the former central banker. A Greek exit from the Eurozone looked less likely. Bailout funds were being released, and Greece's fiscal targets were being relaxed. The European Stability Mechanism (ESM), the 700 billion euro rescue fund for Greece, Ireland, and Portugal, is now a permanent institution. Mario Draghi did, indeed, seem to have a "magic touch." By stating that the ECB would do "whatever it takes" to stop the euro breaking up, and by stating that the bank was ready to buy "unlimited amounts" of short-dated bonds of indebted countries provided the country met certain conditions, the bank's president reassured the markets. Spain and Italy's borrowing costs quickly fell.

Draghi's plan was a move of "genius," according to the former central banker. "The ECB says it will buy debt, but the conditions the bank has imposed make it next to impossible for it to actually make the purchase. But the market applauds them and says all the problems are solved. This is the ultimate result that a central bank can achieve. You say something, and without doing anything, without spending one cent, you totally change the market sentiment. Every central banker dreams of this. It is close to a miracle."[20]

DRAGHI WAS NOT the only central banker basking in media attention. Central bankers are now the rock stars of the financial crisis. The men—they are nearly all men—in sober suits have "achieved a new prominence and become pivotal members of the policy-making establishments of both national and intergovernmental organizations," noted a report co-authored by Ernst & Young, a financial consultancy, and the Official Monetary and Financial Institutions Forum (OMFIF), a forum for central bankers and regulators.[21] The financial crisis and the subsequent need for rapid, coordinated global responses have blurred the traditional distinction between governments' fiscal policies (taxes and public spending) and the central banks' mandate of monetary policy (interest rates and control of inflation). In many countries, central bank governors are "as well known as the government leaders they serve, and their words and deeds are the subject of heated debate in newspapers, bars, and taxicabs."[22]

When Mark Carney, the governor of the Bank of the Canada, was appointed governor of the Bank of England in November 2012, he received the kind of media coverage usually reserved for royalty and soccer players. The *Sunday Times* newspaper ran a hagiographic profile, under the headline "A Superhuman to Push the Old Lady," meaning the Old Lady of Threadneedle Street in the City of London, a synonym for the Bank of England. Carney, who is trim and photogenic, was the first foreigner to be appointed to the job since the bank was founded in 1694. The article enthused that he had "charm, talent, and [George] Clooney looks." He even had a social conscience and had made understanding noises about the Occupy Wall Street movement.[23] This winning combination brought Carney a salary package worth around $1.4 million per year, and he will enjoy a substantial expansion of powers: the bank will now have regulatory control over Britain's commercial banks and insurers.[24]

Carney is a well-known figure at the BIS. He is a member of the board, representing the Bank of Canada. He has served as chairman of the BIS Committee on the Global Financial System, which is a forum for central banks to coordinate polices on monetary and financial stability. He is also chairman of the Financial Stability Board (FSB), which coordinates international financial supervisory and regulatory policies. The BIS hosts the FSB, and insiders say it is likely to assume increasing importance, reflecting the growing mandate of central bankers. Some are now required to supervise national commercial banks, oversee risk management and national financial systems, and stand ever ready as a backstop should disaster strike. "The idea that central bankers should have a primary responsibility for financial stability, as well as price stability, was considered a pretty dramatic break with orthodox central bank thinking, especially in the United States," said Malcolm Knight.[25]

Carney's years at the BIS have brought him a priceless network of personal relationships, nurtured at the bank's dinners and lunches. These connections and the mutual trust that grows between the central bankers fostered by the BIS "matter a great deal," said Sir Mervyn King. "They bring personal trust and confidence, which is very important. Finance ministers do not have the same length of tenure and so do not get to know each other so well."

The governors' personal relationships are crucial in times of crisis. When President Kennedy was shot in 1963, Charles Coombs, of the New York Federal Reserve, was able to take immediate, decisive action to save the dollar, knowing he would be supported by his European counterparts. The same held true after the terrorist attacks on September 11, 2001. King recalled, "We can say things to each other, knowing they won't be leaked. You can do things without going through all the formalities. After 9/11, Alan Greenspan was out of the United States, and Roger Ferguson was in charge of the Federal Reserve. He and I were able to negotiate a swap agreement to supply liquidity in dollars for banks that needed them but could not get them at the Fed. The fact we could do that personally because we trusted each other enabled us to give confidence to our banks that they would be able to get dollars. That is a good example of where an informal connection can make a connection in practice, and that cannot happen unless you have had a long period of personal contact and interaction.

"Normally in that sort of situation, without that personal trust you would have to wait until all the legal details had been sorted out before you can tell someone it can go ahead, by which time it would be too late. Our ability to step in and say, 'Don't worry—it's going to be all right,' was very important."

The governors' weekends are a kind of sanctuary, says Nathan Sheets, who served as head of the Federal Reserve's division of International Finance from 2008–2011. "You are there with like-minded people, and there really is a sense of central bankers' brotherhood. At many other international meetings there is a sense of 'You Americans are doing this' and 'You Europeans are doing that.' At the BIS, the questions are what kind of challenges do we face? And how can we solve these together? Those relationships make it easy to pick up the telephone and call counterparts abroad. The governors know each other, they like each other and they know how each other think, thanks to these meetings."[26]

The BIS gatherings can bring constructive criticism, said Peter Akos Bod, a former governor of the National Bank of Hungary. "If something happened in your country, and you did or did not do something, the others raised questions. You had to face some friendly criticism if your inflation was out of line. The Bundesbank president, for example, would say, this measure that you have taken, why didn't you do that instead? And you would go home, and ask your staff, 'Why didn't we do that?'"[27]

The influence of the BIS is indirect but real, said a former central banker. "You hear things, they stick in your head, you come home, and you use them. Central banking is a very special business because you don't have competitors. If you are a car producer and you meet another car producer, you hide your cars. If you meet another central banker, you ask questions because you have a hell of a lot to learn, and he has no reason to hide from you. From that point of view, these discussions are extremely useful."[28]

The governors' sense of common interest and their mutual trust has proved especially important during the crisis. King said, "We have adopted different forms of communication with the markets, and learned from the experience of others about what worked and what didn't work. The BIS meetings have helped us to formulate views about what we should do, and about the financial instruments we use. All the governors feel they benefit from sharing experiences, which is different from just getting documents."

Nonetheless, the governors' meetings are still dominated by a tight-knit, inner-core of the governors of the Federal Reserve, the ECB, and the Bank of England, who share decades-old connections. Ben Bernanke, Mario Draghi, and Sir Mervyn King all spent time at the Massachusetts Institute of Technology economics department. Bernanke and Draghi earned their PhDs there, while King taught there for a short time in the 1980s and shared an office with Bernanke.[29] The emphasis on status and hierarchy adds to the mystique of the BIS, said Pennant-Rea. "When you strip down the membership, only a relatively small number really matter. The United States above all, Germany and Britain to a minor extent. There is a very strong sense of pecking order."

But like all self-referential groups that rely on each other for mutual advice and reinforcement, the central bankers, cocooned in luxury and discretion at the BIS, can easily forget that they are public servants, said Andrew Hilton, the director of the Centre for the Study of Financial Innovation, a think-tank based in London. "It's a tricky one because you don't want them to be affected by day-to-day populist pressures. On the other hand, you do want them to know how much a pint of milk costs. The fine line you have to draw is between not being pressured by what's happening on the street, but also being aware of it. It's all too easy as a central banker to float over the political economy and throw bread to the masses. Central bankers should probably never be allowed to go anywhere in a limousine. They should take the Basel tram."[30]

Those central bankers who implement austerity programs do not personally suffer the consequences. Jean-Claude Trichet served as president of the ECB from 2003 to 2011. Europe's economies have slid into recession in part because of the ECB's relentless demands to keep inflation below 2 percent. Despite his role in the unfolding Eurozone crisis, Trichet is now a much sought-after speaker on the international conference circuit.

In May 2012 Trichet spoke at the Peterson Institute for International Economics in Washington, DC, offering his thoughts on the "Lessons from the Crisis." To an outsider the scene seemed an extraordinary spectacle: as Spain's economy began to collapse, neo-Nazis patrolled the streets of Athens, beating immigrants, and an entire generation of young Europeans faced years of unemployment and poverty. Trichet, however, was garlanded with praise and lauded for his insight. The French banker, said Peter G. Peterson, "played a decisive role in the Europe crisis as president of the European Central Bank until he stepped down last fall," which was indeed true, although not in the sense that Peterson intended.

The solution to the Eurozone crisis, argued Trichet, was not less supranationalism and technocratic rule, but much more. Trichet called for what he described as "a quantum leap" of economic governance, to accelerate the next stage of European integration. If a Eurozone member refused to obey instructions "coming from the center"—meaning European authorities—there should be the "activation of a federal government by exception." This policy, which even Trichet admitted would be at the "very, very, limit" of what would be acceptable, would mean that if "Your parliament is not behaving properly, we fine the country."[31]

Apparently oblivious to Europe's growing backlash against rule by technocrats, Trichet will have plenty of time to further hone his ideas for the end of national sovereignty in his new position as chairman of Bruegel, one of the foremost think tanks on European economic integration. The first president of the ECB retired having wreaked "the sort of destruction on the European economy that hostile powers could only dream about," said Dean Baker, of the Centre for Economic and Policy Research, a liberal think tank. Trichet embodies the type of central banker who sees the economic crisis as something quite distinct from their responsibilities, said Baker. "Their job is to get inflation down, to 2 percent. The economic crisis is something bad that happened. It would have been nice if it did not happen, but it was not their responsibility, you cannot hold them accountable for it, and they don't have the tools to deal with it."[32]

Central bankers strongly reject this argument. Inflation, they say, is not a tap to be turned on and off when governments like to stimulate growth. "This is not something that you toy with," said one former central banker. "It is very easy for politicians to basically rob people of their savings by creating inflation. It is immoral, and anyway capital is much more mobile than it was ten or thirty years ago. The money will say you are creating inflation, goodbye, we are going to China or wherever, in a few seconds. It is much cleaner if we deal with the problem head on and do the painful things."[33]

Or as Stephen Cecchetti, the head of the BIS Monetary and Economic department, said, high debt levels are a "drag on growth." There can be no growth without structural repair and a gradual but credible reduction in debt levels. "As we have learned from years of experience with crises in both emerging market and advanced economies, the choice between austerity and growth is a false one. The true choice is between austerity and collapse. And that really is no choice at all."[34]

But the BIS's view is outdated. There is a choice, as even the IMF now argues.

CHAPTER SIXTEEN

THE CITADEL CRACKS

"And they said, 'Come, let us build a city, and a tower with its top in the heavens, and let us make a name for ourselves, lest we be dispersed across the whole earth.'" [1]

— Genesis 11.3, The Tower of Babel

The story of the Tower of Babel is often read as a parable of the price of arrogance. Its builders started to construct the tallest building in the world, one that would reach to the very heavens as a physical manifestation of their greatness and ambition. Things ended badly.

The BIS tower, at Centralbahnplatz 2, in Basel does not reach to the heavens, but many of those working inside believe themselves possessed of a near-celestial mandate. Now seventy-three years old, the bank has evolved into one of the world's richest and most influential anachronisms. Montagu Norman's "cozy club" has sixty members. They circle the globe, from Colombia to the Philippines, Iceland to the United Arab Emirates, although the developing world remains underrepresented. The BIS employs around six hundred staff from more than fifty countries. Thousands of central bankers and their officials flock every year to the bank's numerous committees, meetings, and conferences.

Since 2007 the ongoing financial crisis has neither reduced the value of the BIS's assets nor dented its profits and prestige. The bank makes much of its money from the fees and commissions that it charges central banks for its services, such as short-term liquidity and credit, gold swaps, and by providing a range of investment opportunities and instruments. The BIS is a much sought after commercial partner. Its record is solid and conservative, its credit rating superb.

In Basel at least, the crisis has, overall, been good for business. For the financial year ending in March 2009 the bank made net, tax-free, profits of 446.1 million Special Drawing Rights, the equivalent of around $650 million.[2] Its total equity was valued at the equivalent of almost $20 billion.[3] By the end of March 2012, profits had nearly doubled, to the equivalent of around $1.17 billion—almost $100 million a month—and the bank's total equity had increased by 40 percent to around $28 billion.[4] These are extraordinary sums for a single financial institution with just 140 clients and two local offices, in Mexico City and Hong Kong.

Even at a time when the IMF, not usually an advocate of generous public spending, has warned publicly and repeatedly against excessive austerity, at the BIS the legacy of Hjalmar Schacht, Montagu Norman, and Per Jacobssen endures.[5] The bank's managers regularly warn against the dangers of excessive lending and inflation. Austerity is seen as a necessary medicine, no matter how unpleasant its consequences. Such warnings are listened to.

The bank's influence is profound: the BIS is one of the world's most effective instruments of soft power. The bimonthly governors' meeting gathers central bankers from countries that control more than four-fifths of the world's GDP. The discussions at the Basel weekends have shaped the debate about the global financial crisis and the world's response to it. The committees hosted at the BIS are rebuilding the world's financial architecture and coordinating regulatory and supervisory policies. The Basel Committee on Banking Supervision oversees the capital requirement of commercial banks. Its work, wrote Ezra Klein, a columnist for the *Washington Post*, "will shape the future of global finance, and, by extension, the economy." Klein awarded the committee the title of the "Most Obscure-Yet-Important Regulatory Agency of the Year," noting, "its actions may only rarely make the front pages, but the work done in Basel is crucial to creating a more stable world economy."[6] "Obscure yet important" surely brought knowing looks and quiet smiles at the BIS headquarters.

The bank's annual reports are regarded as essential reading in the world's treasuries and governments. The head of the bank's Monetary and Economic Department, who writes and oversees the annual reports, is one of the world's best read and most influential financial and economic analysts and commentators. The BIS hosts one of the world's largest restricted databases of banking information. Its mainframe computers sweep up data about the flow of transnational finance, including money flows in and out of offshore domiciles. Such information is of great interest to governments. Three months after 9/11 the Basel Committee on Banking Supervision hosted a meeting to coordinate central banks' and regulatory authorities' strategies on the prevention of terrorist financing and the sharing of records to prevent terrorist financing.[7]

The Financial Stability Board, hosted at the BIS, is likely to become the fourth pillar of the global financial system, after the BIS itself, the IMF, and the World Bank. The FSB coordinates national financial authorities and regulators. Its members include the Federal Reserve, the ECB, the Bank of England, and the national banks of China, Saudi Arabia, Switzerland, Russia, Japan, and Korea. The IMF, the World Bank, the European Commission, and the BIS itself are also members of the FSB, as are three of the most powerful committees hosted at the BIS: the Basel Committee on Banking Supervision, the Committee on the Global Financial System, and the committee dealing with payment and settlement systems. The writer Matt Taibbi once memorably described Goldman Sachs, the giant investment bank, as a "vampire squid."[8] The BIS is now the vampire squid of the regulatory world, hosting a myriad of committees that in turn spawn a raft of subcommittees, many of which are composed of the same central bankers and officials, each producing reams of reports that are passed back and forth from Basel to national central banks and governments in an endless merry-go-round of resolutions and recommendations.

Others argue that the answer to the banking crisis is not more insider committees and regulatory bodies hosted at the BIS, or anywhere else, but much less, or none at all. "Banking should become a normal industry, like manufacturing bicycles," said Andrew Hilton, of the Centre for the Study of Financial Innovation. "Banking should be regulated to protect against fraud, to protect consumers, and to protect the banks' integrity, but nothing else. That sounds crazy because everyone says that banking is special. Banking is only special because the sums of money flowing through these institutions are so large they can bring society down. If the banks were smaller, if they did simpler things and they were not a systemic threat, either individually or within a cluster, you would not have to regulate them. The banks would take out insurance and the system would be protected."[9]

Such views are regarded with horror in Basel. Yet, the heart of the matter is that BIS is an opaque, elitist, and anti-democratic institution, out of step with the twenty-first century. The BIS should have been closed down in the early 1930s, after the collapse of the German reparations program. Instead it funded the Holocaust and the Nazi war machine. Its staff members, such as Thomas McKittrick and Per Jacobssen, passed vital economic intelligence to the Nazis—often with the knowledge of the Allied authorities. The bank embodied the most cynical kind of capitalism. While millions died, it kept financial channels open across the frontlines.

After 1945 the BIS and its allied committees shaped much of the postwar financial world. Behind the scenes the BIS provided the necessary financial mechanisms, support, and technical expertise for the financial aspects of the Euro-integrationist project. Without the BIS the euro would not exist. The BIS gave birth to the European Central Bank, a bank that is accountable neither to the European Parliament nor to any government, even though it controls the monetary policy of seventeen countries. The BIS has survived through the decades just as it was born—by opacity, secrecy, and by hiding behind a carapace of legal immunities. These protections perpetuate the technocrats' belief that a tiny, self-selecting elite, unaccountable to everyday citizens, should manage global finance. The BIS's privileges are a hangover from a thankfully vanished age of deference to authority, at least in the developed world.

Andrew Crockett, the bank's general manager from 1994 to 2003, did peel back some of the bank's obsessive secrecy. When the BIS was drawn into the torrent of revelations about Swiss banks, looted gold, and collaboration with the Nazis that erupted in 1996–1997, Crockett opened up the bank's wartime archives. It was a sensible decision and a boon for historians and investigators. "Our view was that if anyone had done anything bad it was a long time ago, so there was nothing in it for us to hide it. We decided that the only answer was complete transparency," recalled William White.[10] The bank spent two hundred thousand Swiss francs on specialized computers to digitize and microfilm the records, which had been neglected for decades, and hired a specialist historian, Piet Clement. (Crockett also made himself available for interview on the BIS's wartime record and spoke at length to the author, which is included in the author's 1998 work *Hitler's Secret Bankers: The Myth of Swiss Neutrality During the Holocaust.*) The bank's archives, which are open under the thirty-year rule, are a valuable resource for historians.

But the BIS is far less forthcoming about its present-day governance. The bank's annual reports and other documents are available on its website, and it has a Twitter feed: @bis_org. In February 2013, it had more than thirteen thousand followers. The bank often tweets several times a day, with links to speeches by central bankers as well as studies and working papers published by the bank, thus providing a continuous update to the documents available on the bank's website. But this information is already in the public domain. Information about the bank's internal operations, such as the agenda and themes of the governors' meetings, the elite Economic Consultative Committee, or the attendance list, and the transactions the BIS carries out with the public funds held by central banks whose reserves it manages are not tweeted and nor, at least for the foreseeable future, are they ever likely to be. Rather, the emphasis remains firmly on confidentiality. When the author asked Stephen Cecchetti, the bank's economic adviser, about the high level of secrecy around the governors' meetings and the BIS's activities, he replied, "Banks have confidentiality agreements that bind them not to disclose information about their customers. In the conduct of its banking business, the BIS strives to exceed best practice in its customer relationships."[11]

There is usually no press conference or press statement after the governors' meetings, but the BIS has for years held a press conference after the Annual General Meeting and the release of the annual report. The 2011 gathering, which can be viewed online, was a low-key, even desultory affair.[12] Jaime Caruana, the general manager, read a prepared statement. He and Cecchetti then invited questions from the handful of journalists present. There were four questions: three about the work of the Basel Committee and one about monetary policy. Cecchetti did not speak. The press conference lasted seventeen minutes. The journalists were specialist correspondents. There was no press conference in 2012. The journalists covering the BIS told the bank it was not necessary as the bank releases the annual report with a long embargo and also organizes a teleconference. Had there been a press conference in 2012, a general reporter would have honed in on a much stronger story—one which raises profound questions about the bank's tradition of secrecy, its legal immunities and their implications for the bank's future.

IN 1991 ARGENTINA went bust and defaulted on almost $81 billion worth of debts. The Argentine government eventually offered creditors thirty-five cents on the dollar—previously bankrupt countries had offered fifty to sixty cents. Nonetheless, by 2010 93 percent of creditors had accepted the offer. The remainder, however, were still holding out, demanding a higher payout for their $6 billion worth of debt, including accrued interest. The two main groups are around sixty thousand people in Italy, some of whom bought Argentine bonds to fund their retirement, and a pair of investment funds—Elliott Management and an affiliate, NML Capital—known as "vulture funds," which chase countries in default and which bought many of the bonds in secondary markets. Elliott has chased the Argentine central bank through the American courts. The Italian bondholders are fighting their case at the International Centre for Investment Disputes, which is part of the World Bank group. Both the funds and the Italian investors have won several legal victories.[13]

However, the Argentine central bank has shipped a substantial part of its reserves to the BIS, where the monies are out of the creditors' reach. The funds are now suing the BIS and drawing unwelcome attention to the bank's hyper-privileged legal immunities. The funds allege that the BIS has allowed the Argentine central bank to store between 80 and 90 percent of its $48 billion in foreign reserves in Basel (most central banks keep a small proportion of their reserves there). Lisa Weekes, the bank's head of press, declined to answer detailed questions from the author in December 2012 about the Argentine reserves but pointed to a letter she had published in the *Wall Street Journal* in July 2011.[14]

Weekes confirmed in that letter that the Argentine central bank holds an account at the BIS. The BIS will not disclose the actual sum deposited by the Argentine central bank, citing client confidentiality, but said that the figure of around $40 billion is "grossly overstated." The letter noted that the Swiss Federal Tribunal, Switzerland's highest court, rejected the funds' action and upheld the BIS's immunities, noting that "accepting central banks' deposits is part of the BIS's mission, enabling it to fulfill its statutory function as an international settlement hub for central banks." The BIS, wrote Weekes, like other international organizations, is "protected by immunities that that allow it to carry out its functions in the public interest."

The definition of "public interest," however, looks rather different to the holders of Argentine bonds. The Argentine BIS deposits are a "clear deviation of the bank's standards," wrote Claudio Loser, a former director of the Western Hemisphere Department of the IMF. "The BIS has a serious conflict of interest: it is playing the interests of one national depositor against the interests of many others."[15] In December 2012 the Swiss Federal Council (the Swiss federal government) confirmed that the funds cannot sequester any of the Argentine deposits held at the BIS. The council ruled that there had been no abuse of immunity of the 1987 headquarters agreement between the BIS and the Swiss Federal Council, which governs the bank's legal statues and immunities.

So for now, at least, the BIS seems to have won the battle over the Argentine reserves. But the wider questions remain. What if other countries seek to use the bank as a refuge from their creditors? "Argentina is a big question for the bank," says one former BIS official. "Is the government depositing with the BIS because it is a good place to put its money, or because its deposits are immune and the BIS cannot be sued and forced to surrender them?"[16] The BIS has also helped to repatriate looted money. After the death of the Nigerian dictator Sani Abacha in 1998, the Nigerian authorities pursued hundreds of millions of dollars that had been looted and deposited in Swiss banks. In 2004 the Swiss authorities ordered that almost $500 million be transferred from Swiss banks to a holding account at the BIS for Nigeria, before being transferred to the country's central bank.

The Argentine reserves and the Nigerian looted assets highlight how the BIS's immunities are a double-edged sword: they arguably provide safe haven for a country fleeing its creditors but also ensure that the BIS is the bank of choice for diplomatically sensitive transactions such as the return of looted assets. "It's very important that an institution that is mainly dealing with the central banks of sovereign countries should have full immunity in its financial transactions from the jurisdiction of national legal systems, as do the IMF and World Bank," said Malcolm Knight.[17] Every country dealing with the BIS should be required to sign a single, consistent agreement similar to that required by the IMF, that would provide immunities for all the financial transactions of the BIS with residents of that country, as well as other immunities necessary for the operation of an official international institution, such as immunities for its staff while traveling, said the former BIS general manager.

The BIS "has not become a refuge in any sense at all," said King.

It's very important that in the future sovereign debt issues will not lead a sovereign debtor into a position where it can be exploited by a small minority of creditors who will not go along with the restructuring. The BIS is not special in this debate. This is a much broader debate about how we deal with sovereign debt restructuring. Should creditors such as vulture funds be able to buy their way into sovereign debt and then try and extract a position that is much more favorable to themselves than any other creditor? In the future, sovereign debt should be issued with "collective action clauses" to prevent such holding out behavior, but in a way that is part of the legal rules of the game. The BIS is no different to the IMF or any other international body that has a degree of legal exemption.[18]

The bank's belief that it should be so rigorously protected embodies its central contradiction: that it is shaping the regulatory future of global finance and calls for good governance, yet its own affairs are kept firmly hidden behind a thicket of legal immunities and protections.

THE BIS PROGRESSES through the twentieth-first century with ever more confidence, even though there is no need for it to exist. Its banking services could be carried out by commercial banks, which would be legally bound to observe the necessary confidentiality to prevent market speculation on the central banks' interventions. Its research department and its databases could be relocated to any decent university. Its famed hospitality could be easily replicated in any number of luxury hotels or conference centers. The committees hosted by the BIS that regulate banking and the international financial system could be relocated to the IMF or housed in a new think tank, with open and transparent governance. Breaking down the bank into its constituent parts would help democratize global finance.

Yet the bank is not worried. It has powerful friends, who, it believes, will ensure its inviolability and survival. The Swiss Federal Council, the governing body of the country where the bank is based, has strongly re-affirmed its commitments to the BIS's legal inviolability. The board of directors, which manages the bank's affairs, reads like a who's who of the world's most powerful central bankers. It includes Ben Bernanke, Sir Mervyn King, Mark Carney, Mario Draghi, Jens Weidemann of the Bundesbank, and Zhou Xiaochuan of the Bank of China. The bank's management can reach any one of these with a telephone call, knowing that the governors will make time for them.

The bank's collective memory is reassuring too: in 1945, the BIS outmaneuvered powerful enemies, such as Henry Morgenthau, the US Treasury secretary who wanted the bank to be closed down for collaborating with the Nazis. Whatever legal or political travails may lie ahead, such as the breakup of the Eurozone, a deepening of the financial crisis, or even a new war, banking insiders say there will always be a need for a financial intermediary operating across the lines and behind the scenes.

The BIS helped give birth to the euro and will also be ready to step in should it fail. If the euro crisis worsens and the single currency breaks up, the BIS's expertise will be deemed essential to ensure that the fallout is contained. In early 2013, as this book went to press, there were signs that the Bundesbank, which had been forced against its will to adopt the single currency, was now placing its faith in the oldest store of value of all: gold. The Bundesbank announced that it plans to repatriate 300 tons of the gold it holds in the vaults of the New York Federal Reserve. Germany stores more than two-thirds of its gold reserves, which are worth $183 billion, in New York, Paris, and London. All 374 tons will be removed from Paris, although the German holdings will stay in at the Bank of England.

The decision to move the gold out of Paris but leave it in London was immediately interpreted as a loss of faith in the euro and the supranational project. As the Eurozone and European superstate project totters, gold mania is sweeping through Germany. Humanity's favorite store of value is seen as a safer bet than a currency barely a decade old. In 2012 the German state auditing agency demanded that the Bundesbank carry out an inventory of all German gold stored abroad. Bundesbank officials said that they personally checked all the holdings, which were accounted for. The gold mania would seem very familiar to Hjalmar Schacht and Montagu Norman. Folk memories run deep, especially in Germany, which has twice faced economic meltdown in the last century—in 1918 and 1945. The much-vaunted German economic miracle was always rooted in massive injections of foreign capital, by Wall Street in the 1920s and by the United States government after 1945. Such largesse is unlikely to be repeated nowadays. If the euro collapses, gold is a safer bet than hoping for another transatlantic bailout.

The new emphasis on gold can only be good news for the BIS, and is a return to the bank's roots. As Gianni Toniolo, the author of the BIS official history, notes, the gold standard—fixing the value of a currency to a weight of gold—

was "embedded in the very DNA" of the BIS.[19] The gold standard is long gone, but gold prices continue to rise, and gold still has a powerful hold over investors' psyches. It is certainly ever more central to the BIS's banking operations, so much so that the *Financial Times* has described the bank as "the ultimate bullion pawnbroker."[20] The BIS 2012 annual report revealed that the bank holds 355 metric tons of gold (worth almost $19 billion) in connection with its gold swap contracts, meaning that the bank exchanges currencies for gold, which it returns at the end of the contract.[21]

The BIS would be an essential part of any rescue operation if the euro fell apart, said Rudi Bogni, a veteran international banker. "The BIS could certainly help technically; it has the skills required for any intervention in the markets, should it be required." The BIS could also prove useful in darker scenarios, such a major new war. And it certainly has extensive experience of keeping financial channels open between warring parties. In the modern, globalized economy, pre-serving those links would be judged even more important than in the Second World War. "When people start shooting at each rather than talking to each other, the economies and trade still continue. There is always an interest that is bigger than war," said Bogni. "Even in death you have financial interests that continue after the death of the individual. So in a war where the parties are not dead, they will want to continue those interests after the war."[22] Basel would doubtless, once more, be the place of choice to keep those channels open.

Yet the second decade of the twenty-first century could yet turn out to be the most challenging, even perilous, for the bank. The bank has profited immea-surably from the rapid pace of globalization and economic development and will further do so as new members join from the developing world, all eager to profit from the BIS's expertise and banking services. "There are many emerging market economies for whom the BIS banking operations have real value," said King. "They would feel they would lose something without a bank for central banks."[23]

But the ongoing financial crisis has changed more than banks' balance sheets. Citizens and activists around the world are demanding accountability and transparency from banks and financial institutions. Yet, most have never heard of the BIS, an information deficit that this book has hopefully filled. The bank's management views the BIS's legal inviolability, which is protected—like that of the United Nations and the European Central Bank—by international treaties, as its greatest strength and believes the BIS to be protected in perpetuity. Yet the bank's statutes, written in 1930 for another age, of deference and obedience, may turn out to be its Achilles heel.

The question of the Argentinian reserves raises profound questions about the BIS's legal inviolability. The BIS's immunities could soon be tested again. By early 2013 most observers expected Greece to renegotiate its sovereign debt, which would demand that investors holding Greek bonds would have to take a "haircut" and write off some of the value of their holdings. What would happen, then, if Greece, like Argentina, shifted its foreign reserves to the BIS to avoid angry creditors? If Greece followed Argentina, perceptions of the bank will shift. The BIS's claims of moral probity and of acting in the "public interest" will start to appear decidedly shoddy. For now, the bank has the protection and support of the Swiss courts and the Federal Council. But even in the land of the anonymous, numbered account, public—and legal—opinion is shifting about the country's reputation as a refuge for those seeking legal inviolability. Switzerland is under sustained pressure from the US and European authorities to ease its secrecy and guarantees of anonymity.

As long as Argentine foreign reserves remain out of the creditors' reach, the BIS sets a unsettling precedent: that if a BIS member country defaults, or is about to, it could ship its national reserves to Basel for safekeeping. There are the beginnings here of uncomfortable—for the BIS—parallels with the 1930s and '40s. In March 1939 Montagu Norman, one of the bank's founders and most powerful directors, and Johan Beyen, the BIS's president, refused to stop an order from the National Bank of Czechoslovakia to transfer some of its gold holdings from its BIS subaccount at the Bank of England to the Reichsbank BIS subaccount. It was obvious that the transfer order, given after the Nazis had invaded Czechoslovakia, had been issued under duress. Yet Norman deliberately took the view that the interests of the BIS and the new, transnational financial system were more important than refusing, or even delaying the request. Beyen went along with this decision. The gold was credited to the Reichsbank's account. During the Second World War years, the bank acted as a depositary for looted Nazi gold, even though Thomas McKittrick, the president, was specifically warned that the gold might be stolen. He believed that the bank had no business asking where the gold came from and was anyway protected by its statutes. But even with its powerful allies, the bank still had to fight hard to escape being closed down because of its acceptance of looted gold.

For now, the BIS's statutes and the support of the Swiss legal system ensure that its reserves are untouchable. But laws—and treaties founding international banks—are made in a political context and can be changed. Legal and political pressure could mount. The change in perception of the bank is already happening. Influential analysts and economists, such as Claudio Loser, cited above, are questioning the bank's ethics, behavior, and legal inviolability. In the age of Twitter and Facebook, the BIS, once its central role and importance is known, could yet find itself at the center of a global firestorm.

The BIS's assets may remain untouchable, but as more activists understand the bank's role in the global financial system, its secrecy and elitism, they will increasingly question its operations, role, and need to exist. Such a shift in global perception of the BIS, and the demands to make it more accountable, will bring pressure on politicians, which will then be passed on to the central bank governors, who are independent but still appointed by governments. The controversy over the Argentine reserves could, in turn, corrode the basis of the bank's soft power: its regulation and supervisory frameworks. Commercial banks, might, for example, ask why they should adhere to the Basel Committee's banking rules, when the host bank itself is arguably protecting a central bank against its creditors?

For now, at least, the BIS can rely on its powerful friends. But if the political climate continues shifting toward transparency and accountability, the bank's managers may find that their calls take longer to be returned and are briefer in duration. The bank needs to reform in three areas to ensure its survival: transparency, accountability, and corporate social responsibility.

The first is the simplest. The BIS should hold a press conference after the bimonthly governors' weekends and make it available on the Internet. The bank should publish the attendance list and the broad themes of discussion at the weekend meetings, in particular of the elite Economic Consultative Committee that meets for dinner on Sunday evenings; the Global Economy Meeting the next day, the BIS directors' meeting that deals with the bank's governance, and deliberations of the Markets Committee, which deals with the international financial markets.

The BIS and the central bankers argue that such a move would inhibit discussion. King said,

> *The BIS has moved quite a long way to being open about the state of its finances, its legal position, its board membership, and how it works. The membership of the BIS is well known, and from that you can infer that the governors of the member countries will come to the meetings. The themes and subjects of discussion are of value solely because they are confidential. I would contrast the BIS meetings with the G20 and the IMF where communiqués are published, which purport to be transparent and report what is said. But the expectation of publication constrains useful discussion.*
>
> *The whole point of the BIS conversations is that they are private and are confidential. There has to be a role for private conversations for them to be useful. You cannot have every conversation between central bank governors being minuted and reported. Then there are no useful conversations, simply people making public statements at each other.*
>
> *We don't do deals at Basel. It is too strong to say that this is coordination or harmonization as responsibility, for policy making remains with national central bank committees. The BIS meetings do make us much better informed about why people have done various things and maybe what they intend to do in the future.*[24]

It is true that central bankers do need to be able to speak freely to one another. But there is no need to put a camera in the room and post the video on YouTube or even release a transcript. But the bank should publish minutes: the broad themes of discussion, the lines of debate, and the overall conclusions of the meetings. All the central bankers and officials present at the governors' meetings are public servants, charged with managing national reserves, which are public money. The central bankers are accountable to the citizens who pay their salaries and pensions. It is no longer acceptable for them to gather in a secretive cabal and refuse to release even minimal details of their meetings. The US Federal Reserve is a useful model here. Before each meeting of the Federal Open Markets Committee, the bank releases edited minutes of the previous meeting. The Federal Reserve's website already carries detailed information about which bank officials are attending the BIS weekends and their hour by hour itinerary while in Basel. Neither the Federal Reserve nor the dollar nor even the BIS have collapsed as a result.

Central bankers argue that the comparison is not valid as the BIS is not a decision-making body. King said, "We publish minutes at the Bank of England because we take a formal decision that we have been mandated to take by the UK government. There are no formal decisions like that taken at the BIS. If the BIS was taking interest rate decisions, it would be right to have that degree of transparency. We don't generate decisions at the BIS. We have informal discussions, then we go home and we take our decisions."[25]

Secondly, the BIS should be stripped of its legal inviolability. The BIS is a bizarre hybrid—an extremely profitable commercial banking operation protected by international treaty. Its founding statutes are certainly out of step with the modern age. The statutes provide unnecessary levels of legal protection for a bank dealing in public funds, and they warp the psychology of the BIS. They fuel the peculiar arrogance of much of its senior management. The bank claims to have a mission of public service, yet is structured in such a way that the public is kept as distant as possible, behind the bank's wall of legal immunities. Such a change would demand an Extraordinary General Meeting (EGM). There is a precedent here. In recent years, EGMs were called to change the bank's unit of account from the gold franc to the Special Drawing Right, to forcibly buy back the shares held in private hands, and to distribute the shares held by the former Yugoslavia to its successor states. Voting is decided at EGMs by member central banks. If the governors and officials of the member central banks were mandated by their national governments to vote for the change and modernization, the bank would have to accede to the changes.

Thirdly, such an EGM could also mandate the bank to spend some of its profits on corporate social responsibility and philanthropy. The bank has for decades reaped rich rewards of its stewardship of public funds. In the financial year 2011–2012 the BIS made tax-free profits of almost $100 million each month. It is time to return some of those profits to a wider society, beyond the annual dividends paid to the central bank shareholders. The bank refused to answer questions from the author on how much it spends on charity and philanthropic projects. The words "philanthropy" and "charity" do not appear in the 2011–2012 annual report. Lisa Weekes, the bank's head of press, said that as most of the bank's staff live in or near Basel, the BIS provides "modest financial support for selected initiatives or institutions within the Basel region . . . with a social or cultural purpose."[26] The bank also makes ad hoc donations in response to major natural disasters, such as for the typhoon victims in the Philippines in December 2012, but refuses to say how much.

This is feeble. It is time for the BIS's much-vaunted globalism to extend to its social conscience. The bank should set up a charitable foundation—George Soros's Open Society Institute could be one model—to support global training, education, internship, and development programs for young business people and bankers. One day's worth of annual profit—$3.2 million—would be enough to kick-start such a program, which with the BIS's imprimatur would soon attract corporate sponsorship. The bank's staff could be encouraged to contribute, in lieu of the income tax they are spared. The foundation should be given a block of shares to ensure that civil society has a vote at the bank's annual general meeting. A group of real people at the meeting, outside the charmed circle of the central bankers and their officials, would provide a useful and refreshing reminder that the central bankers' policies and decisions, and those of the BIS, have consequences in the outside world.

Central bankers counter that the BIS already gives something back to society through its numerous seminars and meetings, and by hosting the Financial Stability Institute, which was set up by the BIS and the Basel Committee on Banking Supervision in 1999 to work with financial sector supervisors. King said,

> They do a lot of good work in providing opportunities for smaller members of the BIS to come and learn. There is an informal workshop about governance and the challenges of running a central bank, and smaller members of the BIS have found this of immense value. They belong to a club where they have a chance to quiz their central bank colleagues. At home there was no one to ask for advice. That kind of exchange is invaluable. That is the BIS using the resources of bigger countries to put something back into emerging markets and developing countries.[27]

There are small but encouraging signs that some central bankers understand that with great financial power comes social responsibility. In October 2012, Andrew Haldane, executive director for financial stability at the Bank of England, gave a speech on "Socially Useful Banking" at a meeting hosted by Occupy Economics, the London branch of the social protest movement.[28] The Occupy movement, he said, had helped trigger the first stages of a "reformation of finance." Policymakers were listening to criticism and were acting to close the "fault lines" in the global financial system. "Occupy has been successful in its efforts to popularize the problems of the global financial system for one very simple reason: they are right." Over the years, there had been a "great sucking sound" as "people and monies" were drawn into banking, especially investment banking, draining human and financial resources from the rest of the economy. Even the BIS agrees. Haldane quoted recent research by the bank, which found that when the financial sector reaches a certain level it impedes growth because the financial sector competes with other parts of the economy for scarce resources. "More finance is definitely not always better," wrote Stephen Cecchetti and Enisse Kharroubi.[29]

WHAT THEN DOES the future hold for the BIS? Over the decades, from the Schacht-Norman era, through the Second World War and the birth of the euro, to the present-day jamboree of regulatory committees, the bank has demonstrated an extraordinary ability to make itself essential to the times, repeatedly jettisoning its historical baggage and re-inventing itself to preserve its central place at the heart of the global financial system.

Keenly aware of the growing global hostility toward bankers, the BIS now emphasizes its status as an international organization and its contribution to the common good. This is certainly an effective recruiting tool. "The quality of the people working at the BIS is very high," said King. "It helps, when recruiting really good individuals, to say this is an international institution for which you work, not just a think tank. People like to feel they are working in public service."[30]

But the bank's latest evolution, into a socially responsible institution, may prove the most difficult. Secrecy, opacity, and unaccountability—like gold—are embedded in the bank's DNA. The bank will find it difficult to adjust to the new demands, outlined by Andrew Haldane, that financial institutions be accountable and socially responsible. Yet to survive, it will have to. In an age when information flows as fast as capital, when citizens demand ever more transparency and accountability from the institutions that have power over their lives, when even Wall Street can be occupied for weeks, the Tower of Basel is no longer inviolable.

Unlike its biblical predecessor, the Tower of Basel reaches only eighteen stories above the city skyline. But the fate of the biblical tower-builders should give the bankers pause. For when God saw their work, he confounded their speech and introduced a multitude of tongues. The builders could no longer understand one another. The construction work stopped, they were dispersed, and their tower vanished into history.

Acknowledgments

T his book was born out of a conversation in New York with Clive Priddle, the publisher of PublicAffairs. Clive has been the best editor a writer could hope for: encouraging, insightful, and deeply knowledgeable. My brilliant agent, Elizabeth Sheinkman, of William Morris Endeavor, was an enthusiastic advocate of this project, and Jo Rodgers was always there to help. Numerous friends and colleagues provided encouragement, advice, and ideas, especially Roger Boyes, Justin Leighton, Erik D'Amato, and Nicholas Kabcenell. In New York, Peter Green, Bob Green and Babette Audant were warm and welcoming hosts, while Matt and Emmanuelle Welch in Washington, DC, provided a home from home. In Budapest, I am especially grateful to Flora Hevesi, who diligently transcribed many hours of interviews and never once complained about technical and banking terms. Many thanks to Lori Hobkirk for her production, organization, and editing expertise, to Daisy Bauer for her elegant design, and to Beth Fraser for her diligent copyediting.

Tower of Basel is a book about networks, connections, and the exercise of covert power. Mapping those links is always easier when insiders and former insiders are ready to share their expertise and knowledge. I spoke to numerous sources with firsthand knowledge of the Bank for International Settlements, the world of central banking and related themes. Some prefer to remain anonymous; they know who they are and I am very grateful for their insight. Others did agree to speak on the record. My thanks to Dan Alamariu, Peter Akos Bod, Dean Baker, Geoffrey Bell, Rudi Bogni, Stephen Cecchetti, William de Gelsey, Charles de Vaulx, Adam Gilbert, Richard Hall, Frigyes Hárshegyi,

Andrew Hilton, Zsigmond Járai, Karen Johnson, Sir Mervyn King, Malcolm Knight, William McDonough, Laurence Meyer, Ron Paul, Rupert Pennant-Rea, Nathan Sheets, Paul Volcker, and Peregrine Worsthorne. William White was especially informative and helpful. Thanks also to Sarah Ashley at the Bank of London press office, Gillian Tett, Ralph Atkins, David Dederick, Paul Elston, Barbara Wyllie, Steve Bloomfield at *Monocle*, Jonathan Brandt, John Hubbel Weiss, Peter Grose, John Lloyd, Greg Ip, Peter Rona, William Clothier at Brody House in Budapest, Paulina Bren, Zoltan Markus, Mark Milstein at Northfoto, Alex Kuli, and the folks at the Federal Reserve Press Office. Ryan Avent read the manuscript and shared his insight into the world of central banks while John Shattuck kindly gave me access to the Central European University's library in Budapest. Lee Goddard built me a fine website at www.adamlebor.com.

I am especially grateful to the staff of the following archives: Bank of England; Columbia University Rare Book and Manuscript Library; Federal Reserve Bank of New York; Franklin D. Roosevelt Presidential Library; Seeley G. Mudd Manuscript Library at Princeton University; National Archives, London, and the US National Archives and Records Administration at College Park, Maryland. Special thanks go to my team of researchers. In London, Rosie Whitehouse found valuable material in the Bank of England archives. Elysia Glover diligently searched the records of the Federal Reserve Bank of New York, the archives at Columbia University Library and the Henry Morgenthau diaries, which are held at the Franklin D. Roosevelt Presidential Library in Hyde Park. In Washington, DC, Emmanuelle Welch at French Connection Research (www.frenchpi.com), located a number of valuable documents at the US National Archives. Andras Lengyel and Esther Judah deftly translated from German and French into English.

This book is an unauthorised investigative history of the BIS and has not been read or vetted by any staff member or bank official. However I would like to extend my thanks to several people at the BIS. Edward Atkinson was always insightful, and good-humored as he guided me through the archives. Dr. Piet Clement, the bank's historian, readily shared his knowledge of historical matters, no matter how arcane. Margaret Critchlow and Lisa Weekes at the BIS press office kindly added me to the bank's media mailing list, answered a good number of my questions, provided numerous photographs, and arranged an interview with Stephen Cecchetti, the head of the Monetary and Economic Department.

All works of historical enquiry draw on their predecessors. I am glad to acknowledge the contribution of Professor Gianni Toniolo and Dr. Piet Clement. Their authoritative study of the BIS, *Central Bank Cooperation at the Bank for International Settlements 1930–1973*, is an invaluable work of reference. I am especially grateful to Christopher Simpson, professor of journalism at American University, and to Jason Weixelbaum, a very talented, young historian. Professor Simpson, a pioneer in researching the connection between big business and genocide, was extraordinarily generous with his time and expertise, guiding me through the US National Archives and sharing original documentary material from his own archive. Jason Weixelbaum, an expert in the links between American companies and the Nazis, shared a number of documents about the BIS and allied themes and was also a tenacious researcher. Professor Harold James was generous with his insight into the BIS and the historical backdrop to this book. Donald MacLaren kindly shared his insight into his father's life and work. I am grateful to Helen Scholfield who first contacted me about the extraordinary story of how British secret agents worked against Nazi economic interests in the United States. That episode, like much wartime cross-border economic intrigue, leads back to the BIS.

Thanks most of all to Kati, Danny, and Hannah, for putting up with my long absences, and for daily reminding me that there is indeed life outside the *Tower of Basel*.

Notes

INTRODUCTION

1. Gates McGarrah, "A Balance Wheel of World Credit," *Nation's Business*, March 1931, 24. BIS archive, File 7.18 (2), MCG8/55.

2. Jon Hilsenrath and Brian Blackstone, "Inside the Risky Bets of Central Banks," *Wall Street Journal*, December 12, 2012.

3. Sir Mervyn King interview with the author, in London, February 2013.

4. Paul Volcker, interview with the author, in New York, May 2012.

5. Peter Akos Bod, interview with the author, in Budapest, October 2011.

6. Laurence Meyer interview with the author, in Washington, DC, May 2012.

7. Agreement between the Swiss Federal Council and the Bank for International Settlements to determine the bank's legal status in Switzerland, February 10, 1987, amended effective January 1, 2003. Available for download at http://www.bis.org/about/headquart-en.pdf.

8. Memorandum A, "Benefits which the US might be expected to derive from representation on the board of the BIS," October 16, 1935, NARA, MD. RG 82—FRS, NWCH, box 13.

9. Charles Coombs, *The Arena of International Finance* (New York: John Wiley, 1976), 26.

10. "King: Ace or Joker," *Economist*, March 31, 2012.

11. Harold Callender, "The Iron-Willed Pilot of Nazi Finance," *New York Times*, March 4, 1934.

12. Coombs, op. cit., 26.

13. http://www.bis.org/about/index.htm.

14. The International Monetary Fund, as its name indicates, is a fund, rather than a

bank. The IMF supplies credit to its 188 member countries and imposes strict conditions on the loans, often demanding changes in governments' economic and fiscal policies. The World Bank Group is composed of five agencies, including the International Bank for Reconstruction and Development, and lends money to poor, low, and middle-income countries. The World Bank Group's aim is to relieve poverty, not to make a profit.

15. http://www.investopedia.com/terms/b/basel_i.asp#axzz2JIIsrfcm.

16. Gianni Toniolo, *Central Bank Co-operation at the Bank for International Settlements 1930–1973* (London: Cambridge University Press, 2005), xiii.

17. World Gold Council, World Official Gold Holdings, February 2012.

CHAPTER ONE: THE BANKERS KNOW BEST

1. Gianni Toniolo, *Central Bank Co-operation at the Bank for International Settlements 1930–1973* (London: Cambridge University Press, 2005), 30.

2. Kathleen Woodward, "Montagu Norman: Banker and Legend," *New York Times*, April 17, 1932.

3. Peregrine Worsthorne interview with Rosie Whitehouse, carried out for the author in Hedgerley, England, March 2012.

4. John Weitz, *Hitler's Banker* (London: Warner Books, 1999), 71.

5. Op. cit., 73.

6. Liaquat Ahamed, *Lords of Finance* (London: Windmill Books, 2010), 216.

7. Op cit, 327.

8. Ibid, 332.

9. Hjalmar Schacht, *Confessions of the Old Wizard* (NY: Houghton Mifflin, 1956), 232.

10. Op cit., 235.

11. Andrew Boyle, *Montagu Norman* (London: Cassell, 1967), 247.

CHAPTER TWO: A COZY CLUB IN BASEL

1. Peter Grose, *Gentleman Spy: The Life of Allen Dulles* (Boston: Houghton Mifflin, 1994), 30.

2. Op. cit., 101.

3. Allen Dulles to Leon Fraser, September 3, 1930. BIS archive, File 7.18 (2) MCG, 10/76.

4. Paul Warburg to Leon Fraser, May 28, 1930. BIS archive, File 7.18 (2) MCG, 10/76.

5. Ronald W. Preussen, *John Foster Dulles: The Road to Power* (NY: The Free Press, 1982), 70–71.

6. Op. cit., 72.

7. Gianni Toniolo, *Central Bank Co-operation at the Bank for International Settlements 1930–1973*, 49.

8. Op. cit., 51.

9. Clarence K. Streit, "A Cashless Bank That Deals in Millions," *New York Times Magazine*, July 27, 1930.

10. Gates McGarrah to H. C. F. Finlayson, February 9, 1931. BIS archive, File 7.18 (2) MCG, 4.23.

11. Op cit.

12. Ibid.

13. John Weitz, *Hitler's Banker* (London: Warner Books, 1999), 110.

14. Nancy Lisagor and Frank Lipsius, *A Law Unto Itself: The Untold Story of Sullivan and Cromwell* (NY: William Morrow and Company, 1988), 120.

15. Gates McGarrah to George Harrison, September 22, 1930. BIS archive, File 7.18 (2) MCG, 6/48.

16. Op cit.

17. BIS, *First Annual Report* (Basel: 1931), 1.

CHAPTER THREE: A MOST USEFUL BANK

1. Quoted in Toniolo, *Central Bank Co-operation at the Bank for International Settlements 1930–1973*, 59.

2. Op. cit., 58.

3. Ibid., 59.

4. Ibid., 59.

5. Ibid., 106.

6. Hew Strachan, *Financing the First World War* (NY: Oxford University Press, 2004), 28.

7. Niall Ferguson, *Paper and Iron: Hamburg Business and German Politics in the Era of Inflation, 1897–1927* (London: Cambridge University Press, 2002), 117.

8. Pierre Mendes-France, *La BRI Son rôle dans la vie économique mondiale*, published in *L'Espirit International*, July 1, 1930, 362.

9. Ibid.

10. Toniolo, 46.

11. Gates McGarrah to John Foster Dulles, October 14, 1930. BIS archive, File 7.18 (2) MCG, 7/53.

12. Eleanor Dulles, *The BIS at Work* (NY: Macmillan, 1932), 480.

13. Weitz, *Hitler's Banker*, 106.

14. Gates McGarrah to Leon Fraser, BIS archive, File 7.18 (2) MCG, 12/20a.

15. Interrogation of Kurt Freiherr von Schröder, November 13, 1945. Charles Higham collection, "Trading with the Enemy" Collection, Box 3, Folder 6, University of Southern California Cinematic Arts Library.

16. Op cit.

17. This document, in German, can be accessed at http://www.ns-archiv.de/krieg/1933/04-01-1933.

18. Donald MacLaren, British intelligence dossier on Hermann Schmitz, part of "Brief for the De-Nazification of the German Chemical Industry," December 1, 1945. Author's collection.

19. Joseph Borkin, *The Crime and Punishment of IG Farben* (New York: The Free Press, 1978), 51.

20. Ronald W. Pruessen, *John Foster Dulles* (New York: The Free Press, 1982), 129.

21. Toniolo, 154.

22. Gates McGarrah to Johan Willem Beyen, June 27, 1935. BIS archive, 7.18 (2) MCG, 12/79a.

23. Op. cit.

24. Ibid.

CHAPTER FOUR: MR. NORMAN TAKES A TRAIN

1. Paraphrase of telegram received, from Cochran, American Embassy, Paris, May 9, 1939, no. 907. Franklin D. Roosevelt Presidential Library, Hyde Park, NY. Henry Morgenthau Papers. Book 189, 1–3.

2. Toniolo, *Central Bank Co-operation at the Bank for International Settlements 1930–1973*, 131.

3. Gates McGarrah, "A Balance Wheel of World Credit," *Nation's Business*, March 1931, 24. BIS archive, File 7.18 (2), MCG8/55.

4. Henry M. Christman, editor, *Essential Works of Lenin: "What Is to Be Done?" and Other Writings* (NY: Dover Publications, 1987), 202–203.

5. "Watch Mr. Norman," *News Chronicle*, January 5, 1939. Press cuttings file, Bank of England Archives.

6. "Public Should Know What He Is Doing There," *Daily Herald*, January 6, 1939.

7. Frederick T. Birchall, "Schacht Honored on Sixtieth Birthday," *New York Times*, January 23 1937.

8. The Nikor Project, "Nazi Conspiracy and Aggression: Individual Responsibility of Defendants, Hjalmar Schacht," part three of thirteen, accessed at http://www.nizkor.org /hweb/imt/nca/nca-02/nca-02-16-responsibility-12-03-01.html.

9. H. R. Trevor-Roper, *Hitler's Secret Conversations, 1941–1944* (NY: Farrar, Straus and Young, 1953), 432–433.

10. Hjalmar Schacht, *Confessions of the Old Wizard* (Boston: Houghton Mifflin, 1956), 356.

11. Op. cit, 304.

12. Ibid., 357, 358.

13. Paraphrase of Sections Six and Seven, from Cochran, American Embassy, Paris, May 9, 1939, no 907. FDRPL. Henry Morgenthau Papers. Book 189, pp. 6-11.

14. W. Randolph Burgess notes for meeting of the Federal Reserve Board, October 30, 1931. NARA, RG 82- FRS, NWCH.

15. Andrew Boyle, *Montagu Norman* (London: Cassell, 1967), 281.

16. Op. cit, 281.

17. Diarmuid Jeffreys, *Hell's Cartel: IG Farben and the Making of Hitler's War Machine* (London: Bloomsbury, 2009), 210.

18. Quoted in Toniolo, 195.

19. Bretton Woods Conference, Reel 216, Book 755, page 117. FDRPL. Henry Morgenthau Papers.

20. Tereixa Constenla, "How Franco Banked on Victory," *El Pais* (English), June 13, 2012.

21. Pablo Martín-Aceña, Elena Martínez Ruiz, and María A. Pons, "War and Economics: Spanish Civil War Finances Revisited," Working papers on Economic History, Universidad de Alcala, in Madrid, WP-04-10, December 2010.

22. BIS, *Seventh Annual Report* (BIS: Basel, 1937), 49.

23. Constenla, "How Franco Banked on Victory."

CHAPTER FIVE: AN AUTHORIZED PLUNDER

1. Paul Elston, "Banking with Hitler," *BBC Timewatch* documentary, 1998. Accessed online at http://www.youtube.com/watch?v=YauM5dHLn1s.

2. Douglas Jay, "£10,000,000—And Norman's Fault," *Daily Herald*, June 21, 1939.

Press cuttings files, Bank of England Archives.

3. Elston, "Banking with Hitler."

4. Toniolo, *Central Bank Co-operation at the Bank for International Settlements 1930–1973*, 209.

5. Op. cit., 208.

6. Ibid., 210.

7. Montague Norman to Johan Beyen, May 25, 1939. BIS archive, File 2.22e, Vol 1.

8. George Harrison to Marriner Eccles, April 6, 1939. Columbia University, Harrison, Volume 57. Miscellaneous letters and reports, Volume V, 1940.

9. Op. cit.

10. Ibid.

11. Extract from the minutes of the ninety-third meeting of the Board of Directors held in Basel, June 12, 1939. BIS archive. File 2.22e, Vol. 1.

12. Josef Malik to Thomas McKittrick, June 16, 1945. BIS archive, File 2.22, volume 1.

13. "Sees British Hands Tied on Czech Gold," *New York Times*, June 6, 1939.

14. Toniolo, 187.

15. Milton Friedman, "The Island of Stone Money," Working Papers in Economics, E-91-3. The Hoover Institution, Stanford University, February 1991.

16. Op. cit.

17. John Weitz, *Hitler's Banker* (London: Time Warner, 1999), 244.

18. Andrew Boyle, *Montagu Norman* (London: Cassell, 1967), 309.

CHAPTER SIX: HITLER'S AMERICAN BANKER

1. Winant to State Department, July 10, 1941. Telegram 2939. NARA. Author's collection.

2. Cochran to the State Department, May 9, 1939. Telegram 907. FDRPL. Henry Morgenthau Papers, Book 189, 1–9 and 11–14.

3. Thomas McKittrick interview with R. R. Challener, July 1964. John Foster Dulles Oral Collection at Seeley G. Mudd Manuscript Library, Princeton University Library, 7.

4. Higginson & Co., Paris Office, Copies of Cable & Telegraphic Correspondence—German Gov't Short Term Financing, September 19, 1930. Thomas H. McKittrick Papers. Harvard University Business School, Baker Library Series 2, Carton 6, Folder 13, Reel 10.

5. Gates McGarrah to John Foster Dulles, October 14, 1930. BIS archive, File 7.18

(2) MCG, 7/53.

6. McKittrick interview, 9, 10.

7. McKittrick correspondence with Kenneth Brown Baker, September 25, 1939, and October 19, 1939. Thomas H. McKittrick Papers. HUBL, Baker Library, Series 2, sub-series 2.1, Carton 5, file 18.

8. Mattuck to McKittrick, November 23, 1938. Thomas H. McKittrick Papers. HUBL, Baker Library, Series 2, sub-series 2.1, Carton 5, file 17.

9. McKittrick to Harrison, August 28, 1942. Thomas H. McKittrick Papers. HUBL, Baker Library, Series 2, sub-series 2.1, Carton 6, file 1.

10. McKittrick memo to staff, June 11, 1940. BIS archive, McKittrick papers. Series 2, Business papers 2.2, Carton 10, f.11 Neutrality file.

11. McKittrick to Baranski, May 1, 1940. Thomas H. McKittrick Papers. HUBL, Baker Library, Series 2, Carton 6, Folder 20, Reel 12.

12. McKittrick interview, 19.

13. McKittrick to Cochran, September 2, 1940. FDRPL. Henry Morgenthau Papers. Reel 83, Books 302, 3–5.

14. McKittrick interview, 13–15.

15. Ibid.

16. Winant to the State Department, telegram 2939, July 10, 1941. NARA. Author's collection.

17. Ibid.

18. McKittrick interview, 37.

19. Quoted in Toniolo, 225.

20. Ibid., 229.

21. Currently, there are no figures available for the total amount of foreign exchange bought and sold by the BIS to its various counterparties, including the Reichsbank, during the war years. The information is available in the BIS archives in the files dealing with BIS- Reichsbank transactions, and the BIS's foreign exchange records, but has not been compiled. Most of the transactions involve the Reichsbank, selling Swiss francs to the BIS to cover the interest payments on the bank's investments in Germany. These transactions were usually in the range of 200,000 to 300,000 Swiss Francs, but they ended in January 1943 when the Reichsbank began paying its obligations to the BIS in looted gold. The author is grateful to Piet Clements, the BIS historian, for this information.

22. Erin E. Jacobssen, *A Life for Sound Money: Per Jacobssen, His Biography* (Oxford: Clarendon Press, 1979), 165.

23. Toniolo, 227. Toniolo references the final report by the Swiss Independent Commission of Experts on Switzerland in the Second World War, published in 2002.

24. Interrogation reports, Devisenschutzkommando, May 29, 1945. United Kingdom National Archives, London. FO 1046/763, German Loot.

25. Op. cit.

26. Lucas Delattre, *A Spy at the Heart of the Third Reich* (London: Grove Press/Atlantic Monthly Press 2006), 198.

27. Elizabeth Olson, "Report Says Swiss Knew Some Nazi Gold Was Stolen," *New York Times*, May 26, 1998.

28. Schmitz to Thomas McMittrick, January 3, 1941. Thomas H. McKittrick Papers. HUBL, Baker Library, Series 2, Carton 5, Folder 25, Reel 9.

29. Fraser to McKittrick, November 20, 1940. Thomas H. McKittrick Papers. HUBL, Baker Library, Series 2, Carton 8, Folder 18, Reel 18.

30. Ibid.

31. Ibid.

32. Quoted in Toniolo, 227.

33. Norman to McKittrick, June 12, 1942. Thomas H. McKittrick Papers, HUBL, series 2.2, carton 8, folder 1–2, Correspondence Bank of England 1939–1946.

34. Ibid.

35. Rooth to Norman, September 17, 1942. BIS archive, Thomas H. McKittrick Papers. Series 2, Business papers, 2.2 Carton 10, f.11 Neutrality file.

36. McKittrick memorandum of conversation with President Weber at Swiss National Bank, in Bern, June 7, 1940. HUBL. Thomas H. McKittrick Papers Series 2, Carton 6, Folder 21, Reel 11.

37. Quoted in Toniolo, 225.

38. Ibid.

39. Memorandum from Marcel Pilet-Golaz, October 2, 1942. BIS archive, McKittrick papers. Series 2.2, Business papers, Carton 10, f.11 Neutrality file.

40. Op. cit.

41. Ibid.

42. Ibid.

43. Ibid.

CHAPTER SEVEN: REASSURING WALL STREET

1. Lithgow Osborne to William Donovan, Conversation with McKittrick. December 14, 1942, December 14 1942. NARA. RG 226 OSS records. Entry 92, box 168.

2. McKittrick memo, Trip Basel to Lisbon (undated). BIS Archive, Thomas H. McKittrick Papers, Series 2 Business Papers, 2.2, Carton 9, journeys.

3. Thomas McKittrick interview with R. R. Challener, July 1964. John Foster Dulles Oral History Collection at Seeley G. Mudd Manuscript Library, Princeton University Library, 24.

4. McKittrick interview, 22.

5. Choles to Huddle, February 17, 1943. NARA, RG 84, American Legation, Bern, General Records, 1936–1949. 1943: 850–851.6, Box 92.

6. McKittrick to Harrison, November 15, 1943. NARA, RG 84, American Legation, Bern, General Records, 1936–1949. 1943: 850–851.6, Box 92.

7. Foley to Morgenthau, June 2 1942. NARA Treasury Department. Author's collection.

8. McKittrick interview, 34.

9. McKittrick interview, 31.

10. McKittrick to Fraser, April 22, 1941. Thomas H. McKittrick Papers. Harvard Business School, Baker Library Series 2, Carton 8, Folder 18, Reel 18.

11. McKittrick interview, 31.

12. Osborne to Donovan, op cit.

13. McKittrick memo on conversation with von Trott zu Solz, June 10, 1941. BISA Series 2.2 Business papers. Carton 9, confidential memoranda, f.19.

14. Osborne to Donovan, ibid.

15. Acceptances for Fraser Dinner for Mr. T. H. McKittrick at the University Club, December 17, 1942. Thomas H. McKittrick Papers. Harvard University Business School, Baker Library, Series 2, Carton 8, Folder 18, Reel 17. See also the work of Jason Weixelbaum, in particular "The Contradiction of Neutrality and International Finance: The Presidency of Thomas H. McKittrick at the Bank for International Settlements in Basel 1940–46," May 2010, available at http://jasonweixelbaum.wordpress.com /tag/thomas-h-mckittrick, and "Following the Money: An Exploration of the Relationship between American Finance and Nazi Germany," December 2009, available at http://jasonweixelbaum.wordpress.com/2009/12/21/following-the-money-an-exploration-of-the-relationship-between-american-finance-and-nazi-germany.

16. William M. Tuttle Jr., "The Birth of an Industry: the Synthetic Rubber 'Mess' in World War II," *Technology and Culture*, January 1981, 40.

17. Ibid., 41.

18. *The United States of America vs. Carl Krauch et al* (IG Farben trial). U.S. Military Tribunal, Nuremberg, July 30, 1948, 146. Available at http://www.werle.rewi.hu-berlin.de/IGFarbenCase.pdf.

19. Donald MacLaren, "Description of Work," undated, ca.1943–1944, author's collection.

20. Ibid.

21. The Standard Oil Company of New Jersey renamed itself Exxon in 1972. Exxon merged with Mobil in 1999 to become Exxon Mobil. The firm's international trade name is Esso—the phonetic transcribing of S-O, the initials of Standard Oil. Standard Oil's archives are held at the Exxon Mobil Historical Collection at the Briscoe Center for American History at the University of Texas at Austin and doubtless contain much of interest.

22. Rudy Kennedy interview with author, November 12, 1999.

23. Ibid.

24. "Rudy Kennedy: Holocaust Survivor, Scientist and Campaigner," *The Times* (of London), March 3, 2009.

25. Rudy Kennedy survived in Auschwitz for almost two years. In January 1945 he was moved to Dora-Mittelbau where V-1 and V-2 rockets were manufactured by Werner von Braun, the Nazi rocket scientist whom Allen Dulles later brought to the United States. Kennedy was then sent to Belsen where he was liberated by British troops in April 1945. After the war he settled in Britain and became a successful businessman and campaigner for justice for former slave laborers. Kennedy fought tirelessly for decades against IG Farben, its successor companies, and the German government, demanding that the company accept liability and pay adequate compensation. Under great pressure from the State Department, organizations representing slave laborers eventually signed an agreement in 2000 that paid around $7,000 to each victim. IG Farben's successor companies contributed to the settlement. Those accepting the offer were forced to surrender any future claims. Kennedy refused to sign and carried on campaigning. He died in 2008 at the age of eighty-one.

26. See R. Billstein, *Working for the Enemy: Ford, General Motors and Forced Labor in Germany During the Second World War* (New York: Berghahn Books, 2000). In the

late 1990s Ford opened its archives and commissioned archivists and historians to scrutinize its wartime record. Their findings are compiled in a 208-page report, published in 2001. "Research Findings About Ford-Werke Under the Nazi Regime," is available at http://media.ford.com/article _display.cfm?article_id=10379. The report also notes that Ford and its subsidiaries in Allied countries made a crucial contribution to the Allied war effort, producing vast amounts of aircraft, military vehicles, engines, generators, tanks, and military ordinance.

27. Michael Dobbs, "Ford and GM Scrutinized for Alleged Nazi Collaboration," *Washington Post*, Nov 30, 1998. At this time General Motors opened its archives to the historian Henry Ashby Turner Jr., the author of *German Big Business and the Rise of Hitler*, which downplayed the role of the industrialists in supporting the Nazis. In 2005 Turner published *General Motors and the Nazis: The Struggle for Control of Opel, Europe's Biggest Carmaker*. The book argued that by 1939 General Motors had lost control of its German subsidiary and so had no power over Opel's military production or use of slave labor. This view is not universally accepted.

28. Messersmith to Philips, November 16, 1934. Special Collections Department, University of Delaware Library. Available online at http://www.lib.udel.edu/ud/spec/ findaids /html/mss0109.html.

29. Op. cit.

30. "Thomas J. Watson Is Decorated by Hitler," *New York Times*, July 2, 1937.

31. Christopher Simpson, *The Splendid Blond Beast: Money, Law, And Genocide in the Twentieth Century* (Monroe, ME: Common Courage Press, 1995), 73.

32. Edwin Black, *IBM and the Holocaust: The Strategic Alliance Between Nazi Germany and America's Most Powerful Corporation* (Westport, CT: Dialogue Press, 2008).

33. Messersmith to Geist, December 8, 1938. Special Collections Department, University of Delaware Library. Available at http://www.lib.udel.edu/ud/spec/findaids/ html/mss0109.html.

34. Messersmith to Long, April 7, 1941. Special Collections Department, University of Delaware Library, April 7, 1941. Available at http://www.lib.udel.edu/ud/spec/ findaids/html/mss0109.html.

35. Nuremberg Trial Proceedings, May 6, 1946. William Dodd to Walter Funk. Available at http://avalon.law.yale.edu/imt/05-06-46.asp.

36. Cochran to Morgenthau, October 3, 1940. NARA. US Department of Treasury. Author's collection.

37. Paul Gewirts, US Department of Treasury, Corporate Analysis Unit, "Report on the Activities of the Chase Bank Branches in France," April 3, 1945, 1. University of Southern California Cinematic Arts Library. Charles Higham "Trading with the Enemy" Collection. Box 1, Folder 3.

38. Op. cit.

39. Ibid.

40. Matthew J. Marks, Memorandum for Mr. Ball, US Department of Treasury, "Investigation of Morgan et Cie," April 26, 1945. University of Southern California Cinematic Arts Library. Charles Higham "Trading with the Enemy" Collection, Box 1, Folder 3.

41. Ibid. In December 1998 lawyers acting on behalf of Holocaust victims and their families filed a class action lawsuit in New York against Chase Manhattan bank, J. P. Morgan, and seven French banks, alleging that the US banks' French subsidiaries were complicit in the seizure of the wealth of French Jews who were deported to concentration camps. Chase Manhattan said the suit was "unnecessary" as it was working with Jewish organizations to examine its historical records to identify former customers or their heirs, and pay the customers, or their heirs, with interest. J. P. Morgan soon agreed to settle for $2.75 million. Much of this remained unclaimed and those monies were donated in 2003 to Yeshiva University in New York to endow a center for Holocaust studies. J. P. Morgan and Chase Manhattan merged in 2002 to become J. P. Morgan, Chase & Co. The claims against Chase Manhattan were dealt with by the Drai Commission, a French government organization, which oversaw restitution claims against French banks. The class action lawsuit was one of several targeting American, Swiss, British, and other European banks over their wartime records. Swiss banks eventually agreed to pay restitution of around $1.25 billion. Barclays Bank, in Britain, agreed to pay out $3.6 million to compensate families who had lost assets in France during the Nazi occupation. See: Michael J. Bazyler, *Holocaust Justice: The Battle for Restitution in America's Courts* (New York: New York University Press, 2005).

42. McKittrick to Weber, January 12, 1943. Thomas H. McKittrick Papers. Harvard Business School, Baker Library. Series 2, Carton 8, Folder 18, Reel 17.

43. McKittrick interview, 32.

44. Op cit., 35, 36.

CHAPTER EIGHT: AN ARRANGEMENT WITH THE ENEMY

1. Col. Edward Gamble, Office of Strategic Services, European Theater of Operations, United States Army (Forward), June 15 1945. BIS Archive. Thomas H. McKittrick Papers. Series 2.2, Carton 9, Journeys.

2. Thomas McKittrick interview with R. R. Challener, July 1964. John Foster Dulles Oral History Collection at Seeley G. Mudd Manuscript Library, Princeton University Library, 22.

3. Ibid., 40.

4. Cable from US Legation in Bern, June 23, 1943. NARA. RG 84, American Legation, Bern, General Records. 1943: 850–851.6, Box 92.

5. Neal H. Petersen, *From Hitler's Doorstep: The Wartime Intelligence Reports of Allen Dulles 1942–1945* (University Park, PA: Penn State Press, 1996), 294–295.

6. Ibid., 287.

7. McKittrick to Wallenberg, June 9, 1943. BIS Archive. Thomas H. McKittrick Papers. Series 2.1, Carton 6, f.2.

8. Hewitt report on the Wallenbergs, undated. US National Archives and Records Administration. RG 226, Entry A1-210, Box 345.

9. Ibid.

10. Morgenthau to Grew, "A Summary of Some Information with Respect to the Wallenbergs and the Enskilda Bank," February 7, 1945. NARA. Author's collection.

11. Ibid.

12. Richard Breitman, "A Deal with the Nazi Dictatorship: Hitler's Alleged Emissaries in Autumn 1943," *Journal of Contemporary History*, vol. 30., no. 3, July 1995.

13. Williamson to Dulles, February 1, 1945. NARA. RG 226 OSS, Entry 190, Box 31.

14. Op. cit.

15. Henry Morgenthau diaries, Franklin D. Roosevelt Memorial Library. Book 755, Reel 216, 175.

16. Playfair to Niemeyer, December 6, 1943. Bank of England Archives.

17. Morgenthau diaries, FDRML. July 19, 1944, 9:30 p.m. Book 756, 54.

18. Morgenthau diaries, FDRML. Book 755, Reel 216, 178.

19. Op. cit., 183.

20. Keynes to Morgenthau, July 19, 1944. FRDML. Author's collection.

21. Henry Morgenthau diaries, FRDML, Book 756, July 19, 1944, 7:25 p.m., 134.

22. Toniolo, 271.

23. Ibid., 272.

24. Orvis Schmidt to Henry Morgenthau, March 23, 1945, FDRML. Reel 241, Book 831, 328–333.

25. Op. cit.

26. Ibid.

27. "Survey of the War-Time Activities of the Bank for International Settlements," TWX Conversation between Washington and Berlin, Col. Bernstein, Miss Mayer, Mr. Ritchin, and Mr. Nixon; and Thorson, "Capt. Zap: Investigation by Bernstein's Associates," Donald W. Curtis and William V. Dunkel, December 5, 1945. University of Southern California Cinematic Arts Library. Charles Higham "Trading with the Enemy," Collection. Box 1, Folder 1.

28. Erin E. Jacobssen, *A Life for Sound Money: Per Jacobssen* (Oxford: Clarendon Press, 1979), 163–164.

29. Ibid., 165.

30. Ibid.,178.

31. Ibid.,178.

32. Ibid., 153.

33. Heinz Pol, "IG Farben's Peace Offer," *The Protestant*, June–July 1943, 41.

34. Ibid.

35. Jacobssen, 170.

36. McKittrick to Auboin, January 22, 1946. HUBL. Thomas H. McKittrick Papers. Series 2, Carton 8, Folder 4, Reel 17.

37. McKittrick to Dulles, October 17, 1945.BIS Archive. Thomas H. McKittrick Papers. Series 2.1, Carton 6, f.3.

CHAPTER NINE: UNITED STATES TO EUROPE: UNITE, OR ELSE

1. Oral history interview with W. Averell Harriman, Washington, DC, 1971. Harry S. Truman Library and Museum. Available at http://www.trumanlibrary.org./oralhist /harriman.htm.

2. Thomas McKittrick interview, July 1964. John Foster Dulles Oral History Collection at Seeley G. Mudd Manuscript Library, Princeton University Library, 45.

3. McKittrick to Aldrich, Dec. 12, 1945. Thomas H. McKittrick Papers. Harvard University Business School, Baker Library Series 2, Carton 8, Folder 18, Reel 18.

4. Allen Dulles, "The Future of Germany," *The Commercial & Financial Chronicle*, vol. 163, no. 4458. Author's collection, with thanks to Christopher Simpson.

5. Accessed at http://www.oecd.org/general/organisationforeuropeaneconomiccooperation.htm.

6. McKittrick interview, 45.

7. James M. Boughton, "Harry Dexter White and the International Monetary Fund," *Finance and Development* magazine, September 1998.

8. R. Bruce Craig, *Treasonable Doubt: The Harry Dexter White Spy Case* (Lawrence, KS: University Press of Kansas, 2004).

9. James C. Van Hook, "Review of Treasonable Doubt: The Harry Dexter White Spy Case by R. Bruce Craig," *Studies in Intelligence*, vol. 49, no. 1, April 2007.

10. Accessed at http://usa.usembassy.de/etexts/ga4-mccloy.htm.

11. Robert Taylor Swaine, "The Cravath Firm and its Predecessors 1819–1947," *The Lawbook Exchange Ltd*, New Jersey, 611.

12. Ibid., 610–611.

13. "Alkali Exporters Held Trade Cartel," *New York Times*, August 13, 1949.

14. Rudolf Vrba and Alfred Wexler, two Jewish inmates, escaped from Auschwitz in April 1944. They wrote a detailed, thirty-page report about conditions inside the camp, the operations of the gas chambers, and the preparations for the extermination of Hungarian Jewry. The document, known as the "Auschwitz Protocol," was distributed to the Vatican, the International Committee of the Red Cross, Allied governments, and Jewish leaders. See Martin Gilbert, *Auschwitz and the Allies* (London: Michael Joseph, 1981).

15. David S. Wyman, *The Abandonment of the Jews* (NY: Pantheon, 1948), 296.

16. Harriman interview, ibid.

17. May to J. W. Pehle, Treasury official, August 18, 1941; Examiner's report, October 5, 1942. NARA. Author's collection.

18. Federal Register, Vesting Order 248, November 7, 1942, page 9097, author's collection)

CHAPTER TEN: ALL IS FORGIVEN

1. Major Donald MacLaren, "Brief for the De-Nazification of the German Chemical Industry," Part III, Dossiers of Principal IG Farben Officials, Hermann Schmitz. December 1, 1945. Author's collection.

2. Ron Chernow, *The Warburgs* (NY: Vintage, 1994), 501–502.

3. Ibid., 583.

4. David R. Henderson, "German Economic Miracle: The Concise Encyclopedia of Economics," available at http://www.econlib.org/library/Enc/GermanEconomicMiracle.html.

5. Author telephone interview with Dr. Adam Tooze, author of *The Wages of Destruction: The Making and Breaking of the Nazi Economy* (NY: Penguin, 2009), May 2009.

6. Quoted in Weitz, 314.

7. David Marsh, *The Bundesbank* (London: Heinemann, 1992), 19.

8. Ibid., 137.

9. Tom Bower, *Blind Eye to Murder: Britain, America and the Purging of Nazi Germany* (London: Andre Deutsch, 1981), 18. Bower's information is based on his interview with Hermann Abs.

10. Ibid., 15.

11. Ibid.

12. See Harold James: *The Deutsche Bank and the Nazi Economic War Against the Jews.* (London: Cambridge University Press, 1981).

13. Alfred C. Mierzejewski, *Ludwig Erhard* (Chapel Hill: Univ. of North Carolina Press, 2006), 19–22.

14. John Easton, Economic Warfare Division, to Secretary of State, London, November 27, 1944. NARA. Author's collection.

15. Henry Morgenthau diaries, Book 755, Bretton Woods, July 16–18, 1944, pages 9 and 21.

16. Ibid.

17. Dulles cable, March 21, 1945. NARA. RG 226, Entry 134, Box 162.

18. Donald MacLaren, Brief for the De-Nazification of the German Chemical Industry, Introduction, December 1, 1945. Author's collection.

19. Otto Ambrus, Wollheim Memorial. Available at http://www.wollheim-memorial.de/en/otto_ambros_19011990.

20. Kai Bird, *The Chairman: John J. McCloy and the Making of the American Establishment* (NY: Simon and Schuster, 1992), 369–371.

21. Jeffreys, 346.

22. Chernow, *The Warburgs*, 576–577.

23. Simpson, 146–147.

24. Ibid., 136–137.

25. Murphy to Secretary of State, December 10, 1945. NARA. RG 59, Lot 61, D33, Box 1, file "War Crimes, International Military Tribunal folder A-1."

26. Harrison to Secretary of State, December 13, 1945. NARA. RG 59, Lot 61, D33, Box 1, file "War Crimes, International Military Tribunal folder A-1."

27. Simpson, 228–229.

28. Ibid., 235.

29. Bower, *Blind Eye to Murder*, 347.

30. Priscilla Norman, letter to *The Times (of London)*, July 17, 1981.

31. Peregrine Worsthorne interview with Rosie Whitehouse for author, March 2012.

32. Weitz, 333–334.

CHAPTER ELEVEN: THE GERMAN PHOENIX ARISES

1. Speech by John McCloy, "Germany in a United Europe," *Information Bulletin*, May 1950. Available at http://digicoll.library.wisc.edu/cgi-bin/History/History-idx?type=turn& entity=History.omg1950May.p0041&id=History.omg1950May&isize=text.

2. Paul Hoffman speech to OEEC Council, October 31, 1949. Available at www.let.leidenuniv.nl/pdf/geschiedenis/eu-history/EU_03.doc.

3. Jacobssen, 401.

4. Ibid., 157.

5. David W. Ellwood, "The Propaganda of the Marshall Plan in Italy in a Cold War Context," in Giles Scott-Smith and Hans Krabbendam, eds., *The Cultural Cold War in Western Europe, 1945–1960* (Independence, KY: Frank Cass Publishing, 2004), 225.

7. John Singleton, *Central Banking in the Twentieth Century* (NY: Cambridge University Press), 156–157.

8. Richard Hall, interview with the author, December 2012.

9. Toniolo, 333.

10. See the website of the European Commission at http://eacea.ec.europa.eu/llp/funding/2012 /call_jean_monnet_action_ka1_2012_en.php.

11. Bird, 72.

12. Trygve Ugland, *Jean Monnet and Canada: Early Travels and the Idea of European Unity* (Toronto: Univ. of Toronto Press, 2011).

13. Interview with Albert Connolly. European University Institute, Int 549, Jean Monnet Statesman of Interdependence Collection. Available at http://www.eui.eu/HAEU/OralHistory/bin/CreaInt.asp?rc=INT549.

14. Preussen, 119.

15. Lisagor and Lipsius, 111.

16. Preussen, 309.

17. Ibid., 310–311.

18. Interview with Jelle Zijlstra. European University Institute, Int 534, Jean Monnet Statesman of Interdependence Collection. Available at http://www.eui.eu/HAEU/ OralHistory/bin/CreaInt.asp?rc =INT534.

19. Zijlstra interview, ibid.

20. Richard J. Aldrich, "OSS, CIA and European Unity: The American Committee on United Europe, 1948–1960," *Diplomacy & Statecraft*, vol. 8, no. 1 (1997):208.

21. Speech by McCloy, "Germany in a United Europe."

22. Ambrose Evans-Pritchard, "Euro-Federalists Financed by US Spy Chiefs," *Daily Telegraph*, September 19, 2000.

23. BIS Annual Report, 1956, 229.

24. Ibid.

25. Trial of Walther Funk, May 6, 1946. Available at http://avalon.law.yale.edu/imt/05-06-46.asp.

26. *Banking with Hitler*, from the BBC Timewatch series, produced by Paul Elston, 1998.

27. Donald MacLaren, brief for the De-Nazification of the German Chemical Industry, Introduction, December 1, 1945. Author's collection.

28. Ibid.

CHAPTER TWELVE: THE RISE OF THE DESK-MURDERERS

1. David Marsh, *The Bundesbank: The Bank That Rules Europe* (London: Heineman, 1992), 55. Marsh notes that British officials were less enthusiastic about the German banker, describing him as a "mixed Blessing".

2. Charles Coombs, *The Arena of International Finance* (NY: John Wiley, 1976). All of Coombs quotes are taken from his memoir, mainly from Chapter 3: The Basel Meetings.

3. Ibid., 27.

4. Marsh, 91.

5. Ibid., 54.

6. Bower, 15.

7. Marsh, 52–53.

8. Simpson, *The Splendid Blond Beast: Money, Law and Genocide in the Twentieth Century.* (Monroe, ME: Common Courage Press, 1995), 224.

9. Ibid., 225.

10. Allen Dulles to Joseph Dodge, September 20, 1945. NARA. OMGUS-FINAD. RG260, Box 237. File: Johannes Tuengeler. The extracts from the bankers' biographies are taken from this document. The author is grateful to Christopher Simpson for generously supplying copies of this document, which he unearthed in the US National Archives.

11. Dulles to Dodge, September 20 1945.

12. Petersen, 426–427.

13. Ibid., 628.

14. Toniolo, 377.

15. Coombs, 26.

16. Toniolo, 402.

17. Eric Roll, Obituary of Hermann Abs, the *Independent*, February 8, 1994.

18. Marsh, 51–52.

19. Chernow, 664.

20. "Karl Blessing Is Dead at 71; Led West German Central Bank," *New York Times*, April 27, 1971.

CHAPTER THIRTEEN: THE TOWER ARISES

1. Edward Jay Epstein, "Ruling the World of Money," *Harper's*, November 1983.

2. See Ron Chernow's biography of the Warburg family, *The Warburgs: The Twentieth-Century Odyssey of a Remarkable Jewish Family* (NY: Vintage, 1994).

3. Author interview with Richard Hall, December 2012.

4. Toniolo, 362.

5. Epstein, "Ruling the World of Money."

6. Author interview with Frigyes Hárshegyi, in Budapest, December 2012.

7. James M. Boughton, "Silent Revolution: The International Monetary Fund," (Washington, DC: IMF, 2001), 324.

8. Author interview with Hárshegyi, December 2012.

9. Boughton, 293.

10. Author interview with Richard Hall, December 2012.

11. David M. Andrews, "Command and Control in the Committee of Governors: Leadership, Staff and Preparations for EMU," European University Institute, 2003.

12. Alexandre Lamfalussy interview, Brussels, March 8, 2010. "The BIS, the Committee of Governors of the Central Banks of the EEC, and the Delors Committee," available online at: www.cvce.eu.

13. Ibid.

14. Ibid.

15. Harold James, *Making the European Monetary Union* (Cambridge, MA: Harvard University Press, 2012), 249.

16. Ibid.

17. Boughton, 329.

CHAPTER FOURTEEN: THE SECOND TOWER

1. John Laughlan, *The Tainted Source* (London: Warner Books, 1997), 32.

2. Stephen Haseler, *Super-State: The New Europe and its Challenge to America* (London: I. B. Taurus, 2004), 80.

3. Antony Beevor, "Europe's Long Shadow," *Prospect*, December 2012.

4. Toniolo, 229.

5. Laughland, 17.

6. Ibid.

7. Ibid., 17–18.

8. Walter Funk, "Economic Reorganization of Europe," translation dated July 26, 1940. BIS archives, Thomas McKittrick papers.

9. Op. cit.

10. Ibid.

11. Laughland, 30.

12. Ibid., 33.

13. Heinz Pol, *The Hidden Enemy: The German Threat to Post-War Peace* (New York: Julian Messner, 1943), 256.

14. Ibid., 257.

15. Author interview with Geoffrey Bell, in New York, April 2012.

16. Interview with Alexandre Lamfalussy, in Brussels, March 8, 2010. "The BIS, the Committee of Governors of the Central Banks of the EEC, and the Delors Committee," available at http://www.cvce.eu.

17. Ibid..

18. Bank for International Settlements, 1987 Annual Report (Basel: BIS, 1987), 81.

19. Interview with William White, December 2012.

20. Japan, a founding member of the BIS, had left in 1951. It rejoined in 1970 when the Bank of Canada also became a BIS member.

21. Charles J. Siegman, "The Bank for International Settlements and the Federal Reserve," *Federal Reserve Bulletin*, vol. 80, no. 10, October 1994, 900.

22. Author interview with Karen Johnson, in Washington, DC, May 2012.

23. Ibid.

24. Author interview with Paul Volcker, in New York, May 2012.

25. Ibid.

26. Author interview with Zsigmond Járai, in Budapest, November 2011.

27. Author interview with Rupert Penannt-Rea, in London, July 2012.

28. Ibid.

29. Author interview with Malcolm Knight, in New York, May 2012.

30. Author interview with Nathan Sheets, in New York, April 2012.

31. Ibid.

32. Author interview with Zsigmond Járai.

CHAPTER FIFTEEN: THE ALL-SEEING EYE

1. Author interview with William White, December 2012.

2. White interview.

3. Author interview with Rupert Pennant-Rea, in London, July 2012.

4. Author interview with William McDonough, in New York, May 2012.

5. Ibid.

6. Ibid.

7. "Withdrawal of privately held shares of the BIS: Final decision of the Hague Arbitral Tribunal," BIS, September 23, 2003, available at https://www.bis.org/press/p030922.htm.

8. "A BIS Embarrassed," *Central Banking Journal*, May 13, 2003.

9. Author interview with Charles de Vaulx, December 2012.

10. "Trichet Backs Disputed BIS Share Buyback Plan," *Central Banking Journal*, December 20, 2000.

11. The European Central Bank's monetary policy is available at http://www.ecb.int/mopo/html /index.en.html.

12. Author interview with William White.

13. Patricia S. Pollard, "A Look Inside Two Central Banks: The European Central Bank and the Federal Reserve," *Federal Reserve Bank of St. Louis*, January/February 2003, 24.

14. Prof. Anne Sibert, "Accountability and the ECB," *European Parliament, Directorate General for Internal Policies, Policy Department A: Economic and Scientific Policies, Economic and Monetary Affairs*, September 2009.

15. Ibid.

16. "The Accountability of the ECB," *ECB Monthly Bulletin*, November 2002.

17. Thomas McKittrick to Oliver Knauth, October 30, 1941. BIS archive, Thomas H. McKittrick papers.

18. Author interview with confidential source, 2012.

19. "Australian Central Banker Uncomfortable Over Capital Flow Surge," *Market News International*, Sydney, December 11, 2012.

20. Author interview with confidential source.

21. "Challenges for Central Banks, Wider Powers, Greater Restraints," Official Monetary and Financial Institutions Forum and Ernst and Young, November 2012.

22. Ibid.

23. "A Superhuman to Push the Old Lady," *Sunday Times*, December 2, 2012.

24. Ben Chu, "Why I'm Worried about Mark Carney's Governorship," *The Independent*, December 3, 2012.

25. Author interview with Malcolm Knight.

26. Author interview with Nathan Sheets.

27. Author interview with Peter Akos Bod.

28. Author interview with confidential source, 2012.

29. Jon Hilsenrath and Brian Blackstone, "Inside the Risky Bets of Central Banks," *Wall Street Journal*, December 11, 2012.

30. Author interview with Andrew Hilton, in London, April 2012.

31. Jean-Claude Trichet, "Lessons from the crisis: Challenges for the Advanced Economies and for the European Monetary Union," Eleventh Annual Niarchos Lecture, Petersen Institute for International Economics, Washington, DC, May 17 2012, available at http://www.iie.com /publications/papers/ transcript-20120518niarchos-trichet.pdf.

32. Author interview with Dean Baker, in Washington, DC, May 2012.

33. Ibid..

34. Author interview with Stephen Cecchetti, e-mail to author, December 19, 2012.

CHAPTER SIXTEEN: THE CITADEL CRACKS

1. Rabbi Nosson Scherman, *The Chumash: The Torah, Haftoras and Five Megillos With a Commentary Anthologised from the Rabbinic Writings* (NY: Mesorah Publications, 2001), 49.

2. The BIS replaced the gold franc with the Special Drawing Right (SDR) as its unit of account in 2003. The SDR is not a currency but an international reserve asset and is based on a basket of major currencies: the euro, Japanese yen, British pound, and the US dollar. In January 2013 one SDR was equivalent to $1.53.

3. Profit and loss account for the financial year ended March 31, 2009, *BIS 79th Annual Report*, 182,183.

4. Profit and loss account for the financial year ended March 31, 2012, *BIS 82nd Annual Report*, 135.

5. See the speech of Christine Lagarde, IMF managing director, IMF direct, January 24, 2012, available at http://blog-imfdirect.imf.org/2012/01/24/driving-the-global-economy-with-the-brakes-on.

6. "Presenting the Second Annual Wonky Awards," The Wonkblog Team, *Washington Post* online, December 28, 2012, available at http://www.washingtonpost.com /blogs/wonkblog /wp/2012/12/28 /presenting-the-second-annual-wonky-awards.

7. "Sharing of Financial Records Between Jurisdictions in Connection with the Fight Against Terrorist Financing," BIS, Basel Committee on Banking Supervision, April 2002, available at http://www.bis.org/publ/bcbs89.htm.

8. Matt Taibbi, "The Great American Bubble Machine," *Rolling Stone*, July 9, 2009.

9. Author interview with Andrew Hilton, in London, July 2012.

10. Author interview with William White, December 2012.

11. Author interview with Stephen Cecchetti, e-mail to author, December 17, 2012.

12. The press conference for the BIS 2010–2011 annual report can be seen on webcast at http://www.bis.org/events/agm2011/pcvideo.htm.

13. "Gauchos and Gadflies," *Economist*, October 22, 2011.

14. Lisa Weekes, "The Argentinean Money and Banking Immunity," *Wall Street Journal*, July 27, 2011.

15. Claudio Loser, "Destabilizing Force," Forbes online, available at, http://www.forbes.com /2010/01/20/bank-of-international-settlements-argentina-stagnation-opinions-contributors-claudio-m-loser.html.

16. Author interview, 2012.

17. Author interview with Malcolm Knight, in New York, May 2012.

18. Author interview with Sir Mervyn King, in London, February 2013.

19. Toniolo, 131.

20. Izabella Kaminska, "Apropos Those BIS Gold Swaps," FT Alphaville blog, June 25, 2012, available at http://ftalphaville.ft.com/2012/06/25/1058101/a-propos-those-bis-gold-swaps.

21. *BIS 82nd Annual Report*, 148.

22. Author interview with Rudi Bogni, in London, 2012.

23. Author interview with Sir Mervyn King, in London, February 2013.

24. Ibid.

25. Ibid.

26. Lisa Weekes e-mail to author, January 25, 2013.

27. Author interview with Sir Mervyn King, in London, February 2013.

28. Andrew Haldane, "A Leaf Being Turned," Occupy Economics, London, October 29, 2012, available at http://www.bankofengland.co.uk/publications/Documents /speeches/2012 /speech616.pdf.

29. Cecchetti and Kharroubi, "Reassessing the Impact of Finance on Growth," BIS Working Papers, 381, July 2012, 14.

30. Author interview with Sir Mervyn King, in London, February 2013.

Bibliography

ARCHIVES CONSULTED

Baker Library, Harvard Business School (HUBL)

Bank of England, London (BE)

Bank for International Settlements, Basel (BISA)

Centre for European Studies, Luxembourg (CVCE)

Cinematic Arts Library, University of Southern California, Los Angeles, California (USCCAL)

Columbia University Rare Book and Manuscript Library, New York, New York. (CU)

European University Institute, Brussels (EUI)

Federal Reserve Bank of New York, New York (FRBNY)

Franklin D. Roosevelt Presidential Library, Hyde Park, New York (FDRPL)

Harry S. Truman Library and Museum, Independence, Missouri (HTLM)

Seeley G. Mudd Manuscript Library, Princeton University (SGMML)

Special Collections Department, University of Delaware (UDSCD)

UK National Archives, London (UKNA)

US National Archives and Records Administration, College Park, Maryland (NARA)

BOOKS

Ahamed, Liaquat. *Lords of Finance: 1929, the Great Depression and the Bankers Who Broke the World*. London: Windmill, 2010.

Baker, James C. *The Bank for International Settlements: Evolution and Evaluation*. Westport, CT: Quorom Books, 2002.

Bank for International Settlements, The. *The BIS and the Basel Meetings 1930–1980*. Basel: BIS, 1980.

Bartal, David. *The Empire: The Rise of the House of Wallenberg*. Stockholm: Dagens Industri, 2005.

Bazyler, Michael, J. *Holocaust Justice: The Battle for Restitution in America's Courts.* New York: New York University Press, 2005.

Billstein, Reinhold, Karola Fings, Anita, Kugler, and Nicholas Levis. *Working for the Enemy: Ford, General Motors and Forced Labor During the Second World War*. Oxford, New York: Berghahn Books, 2004.

Bird, Kai. *The Chairman: John J. McCloy and the Making of the American Establishment*. New York: Simon and Schuster, 1992.

Black, Edwin. *IBM and the Holocaust: The Strategic Alliance between Nazi Germany and America's Most Powerful Corporation*. Westport, CT: Dialogue Press, 2012.

Borkin, Joseph. *The Crime and Punishment of I. G. Farben*. New York: Free Press, 1978.

Boughton, James M. *Silent Revolution: The International Monetary Fund 1979–1989*. Washington, DC: IMF, 2001.

Bower, Tom. *Blind Eye to Murder: Britain, America and the Purging of Nazi Germany*. New York: HarperCollins, 1981.

Boyle, Andrew. *Montagu Norman*. London: Cassell, 1967.

Breitman, Richard; Goda, Norman J. W.; Naftali, Timothy; and Wolfe, Robert. *U.S. Intelligence and the Nazis*. Cambridge University Press, 2005.

Chernow, Ron. *The Warburgs: The Twentieth-Century Odyssey of a Remarkable Jewish Family*. New York: Vintage, 1994.

Christman, Henry M., ed. *Essential Works of Lenin*. Mineola, New York: Dover, 1987.

Coombs, Charles. *The Arena of International Finance*. London: John Wiley, 1976.

Delattre, Lucas. *A Spy at the Heart of the Third Reich*. London: Grove Press/Atlantic Monthly Press, 2006

Dulles, Alan. *The Craft of Intelligence*. New York: Harper and Row, 1963.

Dulles, Eleanor Lansing. *The Bank for International Settlements at Work*. New York: Macmillan, 1932.

———. *Chances of a Lifetime: A Memoir*. Eaglewood Cliffs, NJ: Prentice Hall, 1980.

Ellwood, David W. "The Propaganda of the Marshall Plan in Italy in a Cold War Context," in Giles Scott-Smith and Hans Krabbendam, eds., *The Cultural Cold War in Western Europe, 1945–1960*. Independence, KY: Frank Cass Publishing, 2004.

Ferguson, Niall. *Paper and Iron: Hamburg Business and German Politics in the Era of Inflation 1897–1927*. Cambridge: Cambridge University Press, 2002

———. *The Ascent of Money: A Financial History of the World*. London: Penguin, 2009.

Gilbert, Martin. *Auschwitz and the Allies*. London: Michael Joseph, 1981.

Greider, William. *Secrets of the Temple: How the Federal Reserve Runs the Country*. New York, Touchstone, 1987.

Grose, Peter. *Gentleman Spy: The Life of Allen Dulles*. London: Andrew Deutsch, 1994.

Hartrich, Edwin. *The Fourth and Richest Reich: How the Germans Conquered the Post-War World*. London: Macmillan, 1980.

Haseler, Stephen. *Super-State: The New Europe and Its Challenge to America*. London: I.B. Taurus, 2004.

Henderson, David R. *German Economic Miracle: The Concise Encyclopedia of Economics*. Available at: http://www.econlib.org/library/Enc/GermanEconomicMiracle.html.

Higham, Charles. *Trading with the Enemy: An Exposé of the Nazi-American Money Plot 1933–1945*. London: Robert Hale, 1983.

Jacobssen, Erin E. *A Life for Sound Money—Per Jacobssen, His Biography*. Oxford: Clarendon Press, 1979.

James, Harold. *Making the European Monetary Union*. Harvard University Press, 2012.

———. *The Deutsche Bank and the Nazi Economic War Against the Jews*. London: Cambridge University Press, 1981.

Jeffreys, Diarmuid. *Hell's Cartel: IG Farben and the Making of Hitler's War Machine*. London: Bloomsbury, 2009.

Kahn, David. *Hitler's Spies: German Military Intelligence in World War II*. New York: Macmillan, 1978.

Krugman, Paul. *End This Depression Now!* New York: W. W. Norton, 2012.

Laughland, John. *The Tainted Source: The Undemocratic Origins of the European Idea*. London: Time, Warner, 1998.

LeBor, Adam. *Hitler's Secret Bankers: How Switzerland Profited from Nazi Genocide*. London: Pocket Books, 1999.

LeBor, Adam and Roger Boyes. *Surviving Hitler: Choice, Corruption and Compromise in the Third Reich*. London: Pocket Books, 2000.

Lisagor, Nancy and Frank Lipsius. *A Law Unto Itself: The Untold Story of Sullivan and Cromwell*. New York: William Morrow and Company, 1988.

MacMillan, Margaret. *Peacemakers: Six Months that Changed the World*. London: John Murray, 2003.

Mahl, Thomas E. *Desperate Deception: British Covert Operations in the United States 1939–1944*. Dulles, Virginia: Brassey's, 1998.

Marsh, David. *The Bundesbank: The Bank That Rules Europe*. London: William Heinemann, 1992.

———. *The Euro: The Battle for the New Global Currency*. Yale University Press, 2011.

Mierzejewski, Alfred C. *Ludwig Erhard* (Chapel Hill: Univ. of North Carolina Press, 2006)

Mosley, Leonard. *Dulles: A Biography of Eleanor, Allen and John Foster Dulles and their family network*. New York: Doubleday, 1978.

O'Sullivan, Christopher D. *Post-War Planning and the Quest for a New World Order*. Columbia University Press, 2008.

Padoa-Schioppa, Tommaso. *The Road to Monetary Union in Europe*. Oxford: Clarendon Press, 1994.

Partnoy, Frank. *The Match King: Ivar Kreuger and the Financial Scandal of the Century*. New York: PublicAffairs, 2010.

Pauly, Louis W. *Who Elected the Bankers? Surveillance and Control in the World Economy*. Ithaca: Cornell University Press, 1997.

Petersen, Neal H., ed. *From Hitler's Doorstep: The Wartime Intelligence Reports of Allen Dulles 1942–1945*. Penn State University Press, 1996.

Pol, Heinz. *The Hidden Enemy: The German Threat to Post-War Peace*. New York: Julian Messner, 1943.

Roberts, Richard. *Schroders: Bankers and Merchants*. London: Macmillan, 1992.

Sampson, Anthony. *The Money Lenders: The People and Politics of the World Banking Crisis*. London: Viking, 1983.

Schacht, Hjalmar. *Confessions of the Old Wizard*. New York: Houghton Mifflin, 1956.

Scherman, Rabbi Nosson. *The Chumash: The Torah, Haftoras and Five Megillos With a Commentary Anthologised from the Rabbinic Writings,* NewYork: Mesorah Publications, 2001.

Simpson, Christopher. *Blowback: The First Full Account of America's Recruitment of Nazis and Its Disastrous Effect on Our Domestic and Foreign Policy*. New York: Weidenfeld and Nicholson, 1988.

———. *The Splendid Blond Beast: Money, Law and Genocide in the Twentieth Century*. Monroe, ME: Common Courage Press, 1995.

Simpson, Christopher, ed. *War Crimes of the Deutsche Bank and the Dresdner Bank: Office of the Military Government (US) Reports*. Teaneck, NJ: Holmes and Meier, 2002.

Singleton, John. *Central Banking in the Twentieth Century*. Cambridge: Cambridge University Press, 2010.

Stiglitz, Joseph. *Freefall: Free Markets and the Sinking of the Global Economy*. London: Penguin, 2010.

Strachan, Hew. *Financing the First World War*. Oxford: Oxford University Press, 2004.

Sutton, Anthony. *Wall Street and the Rise of Hitler*. West Hoathly, Sussex: Clairview Books, 2010.

Swaine, Robert Taylor. *The Cravath Firm and Its Predecessors 1819–1947*. New Jersey: The Lawbook Exchange Ltd, 1964.

Tarullo, Daniel. *Banking on Basel: The Future of International Financial Regulation*. Washington, DC: The Peterson Institute for International Economics, 2008.

Toniolo, Gianni, with Piet Clement. *Central Bank Cooperation at the Bank for International Settlements 1930–1973*. London: Cambridge University Press, 2005.

Tooze, Adam. *The Wages of Destruction: The Making and the Breaking of the Nazi Economy*. London: Allen Lane, 2006.

Touffut, Jean-Philippe. *Central Banks as Economic Institutions*. Cheltenham: Edward Elgar Publishing, 2008.

Trevor-Roper, H. R. *Hitler's Secret Conversations, 1941–1944*. New York: Farrar, Strauss, and Young, 1953.

Turner, Henry Ashby Jr. *German Big Business and the Rise of Hitler*. New York: Oxford University Press, 1985.

Ugland, Trygve. *Jean Monnet and Canada: Early Travels and the Idea of European Unity*. Toronto: University of Toronto Press, 2011.

Weitz, John. *Hitler's Banker: Hjalmar Horace Greeley Schacht*. London: Warner Books, 1999.

West, Nigel. *British Security Co-ordination: The Secret History of British Intelligence in the Americas 1940–45*. London: Little, Brown, 1998.

Wistrich, Robert. *Who's Who in Nazi Germany*. London: Routledge, 2002.

Wyman, David S. *The Abandonment of the Jews: America and the Holocaust 1941–1945*. New York: Pantheon, 1984.

SELECTED ARTICLES AND PAPERS

Aldrich, Richard. "OSS, CIA and European Unity: The American Committee on United Europe 1948–1960," *Diplomacy and Statecraft*, Vol. 8, No. 1, March 1997.

Andrews, David M. "Command and Control in the Committee of Governors: Leadership, Staff and Preparations for EMU," European University Institute, available at http://aei.pitt.edu/2811/1/078.pdf.

Auboin, Roger. "The Bank for International Settlements, 1930–1955," *Essays in International Finance*, May 1955.

Avent, Ryan. "The Twilight of the Central Banker," *Free Exchange*, *The Economist*, June 26, 2012, available at http://www.economist.com/blogs/freeexchange/2012/06/central-banks.

Bank for International Settlements, The. Annual reports from 1930, available at http://www.bis.org.

Bank for International Settlements, The. "Note on Gold Operations Involving the BIS and the German Reichsbank, September 1, 1939–May 8, 1945," available at http://www.bis.org/publ/bisp02b.pdf.

Beevor, Antony. "Europe's Long Shadow," *Prospect* magazine, December 2012.

Borkin, Joseph and Charles Welsh. "Germany's Master Plan," review by J. Hurstfield, *Economic History Review*, Vol. 14, No. 2 (1944), 206–207.

Boughton, James M. "Harry Dexter White and the International Monetary Fund," *Finance and Development* magazine, September 1998.

Breitman, Richard. "A deal with the Nazi dictatorship: Hitler's alleged emissaries in Autumn 1943," *Journal of Contemporary History*, Vol. 30, No. 3, July 1995.

Cecchetti, Stephen and Enisse Kharroubi. "Reassessing the Impact of Finance on Growth," *BIS Working Papers*, 381, July 2012.

Clement, Piet. "The touchstone of German credit: Nazi Germany and the service of the Dawes and Young Loans," *Financial History Review*, Vol. 11, 1, April 2004.

———. "The term 'macroprudential': origins and evolution," Bank for International Settlements, *BIS Quarterly Review*, March 2010.

Eichengreen, Barry, and Jorge Braga de Macedo. "The European Payments Union: History and implications for the evolution of the international financial architecture," OECD Development Center, Paris, March 2001.

Epstein, Edward Jay. "Ruling the world of money," *Harper's*, November 1983.

Friedman, Milton. "The Island of Stone Money," Working Papers in Economics E-91-3, The Hoover Institution, Stanford University, February 1991.

Funk, Walter. "Economic Reorganisation of Europe," Reichsbank, Berlin, 1940.

Goodhart, Charles. "The Changing Role of Central Banks," BIS Working Paper 326, November 2010.

Hilsenrath, Jon, and Brian Blackstone. "Inside the Risky Bets of Central Banks", *Wall Street Journal*, December 12, 2012.

Haldane, Andrew. "A Leaf Being Turned," Occupy Economics, London, 29 October, 2012, available at http://www.bankofengland.co.uk/publications/Documents/speeches/2012 /speech616.pdf.

Hudson, Manley, O. "The Immunities of the Bank for International Settlements," *American Journal of International Law*, Vol. 32, No. 1 (Jan. 1938), 128–134.

Johanssen, Niels and Gabriel Zucman. "The End of Bank Secrecy? An Evaluation of the G20 Tax Haven Crackdown," Working Paper 2012–04, Paris School of Economics, February 2012.

Keynes, J. M. "The Bank for International Settlements, Fourth Annual Report, 1933–34," *Economic Journal*, Vol. 44, No. 175. September 1934, 514–518.

Kriz, M.A. "The Bank for International Settlements: Wartime Activities and Present Position," (Revised), Federal Reserve Bank of New York, Foreign Research Division, June 11, 1947.

Lamfalussy, Alexandre. "Central banks, Governments and the European Monetary Unification Process," BIS Working Paper 201. February 2006.

Lefort, Daniel. "Bank for International Settlements, Basel, Switzerland," Kluwer Law International, Intergovernmental Organisations—Supplement 36, November 2009.

Martín-Aceña, Pablo, Elena Martínez Ruiz, Maria. A. Pons, "War and Economics: Spanish Civil War Finances Revisited," Working papers on Economic History, Universidad de Alcala, Madrid, WP-04-10, December 2010.

Maes, Ivo. "The Evolution of Alexandre Lamfalussy's Thought on the International and European Monetary System (1961-1993)," Working Paper Research, November 2011, No. 127. National Bank of Belgium.

Official Monetary and Financial Institutions Forum and Ernst and Young. "Challenges for Central Banks, Wider Powers, Greater Restraints." November 2012.

Pol, Heinz. "IG Farben's Peace Offer," *Protestant Magazine*, June–July 1943, 41.

Pollard, Patricia. "A Look Inside Two Central Banks: The European Central Bank and the Federal Reserve," Federal Reserve Bank of St. Louis, January/February 2003.

Sibert, Anne. "Accountability and the ECB," European Parliament, Directorate General for Internal Policies, Policy Department A: Economic and Scientific Policies, Economic and Monetary Affairs, September 2009, available at http://www.europarl.europa.eu/document/activities /cont/200909/20090924ATT61145/20090924ATT61145EN.pdf.

Siegman, Charles J. "The Bank for International Settlements and the Federal Reserve," *Federal Reserve Bulletin*, Volume 80, number 10, October 1994.

Simmons, Beth. "Why Innovate? Founding the Bank for International Settlements," *World Politics*, Vol. 45, No. 3 (Apr. 1993), 361–405.

Taibbi, Matt. "The Great American Bubble Machine," *Rolling Stone*, July 9 2009.

Tuttle, William M. Jr. "The Birth of an Industry: the Synthetic Rubber 'Mess' in World War II," *Technology and Culture*, January 1981, 40.

Van Hook, James C. "Review of Treasonable Doubt: The Harry Dexter White Spy Case by R. Bruce Craig," *Studies in Intelligence*, Vol. 49, No. 1, April 2007.

Weixelbaum, Jason. "The Contradiction of Neutrality and International Finance: The Presidency of Thomas H. McKittrick at the Bank for International Settlements in Basel 1940–1946," May 2010, available at http://jasonweixelbaum.wordpress.com/tag/thomas-h-mckittrick.

———. "Following the Money: An Exploration of the Relationship between American Finance and Nazi Germany," December 2009, available at http://jasonweixelbaum .wordpress.com/2009/12/21/following-the-money-an-exploration of-the-relationship-between-american-finance-and-nazi-germany.

ARCHIVED INTERVIEWS

Connelly, Albert Ray. Conducted in October 1990. Number 549, Jean Monnet Statesman of Interdepence Collection (EUI), available at http://www.eui.eu/HAEU/OralHistory /bin/CreaInt.asp ?rc=INT549.

Harriman, Averell. Conducted in 1971. Harry S. Truman Library and Museum, available at http://www.trumanlibrary.org/oralhist/harriman.htm.

Hoffman, Paul. Conducted in October 1964. Harry S. Truman Library and Museum, available at http://www.trumanlibrary.org/oralhist/hoffmanp.htm.

Lamfalussy, Alexandre. Series of interviews conducted in March 2010, available at http://www.cvce.eu.

McKittrick, Thomas. Conducted in July 1964. John Foster Dulles Oral History Collection, number 172 (SGMML).

Zijlstra, Jelle. Conducted in May 1989. Number 534, Jean Monnet Statesman of Interdepence Collection (EUI), available at http://www.eui.eu/HAEU/OralHistory/bin/CreaInt.asp ?rc=INT534.

SELECTED WEBSITES

Bank for International Settlements, http://www.bis.org

Centre for European Studies, http://www.cvce.eu

Economics resource, http://www.dictionaryofeconomics.com

Economics and finance resource, http://www.econlib.org

The Economist magazine, http://www.economist.com

European University Institute, http://www.eui.eu

Financial Times, http://www.ft.com

Investopedia finance resource, http://www.investopedia.com

New York Times, http://www.nytimes.com

Holocaust research resource, http://www.nizkor.org

Harry S. Truman Library and Museum, http://www.trumanlibrary.org

IG Farben historical resources, http://www.wollheim-memorial.de

US Department of State, Office of the Historian, http://www.history.state.gov

Index

About the Author

Szabolcs Dudas

Adam LeBor is an author, journalist, and literary critic based in Budapest. He writes for *The Economist*, the *Times* (London), *Monocle*, and numerous other publications, and also reviews for the *New York Times*. He has been a foreign correspondent since 1991, covering the collapse of Communism and the Yugoslav wars, and has worked in more than thirty countries. He is the author of seven nonfiction books, including the ground-breaking *Hitler's Secret Bankers*, and two novels.

www.adamlebor.com • Twitter: @adamlebor